The Politics of Economic Reform in Ghana

This book explores the significant economic transformation of Ghana over the three decades since the end of the Cold War, focusing on the role of political–economic change and reform.

The Politics of Economic Reform in Ghana presents a range of perspectives from scholars drawn from both academia and policymaking on the way Ghanaian economic reforms have been shaped by various political and economic actors. First, it establishes and debates the uniqueness of Ghana as a case study in Africa, and the developing world. Second, the book offers a broad account of how global and domestic political or institutional actors have contributed to shaping economic development in Ghana. Drawing on theoretical perspectives, the volume assesses how major political–economic changes have affected Ghana's economic development.

This book will be of interest to students, scholars, policymakers, and organizations interested in the economic and political advancement of Africa, as well as African politics and economics.

Richard Aidoo is Associate Professor of Politics at Coastal Carolina University in South Carolina, USA, where he also serves as Assistant Dean of the Thomas W. and Robin W. Edwards College of Humanities and Fine Arts. In addition to journal articles and book chapters, his work on the sub-Saharan African political economy and Africa–Asia relations has appeared in several media outlets including *CNN*, *Real Clear World*, *The Diplomat*, the *Washington Post*, the *National Interest*, *Yahoo News*, and *Foreign Policy Journal*. He is also the coauthor of *Charting the Roots of Anti-Chinese Populism in Africa*.

Routledge Studies on the Political Economy of Africa

1 **The Political Economy of Energy in Sub-Saharan Africa**
Edited by Lucky E. Asuelime and Andrew E. Okem

2 **The Political Economy of Land and Agrarian Development in Ethiopia**
The Arssi Region since 1941
Ketebo Abdiyo Ensene

3 **The Political Economy of Livelihoods in Contemporary Zimbabwe**
Edited by Kirk Helliker, Manase Kudzai Chiweshe and Sandra Bhatasara

4 **The Politics of Economic Reform in Ghana**
Edited by Richard Aidoo

The Politics of Economic Reform in Ghana

Edited by Richard Aidoo

Routledge
Taylor & Francis Group
LONDON AND NEW YORK

First published 2019
by Routledge
2 Park Square, Milton Park, Abingdon, Oxon OX14 4RN

and by Routledge
605 Third Avenue, New York, NY 10017

First issued in paperback 2021

Routledge is an imprint of the Taylor & Francis Group, an informa business

British Library Cataloguing-in-Publication Data
A catalogue record for this book is available from the British Library

Library of Congress Cataloging-in-Publication Data
Names: Aidoo, Richard, editor.
Title: The politics of economic reform in Ghana / Edited by Richard Aidoo.
Other titles: Routledge studies on the political economy of Africa ; 4.
Description: New York, NY : Routledge, 2019. | Series: Routledge studies on the political economy of Africa ; 4
Identifiers: LCCN 2018061163| ISBN 9781138497337 (hardback) | ISBN 9781351018982 (ebook) | ISBN 9781351018968 (epub) | ISBN 9781351018951 (mobipocket)
Subjects: LCSH: Economic development–Political aspects–Ghana. | Ghana–Economic policy. | Ghana–Economic conditions. | Ghana–Foreign economic relations.
Classification: LCC HC1060 .P66 2019 | DDC 338.9667–dc23
LC record available at https://lccn.loc.gov/2018061163

ISBN 13: 978-0-367-78636-6 (pbk)
ISBN 13: 978-1-138-49733-7 (hbk)

Typeset in Times New Roman
by Wearset Ltd, Boldon, Tyne and Wear

This work is dedicated to the hardworking people of Ghana, many of whom toil from dawn to dusk in often forgotten informal sectors of the economy and rural environments, away from the cities, high-rise buildings, banking halls, and government offices.

And to the memory of our friend, teacher, mentor, and dear colleague Professor Cyril K. Daddieh who is sorely missed for his generous spirit, humor, wit, sharp intellect, and also for his genuine passion and commitment to Ghana's democratic process.

Contents

List of illustrations ix
Notes on contributors x
List of abbreviations xiii

1 **Introduction: The politics of economic reform in Ghana – an overview** 1
RICHARD AIDOO

PART I
Conceptual considerations 29

2 **Politicizing economic reform in Africa: Ghana's political–economic framework** 31
LORD MAWUKO-YEVUGAH

PART II
A world of reforms: Diverse global perspectives 45

3 **Is there a consensus from Ottawa? Canada's role in Ghana's economic reforms** 47
ERNEST OPOKU-BOATENG

4 **EU as a democratic and development partner in Ghana: Credibility, coherence, and consistency in reforms** 67
MARIAM DEKANOZISHVILI

5 **Ghana–Asian partnerships: The scramble for markets, power, and agency** 81
NAABORLE SACKEYFIO

PART III
Lessons from Ghana: Reflections on resource management and reform experiences 93

6 Oil and social responsibility in Ghana 95
ANTOINETTE TSIBOE-DARKO

7 Ghanaian agency in economic engagement in the 21st century: The role of Chinese transnational oil corporations in Ghana 111
ISAAC ODOOM

8 The politics of galamsey and anti-Chinese populism in Ghana 127
RICHARD AIDOO

9 The search for economic self-determination: Senegal and Ghana's destiny 145
SALIOU DIONE

10 The "new Gambia" and Ghana collaboration: Potential lessons from Accra 164
ABDOULAYE SAINE

11 Making democracy and development work in Kenya: Lessons from Ghana 173
FATUMA BORU GUYO

12 Conclusion: Ghana's exceptionalism in economic reforms? Resolve vs. results 191
RICHARD AIDOO

Index 201

Illustrations

Figures

1.1 GDP per capita: Ghana and sub-Sahara Africa 3
1.2 Freedom House scores: Ghana (1998–2018) 4

Tables

7.1 Terms and conditions of the original Master Facility Agreement (2011) 117
8.1 Showing deportations/repatriations by the Ghana Immigration Services 2010–2013 135

Contributors

Richard Aidoo is an associate professor of politics at Coastal Carolina University in South Carolina, USA where he also serves as Assistant Dean of the Thomas W. and Robin W. Edwards College of Humanities and Fine Arts. His research focuses on the political economy of countries in sub-Saharan Africa, particularly diplomatic engagements between these countries and Asian economies, like China. He has written extensively on China–Africa relations, and broadly on economic development issues in sub-Saharan Africa. In addition to journal articles and book chapters, his work has appeared in several media outlets including *CNN*, *Real Clear World*, *The Diplomat*, the *Washington Post*, the *National Interest*, *Yahoo News*, and *Foreign Policy Journal*. Aidoo is also the coauthor with Steve Hessof *Charting the Roots of Anti-Chinese Populism in Africa* (2015).

Mariam Dekanozishvili is an assistant professor of Politics and the Global Studies advisor at the Department of Politics at Coastal Carolina University. She received her M.A. in European Affairs from Lund University, Sweden and another M.A. and Ph.D. in political science from the University of South Carolina. Her area of teaching and research is European/EU politics, with a particular focus on integration and policymaking in the EU, and EU energy policy. She has extensive professional and research experience in her field. Before entering academia, she worked for the Ministry of European Integration of Georgia and the Organisation for Security and Co-operation in Europe. She is the author of *The European Neighborhood Policy: The South Caucasus Dimension* (2011).

Saliou Dione is a lecturer at Cheikh Anta Diop University of Dakar in Senegal. He holds a doctorate in African and postcolonial studies, a postgraduate diploma in American literature and civilization, and a bachelor's degree in British literature and civilization. His main areas of academic interest and research include society, politics, culture, language, discourse, pan-Africanism, postcolonialism, African literature, gender, sexuality(ies), migration, and development issues. He has published a wide range of articles covering these issues. Dione has been a Senior Fulbright Visiting Scholar at Rutgers, the State University of New Jersey (USA). As a Fulbright Scholar, he has delivered lectures at Ohio Wesleyan University and Denison University, in Ohio (USA), and at Rutgers, the State University of New Jersey, in New Jersey (USA), and presented conference papers at the City College of New York and Colombia University, in New York (USA), and Howard University, in Washington, DC (USA).

Fatuma Boru Guyo is a lecturer in history at Pwani University, Kilifi, Kenya. She was previously postdoctoral scholar for the College of Liberal Arts at Wright State University, Dayton, Ohio, USA. She holds a Ph.D. in history from Southern Illinois University, Carbondale. Her current research focuses on colonial and postcolonial East Africa, especially themes with dimensions on policy history, socioeconomic changes, peace and conflict and issues of democratization and development with an approach to historical, gender, and ethnic marginalization.

Lord Mawuko-Yevugah is currently a senior lecturer and Head of Department for Public Management and International Relations at the Ghana Institute of Management and Public Administration. He is also the editor of the Institute's *Greenhill Journal*. He holds a Ph.D. in political science from the University of Alberta in Canada; an M.Phil. in development studies from the University of Cambridge, UK; and a BA in political science from the University of Ghana, Legon. He also held a Royal Netherlands Academy of Arts and Sciences Research Fellowship at the International Institute of Social History in Amsterdam. Mawuko-Yevugah has published widely in the areas of international political economy, aid, and international development cooperation; comparative politics of development in Africa; political economy of Ghana; and postcolonial theory. His major intellectual work, *Reinventing Development: Aid Reform and Technologies of Governance in Ghana* originally published by Ashgate Publishers was republished by Routledge in 2016. He also coedited the highly acclaimed volume, *African Youth Cultures in a Globalized World* (2015).

Isaac Odoom teaches at the Department of Political Science, University of Alberta, Canada where he also obtained his Ph.D. in political science. He has a master's degree in international relations from Brock University, Canada, and a BA in political science from the University of Ghana, Legon. His scholarly interests include Africa's international relations, Africa–China relations, emerging powers, South–South cooperation, and the political economy of development. His research publications have appeared in the *Third World Quarterly*, *Journal of Asian and African Studies*, and the *African Review of Economics and Finance*. He has also contributed several chapters in volumes such as *From Millennium Development Goals to Sustainable Development Goals* (2018). Odoom is a non-resident research fellow of the Centre for Asian Studies, University of Ghana, Accra.

Ernest Opoku-Boateng is a senior policy adviser with the Ontario provincial government in Canada, where he provides advice on international trade, climate change, intergovernmental relations, and regulatory burden reduction. He holds master's and doctorate degrees from the University of Toronto. Prior to joining the government, he was a lecturer at the University of Toronto. He was also a cofounder and Executive Director of the African Public Policy Research Centre. Recently, he launched the Institute for Environment and Social Innovation in Ghana – an organization working with local communities as well as district and municipal assemblies to develop and deploy entrepreneurial solutions to pressing environmental problems.

Naaborle Sackeyfio is an assistant professor of global and intercultural studies at Miami University of Ohio. Her book, *Energy Politics and Rural Development in sub-Saharan Africa: The Case of Ghana* was in 2017. Her research interrogates African political economy with a focus on resource politics and gender, economic empowerment, and sustainable development. Concurrently, future work will explore identity politics, labor and belonging of African migrants in East Asia.

Abdoulaye Saine is University Distinguished Scholar and Professor of political science at Miami University, Oxford, Ohio. He has published widely on elections and democratization in West Africa and the Gambia. He is the author of *Culture and Customs of Gambia* (2012), *The Paradox of Third-Wave Democratization in Africa* (2009), coauthor of *Not Yet Democracy: West Africa's Slow Farewell to Authoritarianism* (2005). Saine is also coeditor of *State and Society in The Gambia Since Independence, 1965–2012* (2013), and *Elections and Democratization in West Africa, 1990–2009* (2011). His work has appeared in, among others, *Journal of Democracy* and *African Studies Review*, and in numerous edited volumes on Africa.

Antoinette Tsiboe-Darko is a social development analyst. She is a research fellow and lecturer at the Centre for Social Policy Studies at University of Ghana, and holds a Ph.D. in development studies from the University of Ghana and an M.Phil. in social change from the Norwegian University of Science and Technology. Her broad research interests include developing appropriate institutions and governance systems in the management of natural resources. She has researched in social mobilization, volunteerism and decentralization, natural resource development in Ghana and Burkina Faso. She has contributed to the development of corporate social responsibility guidelines for private multinational companies. Tsiboe-Darko has been involved in a nationwide community sensitization exercise for the Petroleum Commission of Ghana and partners in coastal communities in Ghana to help policymakers and stakeholders identify the specific needs of communities and to inform fisherfolk about the positive benefits of oil exploration. She teaches graduate-level courses at the University of Ghana. She is a member of the Advisory Board of the Ministry of Lands and Natural Resources in Ghana.

Abbreviations

ACEP	Africa Centre for Energy Policy
ACP	African Caribbean and Pacific [countries]
ADB	African Development Bank
AFRC	Armed Forces Revolutionary Council
AGS	Accelerated Growth Strategy
APIX	Agency for Promotion of Investment and Major Projects
ASALs	arid and semi-arid lands
BCEAO	Central Bank of West African States
BOST	Bulk Oil Storage and Transportation Company Limited
BP	British Petroleum
CAFTTG	Canadian Armed Forces Training Team Ghana
CCAC	Climate and Clean Air Coalition to Reduce Short-Lived Climate Pollutants
CDB	China Development Bank
CFSP	Common Foreign and Security Policy
CIDA	Canadian International Development Agency
CIDP	Canadian International Development Platform
CMB	Cocoa Marketing Board
CNOOC	China National Offshore Oil Corporation
COVE	Corporate Village Enterprise
CPP	Convention People's Party
CSOs	civil society organizations
CSR	corporate social responsibility
CSRM	corporate social responsibility movement
CUSO	Canadian University Students Overseas
DAC	Development Assistance Committee
DEVCO	development and cooperation
DFRD	District Focus for Rural Development
DG	Directorate General
ECF	extended credit facility
ECK	Electoral Commission of Kenya
ECOWAS	Economic Community of West African States
EDF	European Development Fund

EEAS	European External Action Service
EMPRETEC	Empresariou Technologica
EPA	Economic Partnership Agreement
EPA	Environmental Protection Agency
ERP	Economic Recovery Programme
EU	European Union
EUTF	European Union's Trust Fund
FBOs	farmer-based organizations
FDA	French Development Agency
FDI	foreign direct investment
FES	Friedrich-Ebert-Stiftung
FGD	Focus Group Discussion
FINSAP	Financial Sector Reform Programme
FINSSP	Financial Sector Strategic Plan
FPSO	floating production storage and offloading
GAC	Global Affairs Canada
GDP	gross domestic product
GHGs	greenhouse gases
GNPC	Ghana National Petroleum Corporation
GOANA	Grand Agricultural Offensive for Food and Abundance
GoG	Government of Ghana
GOIL	Ghana Oil Company
GPRS	Ghana Poverty Reduction Strategy
GSGDA	Ghana Shared Growth and Development Agenda
GTUC	Ghana Trades Union Congress
HIPC	Heavily Indebted and Poor Country [Initiative]
ICC	International Criminal Court
ICFG	Integrated Coastal and Fisheries Governance
IEBC	Independent Electoral and Boundaries Commission
IFCTU	International Federation of Christian Trade Unions
IFIs	international financial institutions
IMF	International Monetary Fund
IOCs	international oil companies
IPAC	Inter-Party Advisory Committee
JBIC	Japan Bank for International Cooperation
JETRO	Japan External Trade Organizations
KADU	Kenya African Democratic Union
KANU	Kenya African National Union
KP	Kyoto Protocol
KPU	Kenya People's Union
LAPSSET	Lamu Port-Southern Sudan–Ethiopia Corridor Project
LGBT	lesbian, gay, bisexual, transgender
LIBOR	London Interbank Offered Rate
LPG	liquefied petroleum gas
MDGs	Millennium Development Goals

MDRI	Multilateral Debt Relief initiative
METI	Ministry of Economy, Trade and Industry
MFA	master facility agreement
MITI	Ministry for International Trade and Industry
MOF	Ministry of Finance
NAFTA	North American Free Trade Agreement
NARC	National Alliance Rainbow Coalition
NCD	National Commission for Democracy
NDC	National Democratic Congress
NDPC	National Development Planning Commission
NEPAD	New Partnership for Africa's Development
NORPALM	Norwegian Palm Ghana Limited
NPP	New Patriotic Party
NRC	National Redemption Council
ODA	Official Development Assistance
ODAA	Official Development Assistance Act
ODI	Overseas Development Institute
OECD	Organisation for Economic Co-operation and Development
OPEC	Organization of Petroleum Exporting Countries
OPIC	Overseas Private Investment Corporation
PAMSCAD	Programme of Actions to Mitigate the Social Costs of Adjustment
PC	Petroleum Commission
PD	Paris Declaration on Aid Effectiveness
PES	Plan for an Emerging Senegal
PIAC	Public Interest & Accountability Committee
PNDC	Provisional National Defence Council
PP	Progress Party
PRC	People's Republic of China
PRMA	Petroleum Revenue Management Act
PRS	Poverty Reduction Strategy
PRSP	Poverty Reduction Strategy Paper
PSDS	Private Sector Development Strategy
RTAs	regional trade agreements
SAF	Structural Adjustment Facility
SAL	Structural Adjustment Lending
SAP	Structural Adjustment Program
SECAL	Sectoral Adjustment Lending
SDA	social dimensions of adjustment
SDR	special drawing rights
SMC	Supreme Military Council
SME	small-to-medium enterprise
SOEs	state-owned enterprises
SWFs	sovereign wealth funds
TICAD	Tokyo International Conference on African Development

TNCs	Transnational Corporations
UDP	United Democratic Party
UGCC	United Gold Coast Convention
UNDP	United Nations Development Program
UNICEF	United Nations Children's Emergency Fund
UNIGOV	Union Government
WAEMU	West African Economic and Monetary Union
WB	World Bank
WC	Washington Consensus
WTO	World Trade Organization

1 Introduction

The politics of economic reform in Ghana – an overview

Richard Aidoo

Over the past six decades, the project of building a postcolonial Ghana, out of the controversies of exploitation and enslavement of the colonial and precolonial eras in Africa has been founded on some of Kwame Nkrumah's rhetorical visions which serve as continuous inspiration to Ghanaians and Africans, along with years of political and economic uncertainty, and a return to a relatively stable democratic course with some economic gains. After political self-determination was reached in 1957, the more arduous task of economic autonomy has proven rather daunting and elusive, despite some of the ingenious development agenda of successive leaders and administrations, both military and civilian, after Kwame Nkrumah and the Convention People's Party (CPP). Different periods of reported national economic growth and achievements are often interspersed with widespread economic stagnation or strife necessitating reform programs, repeatedly with the initiation of a new political administration. This characteristic start-and-stop feature has impacted Ghana's economic development course as the lack of continuity in economic vision, and external dictates that come with diverse loans, aid, and technical assistance amid other domestic political–economic challenges have combined to slow the progress toward economic self-dependency.

Ghana, the first country to attain political independence south of the Sahara, has spent approximately half of its over six-decade existence in diverse economic reform agenda to right the political–economic unsteadiness created at different times in the post-independent years. Expectedly, results of the diverse economic reforms in Ghana have been largely debated and contested at various levels. Whereas some external organizations and state actors have praised Ghana's political steadiness and long-suffering efforts toward economic progress, domestic rhetoric has been diverse and often criticisms as large segments of the Ghanaian population are yet to experience economic respite from these economic reforms. Different issues and challenges manifested in various sectors of the economy, society, and politics attest to these sentiments.

According to Sandbrook's 1985 portrait of post-independent Ghana with dashed hopes of economic reform, he stated

> The first colony to win independence, Ghana emerged as a sovereign nation in 1957 with living standards, infrastructure and administrative competence

> unequalled in Black Africa. But its economy has been in decline since the 1960s. In 1970s, per capita Gross Domestic Product fell more than three percent per annum. Output declined in all major sectors – cocoa, timber, mining and manufacturing. Annual price inflation averaged 50–100 percent.... While the modern economy collapsed, kalabule – the Ghanaian term for the black market or parallel economy – flourished.
>
> (Sandbrook, 1985, pp. 2–3)

He further argued that this dire socioeconomic scenario was also shared by many other African countries such as Angola, Chad, Mozambique, Sudan, Uganda, and Tanzania but not as marked in selected countries like Botswana, Gabon, Kenya, and Ivory Coast. Obviously, different economic development fortunes have shaped these countries into their present development states. Since Sandbrook's characterization, Ghana has seen upward trends of economic progress, albeit inconsistent and unevenly distributed. These notes of progress have often anchored the claims of exceptionalism and exemplariness of this African state. After recounting Ghana's economic challenges in the 1970s and early 1980s, away from the halcyon days of the early post-independent period, Radelet (2010) notes the economic reform recipe that was adopted by the Jerry John Rawlings regime after 1983, and further highlights the impacts of the reforms on the Ghanaian economy. In his twenty-first-century assessment, Radelet reports

> The result [of the reforms] has been a striking turnaround. The Ghanaian economy today bears little resemblance to the basket case of the early 1980s. Economic growth has averaged 5 percent per year for 25 years, translating into a 70 percent increase in the income of the average Ghanaian. The poverty rate, after dropping only slightly from 53 percent in 1984 to 50 percent in 1993 in the early days of the reform program, fell dramatically to 30 percent.
>
> (2010, p. 72)

These two contrasting images of Ghana from Sandbrook and Radelet are both recognizable within a generation, as the country embraced different economic reforms to resuscitate, stabilize, and grow its economy which at independence was seen as a guidepost to other African economies. A decade after the launch of the Economic Recovery Programme (ERP) by Jerry John Rawlings and the Provisional National Defence Council (PNDC), the World Bank extoled Ghana's reform efforts and characterized it as the beacon on the African continent (see Aryeetey, Harrigan, and Nissanke, 2000). This sense of approval was reechoed in 2011 by the Overseas Development Institute (ODI) (2011) referring to Ghana as a developmental "star performer," years after structural adjustment under the Rawlings regime, and the designation of the country as a highly indebted and poor country (HIPC) in 2001 under John Kufuor and the New Patriotic Party (NPP).

In recent years, these economic development accolades and pronouncements are often supported by Ghana's post-Cold War era stable democracy away from the disrupting effects of military interventions and inconsistent economic development plans from the mid-1960s to early 1980s. Admittedly, there are both causes for celebration and concern. As shown in Figure 1.1, Ghana has made some economic progress, after the reforms in the early 1980s which was significantly characterized by the jolt in GDP per capita from a –7.8% in 1983 to 1.7% two years later. Since then, unlike the whole sub-Saharan African region, Ghana has often stabilized its GDP per capita with some highs like in 2011 and many lows including 2015. However, the dizzying situations of intermittent economic performances have often been overwhelmed by Ghana's image as a democratic reformer with consistently peaceful elections and turnovers that have earned the country a place in the ranks of the world's known stable democracies. This is perceived exemplary as this country is nestled among some struggling democracies that are often an election away from political strife.

Nevertheless, Ghana's praise of exceptionalism is not without immense critique as consistent and pro-poor economic growth has been elusive with insufficient political will to enact and execute policies committed to macroeconomic stability and fiscal discipline – two known objectives in most reform programs that the country has adopted over the decades. This is further compounded by the penchant to access diverse loans from external actors that many argue does very little to change the economic development fate of Ghana. Despite the consistency in political development as shown in Figure 1.2, the country's democratic credentials have also been cautioned over frailties such as the unfair advantage of political incumbency, the feature of underperforming minor political parties, and the often-stated ethnic influences in democratic politics. Thus, this volume is a collection of multiple perspectives to highlight, dissect, and reflect on the political, economic, and social characteristics that have

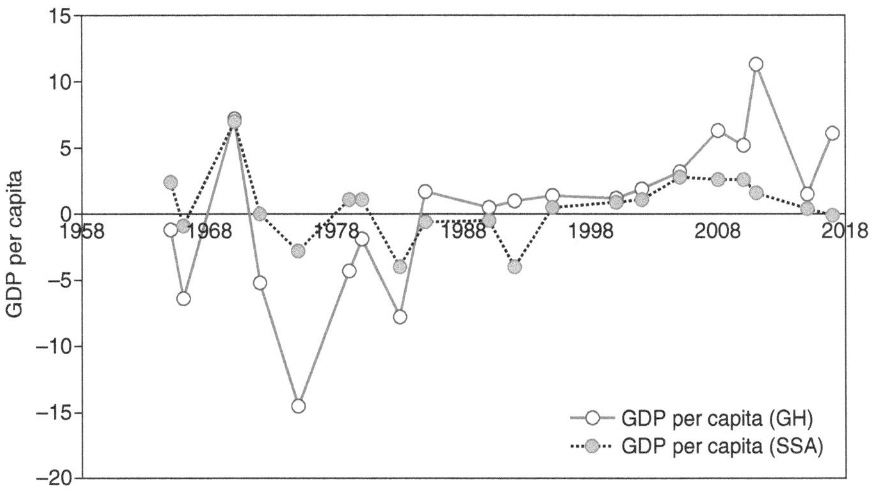

Figure 1.1 GDP per capita: Ghana and sub-Sahara Africa.

Source: Author's construct based on Africa Development Bank, 2018.

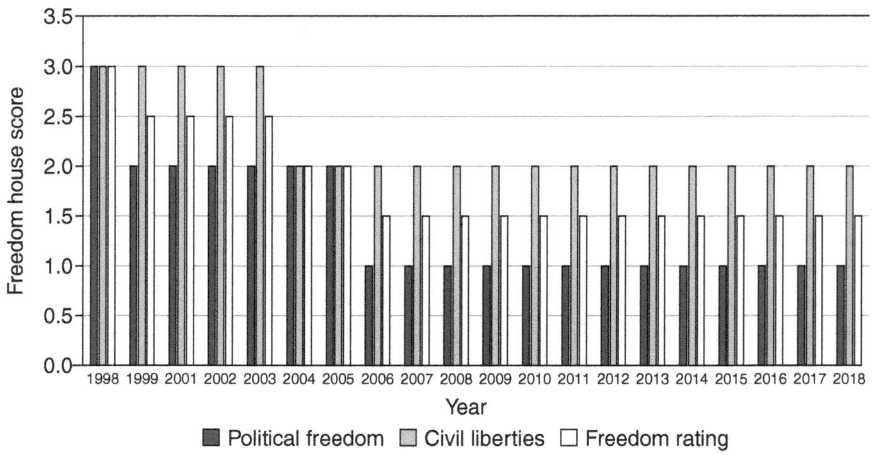

Figure 1.2 Freedom House scores: Ghana (1998–2018).

Source: Author's construct based on Freedom House, 2018.

continuously intrigued, weakened, and undermined the gains of economic reform efforts, if any. With different global, regional, and national inputs from multiple disciplines and expertise, the theoretical thread that connects these perspectives is the dynamic interactions among political actors (both international and domestic) continue to shape and perpetuate economic outcomes in a transitional polity. With over a generation of economic reform experience, is Ghana really exceptional? What has this sub-Saharan African state done that is worthy of emulation, and what needs to be done to assert and perpetuate any gains of economic reform in this century?

The politics of economic reform

In a global economic order often criticized for marginalization of the developing or underdeveloped regions, there is always research effort in a bid to construe the challenges of economic growth and reform in these regions. These attempts are regularly guided by contested western political and economic ideologies. Discussions of the different processes and outcomes of economic reforms and development plans have often leaned largely on rationalist economic explanations and approaches and de-emphasized the core and disciplinary function of politics – in other words, a depoliticization of most of the issues that contribute to the adoption and implementation of the reform agenda. This is particularly important in a region where international financial institutions (IFIs) use economic models, and economists to offer critical advice and policy directives to help shape the needed outcomes. As noted by Jerven (2015), the tale of African economic growth is strongly linked to the history of policymaking on the continent, especially to the role of foreign policy directions and support. Furthermore, to appreciate the nuances of the policy outcomes in economic development, a study of the political interactions and perspectives of both domestic and foreign actors is of immense value. Therefore, there is the need to repoliticize economic reforms in Africa, to better understand the dynamism of the actors, the processes and some of the new but historically laden challenges that have evolved along the way. Hay and Marsh (1999, p. 9) aptly capture this intellectual need as they referenced Richard Higgot's (1985) rejection of the conception of globalization as merely an economic phenomenon, and also considering it as a "politico-ideological rationalization" of a series of emergent tendencies and trends in the governance of the economy. Consequently, to value the scholarly reflections of gains or otherwise made after a generation of economic reforms in Ghana, conceptual considerations of ideology, institutions, regionalization, and globalization are imperative as these have variedly impacted the course of economic development.

Politics of ideology

Economic reforms in Ghana, and Africa have been driven by ideological overtones that date back to the immediate post-independence socialist and statist agenda of Kwame Nkrumah. Nkrumah's attempts to reconstruct Ghana's economy away from the imperialist economic identity led to the infusion of different economic ideas from renowned development theorists such as William Arthur Lewis who helped develop Ghana's first Five-Year Development Plan (1959–1963). In the past generation, two significant ideological strands have characterized political and economic reforms in Ghana. First is the neo-Marxist conceptualization, which has its bedrock in the political and development ideals of Kwame Nkrumah at independence, and further embraced at different interruptive and insurrectionist moments in the country's history by military interventionists. The second ideology is (neo)liberalism which is well entrenched in the Busia-Danquah tradition in Ghana, and also present in various reform agendas through arrangements promoted by IFIs like the World Bank and IMF, and western countries, and variedly supported by both military and civilian Ghanaian administrations.

Beyond the intent of anti-imperialism and support for African nationalism, in the past three decades, neo-Marxist agenda was mainly encountered in Ghana through the Rawlings-led military interventions in 1979 and 1981. This was much in line with the dominant approach of the dependency theory espoused by Latin American intellectuals, which welded together Marxist ideas and structuralism to critique the squelching impacts of developed world policies on underdeveloped countries within a capitalist global order. In addition to the focus on external factors that explain the struggle of underdeveloped and developing economies to access benefits from the global economy, there is also emphasis on the role of internal factors, and the relationship between both internal and external forces. So, as most revolutionaries and reformists in the underdeveloped world were intrigued and energized by the discourse of Andre Gunder Frank's (1966) that centered on the external influences produced by the dominance of the developed North in their global capitalist linkages with the underdeveloped South, analysis by the Henrique Cardoso and Enzo Faletto (1979) also drew attention to the role of elites in the South. According to the latter school of thought, bureaucratic and national bourgeoisies of countries in the South acted through linkages and alliances with capitalists in the developed North to further perpetuate a relationship of dependency which disadvantaged the underdeveloped.

Though the Rawlings-led regimes in Ghana's political history spent most of the almost two decades in political power pursuing a neoliberal ideological agenda mainly at the behest of IFIs and the West, the initial approach to radically reforming a free-falling Ghanaian economy in the early 1980s heavily gleaned from neo-Marxist ideas as the call for a change in the global economic order was juxtaposed with the injection of domestic conversations of class and social justice in the Ghanaian society. This consisted of tapping into the ethos of African nationalism as well as the controversial "domestic house-cleaning" efforts to purge the political and economic system of corrupt elites (compradors) (see Oquaye, 2004). At the World Summit for Social Development in 1995, Jerry Rawlings (n.d.) asserted:

> From our experience in Ghana, we now believe that structural adjustment, to be successful, must be reciprocal. The developed countries must also restructure their economies to reduce excessive consumerism, to pay appropriate prices for primary commodities, and to open up their markets to fair and effective competition. Of course, we have little right to complain unless we can demonstrate that the limited resources available to us are being used equitably and efficiently in the best interests of all our people. But if we are sincerely and effectively making these efforts, and yet it is clearly not enough to address the social injustices in our countries, then are we not justified in questioning the present world order?

The neo-Marxist ideology provides explanation for the initiation and sustenance of the domestic populist fervor that was needed to propel the radical political intervention by Jerry John Rawlings, and to simultaneously help him draw international support from a fraternity of countries and leaders that were intellectually aligned with the neo-Marxist thought and its variants. So, while Rawlings rallied university students and educated urbanites to Ghanaian hinterlands to help transport cocoa beans for export, he trekked around the world to shake hands with leaders like Fidel Castro of Cuba.

Additionally, the (neo)liberalism ideology has considerably shaped Ghana's economic reform agenda over the past three decades. Gyimah-Boadi and Jeffries (2000) state that the study of the politics of economic policy in Africa has been largely dominated by the liberal political economy as they challenge the rationalist argument by Robert Bates's (1981) projection that African leaders and elites are rational actors – maximization of their interests and gains through the fostering of an "urban bias" political economy by ploughing the agricultural resources and gains from rural areas to benefit urban elites, in the interest of political expediency. Bates's thesis seem plausible with a review of post-independent government administrations (including the military ones) that were largely haunted by the enormously high popular expectations and hence will grasp onto any approach to ensure the crucial urban support. As Gyimah-Boadi and Jeffries (2000) counter this line of reasoning and other aspects of Bates's argument, they also elevate the discourse of liberalization – a main feature of the Washington Consensus – in Ghana's reform policy.

The Washington Consensus has featured as market fundamentalism, and many scholars simply perceive it as an embodiment of neoliberal reforms which dominated academic discussions, media and policy domains, and corporate organizations in both developing and developed world (Broad, 2004). As conceptualized by the economist John Williamson, the ideas expressed in the Washington Consensus were politically embraced and further evoked by economic departments, institutions, and agencies in Washington. Though Williamson's conceptualization consists of 10 major policy prescriptions, the list largely captures three dominant areas – liberalization, deregulation, and privatization. From the 1990s, these policy prescriptions were packaged into bilateral and multilateral trade and investment arrangements with developing countries, including Ghana. With the advent of the post-Cold War era, the Washington Consensus became the only way, and the desirability of its policies was presented as an objective economic truth (Broad, 2004, p. 132). In the early 1980s, Ghana's economic reform was introduced with the Economic Recovery Programme (ERP) by the Rawlings and the PNDC administration, in conjunction with IMF and World Bank-sponsored Structural Adjustment Program (SAP). This was an adjoined attempt to combine structural and fiscal reform measures to help an anemic economy from inflationary burdens, balance-of-payment deficits, weak manufacturing sector, and deficiencies in other economic sectors. To help resuscitate the Ghanaian economy after decades of inconsistent economic planning and implementation coupled with an unsettling nature of political regime change, the key neoliberal tenets of deregulation, liberalization, and privatization were embraced to help improve revenue collection, increase manufacturing through increased investment opportunities, deal with a weaken local currency, and diversify the exports to improve the balance-of-payment deficits.

Besides the reintroduction and stability of democratic governance in the early 1990s, there were some notable achievements of the neoliberal economic reform agenda that earned Ghana the references of exceptionalism as a dedicated reformer in Africa. By the mid-1990s, the reforms had marked a reduction of tariffs to a relatively uniform range of 10–25%, lower corporate taxes to 35%, and capital gains tax to 5% (Opoku, 2010). Additionally, state-owned enterprises were privatized and other incentives offered to infrastructure investors to help increase foreign direct investment (FDI) (Opoku, 2010). Such economic reform initiatives enabled Ghana's economy to maintain an average GDP growth of 5.2% from 1983 to 1990 albeit a decline to 4.4% in the 1990s (Hutchful, 2002).

As shown in Figure 1.1, GDP per capita displayed relatively stable and significant improvement since 1985.

That said, neoliberal ideology packaged into the Washington Consensus and delivered through SAPs and other economic reforms to countries like Ghana has not been without protest and blame. The negative impacts of this ideological approach to economic reform have mostly been socioeconomic, chiefly, the inequalities created or deepened as a result of neoliberal policies. Though the global pushback of the Washington Consensus blame neoliberal ideals for fomenting corporate scandals in the developed world (Broad, 2004), the critics have been the harshest from developing and underdeveloped countries in Africa, Asia, and Latin America where liberalization, deregulation, and privatization of economies have contributed to the outcry of workers, companies, environmentalists, and most significantly poverty-stricken populations who aver that the neoliberal agenda has not been pro-poor. John Williamson, the conceptual architect of the Consensus later acknowledged "I deliberately excluded from (my) list (of the 10 areas) anything which was primarily redistributive ... because I felt the Washington of the 1980s to be a city that was essentially contemptuous of equity concerns" (1993, p. 1329, as quoted in Broad & Cavanagh (1999, p. 81)). Despite the accolades mainly from international observers, the impacts of these arrangements on Ghana are perceived to be wide-ranging and long-term as different sectors of the economy have seen various degrees of competition from imports and foreign investments (Opoku, 2010) – a development imputed for deindustrialization. Hence, in the past generation, the ideological insufficiencies have been quite vivid in Ghana's economic reform path, necessitating continuous reform attempts to mainly achieve stabilization of macroeconomic gains.

Evidently, the ideological vacillation between Marxist and liberal approaches to economic development reforms in Africa is one that remains unchanged for two main reasons. First, most countries often lack the political stability and continuity to effectively engineer and implement economic reforms with certainty and consistency. Ghana, the often-cited exemplary economic reformer has existed slightly over two generations with half of its life span exemplifying a political culture of uncertainty characterized by military interventions in politics. Second, to scholars and stakeholders, the (neo)liberal approach to economic reform as espoused through the Washington Consensus and related arrangements such as the SAPs has not lived up to the hype, especially pertaining to resolving inequities in economic growth, addressing issues of environment injustices, and providing respite from many of the socioeconomic challenges that ail societies in the developing world (see Broad, 2004). Hence, for African states like Ghana, despite the spurts of positive economic growth accorded to the neoliberal order, there is still a search for other approaches that will encourage resilient and consistent growth in a rather volatile global economic system. Whether the overall economic reform goal is redistributionist or creation of wealth and opportunities, Ghana may be unique in terms of gaining some of the benefits that accrue to the long-suffering of neoliberal ideological reforms, but not immune from the impacts caused by deficiencies of such an economic approach.

Politics of institutions

Robert Keohane's (1989, pp. 3–4) definition of institutions as "persistent and connected sets of rules that prescribe behavioral roles, constrain activity and shape expectations" underscores the thought that institutions, both formal and informal, can and do change. African leaders have often shown opposition or reluctance to sociopolitical change, particularly when externally induced and with their administrations or states as perceived targets. Thus, they have held on and used the state and other institutions to project power and authority, and, in effect, to either extend their terms of office or shape their legacies. This makes the study of issues of political and economic change a good gauge for the workings of the African state – a tool for improvement of economic conditions and well-being or otherwise in Africa (Herbst, 1993). Second, the health of institutional reforms is also a reliable indication of the sustainability of long-term economic growth. According to Bates (1990), one implication is that those studying developing areas face a subject that stands at the very frontline of the field of political economy: the problem of institutional origins. To appreciate discussions of issues and outcomes pertaining to economic reforms in Ghana in the past three decades, a look at the changing nature of the state and other institutions like the private sector and international organizations is quite useful. If institutional development and reform remains an Achilles heel of many African states, is Ghana an example in sustained economic reform because of good and persistent political institutional reform?

In the post-Cold War era, economic reforms in Africa have generally moved along with political changes, mostly democratization. Most countries in Africa, swept by the third wave of democratization fostered by the dominance of western liberalism, were equally nudged to institute reforms to help with economic progress – an often-assumed outcome of political liberalization. For African states like Ghana, acquiescence to political change was a significant means to achieve economic progress and well-being for suffering populations. Nonetheless, once democracy was established and functional in a state, the continuous promise of economic reform remains a useful campaign platform for political organizations. Even for single-party dominant democratic states like Zimbabwe, Angola, and South Africa, the offer of persistent economic reforms as part of the party agenda is critical to preserving the party base and to avert external criticisms, particularly from the international community. As shown by Figures 1.1 and 1.2, Ghana's progress in political liberalization through the consolidation of democratic norms has moved along with some hopeful signs of economic growth, a detour from the abysmal and highly unstable economic performances that preceded the Fourth Republic democratic dispensation. Arguably, this leaves some trail of evidence for the proposition that political reforms further beget economic reforms and the two are somewhat mutually reinforceable as shown by the Ghana case (see Radelet, 2010).

The success or otherwise of economic reforms in African states is incumbent on the existing or evolving relationship between the state and the private sector.

This relationship has witnessed some positive change, albeit glaring challenges. Herbst (1993, p. 5) points to "the poor and antagonistic relationship between government and the private sector" a principal issue that has troubled African states from independence. He further argues that during decolonization, most of the nationalist leaders arose from control of the strongest political parties, and their subsequent successors mostly emerged from military and populist juntas with the control of weapons. Accordingly, leadership did not emerge from the private sector with the needed expertise to help propel these African independent states to economic self-determination, to go along with their political freedoms, unlike their East Asian counterparts. The underlying cause for this issue was the clear distrust of the private sector, particularly foreign capital which was perceived by these leaders as a threat to their political existence. This character continued to daunt African states well into the 1980s and 1990s as Handley (2008) and Taylor (2007) note that collaboration between African governments and the business community has not impacted policymaking. In Ghana, Opoku (2010) demonstrates this situation by drawing on the extreme anti-private sector measures adopted by the Rawlings and his PNDC government to undermine opposition-aligned capitalist ventures. Even though this proved inimical to the overall national economic growth, similar to the immediate post-independence leaders, it fortified his political position and also enabled clientelism and patronage. Though remnants of this culture still linger as governments often overreach into the activities of the private sector, there has been some progress within the past generation in Ghana. Following Rawlings's economic liberalization arrangements within the ERP and SAP reform packages, deregulation and privatization policies were encouraged to help boost foreign investments, increase revenue flow, and strengthen the local currency – cedi. The foreign capital that trickled in from the 1980s and 1990s along with technical expertise largely from western states and institutions further increased as the Kufuor government that succeeded Rawlings, declared the "Golden Age of Business" in 2001.

President Kufuor and the New Patriotic Party (NPP) administration's resolve to attract more private sector capital, and make the Ghanaian economy more globally competitive included the establishment of a new Ministry for Private Sector Development, and the strengthening of existing reforms such as the Financial Sector Reform Programme (FINSAP), which was initially implemented between 1988 and 1999. In order to position Ghana as the subregional economic gateway, and improve state–private sector relations, a new wave of reforms was launched under the banner of the Financial Sector Strategic Plan (FINSSP) in 2003 (Bawumia, 2010). The roles of the Ghanaian state and the private sector in the past generation were also significant and became more prominent after the 2007 oil discovery. Though post-Kufuor, subsequent government administrations of both the National Democratic Congress (NDC) and NPP have attempted to enhance cordiality and efficiency between the institutions of the state and private sector, which is the key to the success of the economic liberal culture (Kennedy, 1980), the biographical account by George Yaw Owusu titled *In Pursuit of Jubilee: A True Story of the First Major Oil Discovery in Ghana* (2017) alleges several incidents that undermine aspects of this relationship. Nevertheless, over the past three decades, various attempts at economic reform have produced some institutional progress regarding private sector development despite the existing bottlenecks.

The politics of economic reform which encourages structural changes emphasizes the significant role of institutions in fostering economic change rather than the dominant role of personalities which is quite common throughout Africa's post-independent era, as leaders such as Nkrumah, Nyerere, and Kaunda embodied the ideological reforms they directed in their respective states. In the case of Ghana, as in many other African countries, military administrations that succeeded nationalist leaders often charted this approach as these military bureaucracies sought to achieve the whims of the leader, which was also likely in line with the populist demands that have propelled or supported the revolt or regime change. For example, the use of "Junior Jesus" in adulation and support of Jerry John (J. J.) Rawlings on his arrival on the political scene through 1979 and 1981 positioned him as the fulcrum of the entire attempt to roll back years of failed post-independent political and economic provisions. Such endeavors produce Nugent's (1995) conception of "big men" in Ghanaian politics who use existing institutions (e.g., civil service) as patronage resources instead of tools for achieving social and economic goals (Killick, 2005). This personality-driven (or personal rule) change also permeates into the general work environment as Opoku (2010, p. 197) notes that for many years the public sector in Ghana has been characterized by

> the persistence of a bureaucratic ethos of deliberate delays, an aversion to transparency, and the tendency to privatize office for personal gain. Additionally, public officers in Ghana often treat their workplace like their personal domain and make their own rule to undermine existing laid down procedures and rules.

Though such sentiments still persist, however, along with political change in Ghana, economic reforms over the past three decades have been significantly borne by institutions with varied objectives of restructuring or doing so at the prod of international institutions that often precondition resources and donations with such efforts. Thus, there is the general promotion of the role of established institutions (formal and informal) in performing their roles irrespective of the underwhelming results often reported. Intriguingly, after decades of economic reforms to help strengthen the Ghanaian economy and reframe institutions that inefficiently deal with inequities, the proverbial "whom-you-know" as a means to diverse opportunities in Ghana is still pervasive, but often cautioned by the resounding reminder that "Africa doesn't need strongmen, it needs strong institutions" opined Barack Obama in 2009 (White House, 2009).

Related to the above, the roles played by various formal and informal institutions in attempts at reform underscore one significant development – discussion of Ghanaian agency in stimulating and supporting economic reforms and growth.

After years of economic reforms initiated by IFIs such as IMF and the World Bank, scholars and stakeholders often note the relative absence or erosion of African agency in the structure and implementation of such reform packages, hence results are often not attuned with the domestic situation or rather unsustainable as general preconditions of the reform policy undermine the overall goals. Reform programs like the SAPs were heavily criticized for lack of African (in this case Ghanaian) input and initiative, ultimately, eroding the capacity for the state to function in its own varied interests, especially in a competitive globalized market. However, a review of individual economic sectors in the state may provide an alternative view. Buur and Whitfield (2011) conclude that Ghana's cocoa sector reforms in the late 1980s and early 1990s produced some beneficial outcomes through the insistence on partial liberalization by the Rawlings administration, and also represented the administration's effort to stand up to the IMF and World Bank institutions as they monitored structural adjustment reforms. Again, with instances from Ghana, Mohan and Lampert (2012) assert that China's recent resurgence in Africa shows that at various levels, African actors have shaped and driven Chinese engagements in important ways. The value of the Ghanaian agency in its relationships with Asian partners like China is further explored in this volume in Chapters 5 and 7.

Politics of regionalization and globalization

Over the past three decades, discussions related to the exemplariness or otherwise of Ghana's economic reforms are within the context of regionalization and globalization as they often underscore the comparison of cases within Africa, the developing world, and the global economy as a whole. This is quite significant as scholars and other stakeholders in African economies have discussed the lack of pertinent gains from regionalization or continental economic integration. Similarly, globalization has been perceived both as a transformative force as well as possessing weakening tendencies that can erode or challenge gains from economic reform policy in Africa. The discourse of globalization is defined by conceptual cul-de-sacs such as internationalization, liberalization, universalization, and most significant for the post-Cold War era, westernization (see Scholte, 2005) that de-emphasizes political and economic exclusivity. Hence, regionalization with multiple benefits like regional trade agreements (RTAs), and the alignment of security policies to fight the scourge of terror offers a conceptual conduit for the promotion of some uniqueness in an interconnected global system.

Mainly championed by Ghana's Kwame Nkrumah, Africa's attempt at regionalization dates back to the immediate post-independent era when the African nationalism – a potent ideology – was appropriately harnessed to encourage political and economic development in the various independent polities. It was also evident in Nkrumah's attempt to regionalize the liberation struggle against colonial rule by extending political and economic support to other African colonies after Ghana's independence. Needless to say, this garnered more political notoriety for the leaders, but less in economic self-determination for the individual countries. Hence the post-Cold War acceleration of the traits and tendencies of the concept of globalization challenged Africa's unfinished project of regional political and economic harmonization. In terms of globalization, Ghana has developed and maintained productive relationships with most of the global financial institutions such as the IMF and World Bank. Today, would globalization as liberalization or westernization offer a realignment with global powers or reforms within Africa (Ghana) to enable access to the benefits of reform policies as has occurred in other regions like Asia? This query is particularly necessary as contemporary globalization is largely concentrated in the triad of North America, Europe, and East Asia, marginalizing regions like sub-Saharan Africa in an asymmetric global level playing field (Pieterse, 2004). In this volume, Ernest Opoku-Boateng, Mariam Dekanozishvili, Naaborle Sackeyfio, and Isaac Odoom all examine elements from the North America–Europe–East Asia triad as they present various arguments on Canada, the European Union, and other East Asian cases. So, even with conceptual deficiencies with regard to regionalization and globalization in Africa, how has the politics of these concepts shaped the discourse of economic reforms in an African case like Ghana?

First, globalization and regionalization have helped situate the discussions of economic reforms and development in North–South or South–South contexts, which are both pertinent political frameworks for analysis of the benefits or otherwise of these economic reforms. Many scholars that have studied and written on economic reforms in Ghana often begin with the puzzle of unequal development outcomes between Ghana and some Asian countries like South Korea and Malaysia that all achieved political independence around the same period (see Herbst, 1993; Lal & Myint, 1996). This intriguing quandary points to the discussion of difference in ideological and pragmatic approaches to economic reforms despite similarities in the course of political history and development. Since the days of the decolonization struggles in Africa, countries like Ghana drew inspiration from South–South solidarity to build new political and economic systems, away from the structures of colonial rule. Alternatively, the postcolonial aspirations of economic self-determination have been broadly influenced by ideas and arrangements from the global North, making North–South relationships pertinent to the adoption and implementation of economic policies. In the past two decades, while Ghana has continued to accept and attempt economic reform agenda from IFIs and countries in the global North, like other African countries, it has found China's approach to economic reform and development rather appealing and with diverse possibilities for poverty eradication, and acceleration of industrialization. Thus, in terms of reforms to engender economic growth in Ghana, both South–South and North–South linkages have immensely, but diversely shaped Ghana's global and regional favorability.

Globalization and regionalization with the attendant features of internationalization and interdependence are manifestations of the neoliberal economic reforms that Ghana often represents. From the implementation of the SAPs in the 1980s and 1990s through the HIPC initiative and other financial institutional reforms in the early 2000s, to a recent extended credit facility (ECF), the Ghanaian economy has embodied David Harvey's assertion that "neoliberalism has, in short become hegemonic as a mode of discourse and has become incorporated into the commonsense way many of us interpret, live in, and understand the world" (2005, p. 3). In the process of considering neoliberal reforms to either jump-start its decline-bound economy in the 1980s or sustain growth gains made as a result of past reform attempts, Ghana's efforts captured the ideals of globalization. According to Callinicos (2007) the lens through which to view globalization is that of the historical development of capitalism as a world system, and for African countries like Ghana that largely remain in the margins of a global economy for various structural reasons, the path to modernization and hence a place in the contemporary global economic system is to advance neoliberal economic policies. On the other hand, critics argue that Ghana's conformation to forces of globalization through neoliberal economic reforms with emphasis on liberalization, deregulation, and privatization is yet to produce "a single unambiguous success story in the past 30 years" (Opoku, 2010, p. 155). Concurrently, Thomas Risse (2007) points to the structuralist argument that globalization produces anonymous forces through financial markets or global production networks which command the global economy, diminishing the autonomy of states to freely make decisions of social policy and welfare which impacts the local population.

Finally, the concepts of regionalization and globalization contribute to a shared sense of African development. Samuel Huntington (2004) suggests that modernization, economic development, urbanization, and globalization have led people to rethink identities and to redefine them narrower, more intimately, communal terms. Over the past three decades, as Ghana's economic reform experience is offered as exemplary by western institutions and countries other African states have either deepened relations with Ghana or reached out to glean from the country's evolving experiences in political and economic reform. This possibility exists for other African countries as globalization fosters hybridization which is plainly interdependent in different ways (Ferguson and Mansbach, 2012, p. 144) and as stated by Lieber and Weisberg (2002, p. 150) "we are constantly borrowing, imitating and incorporating just as we are distinguishing and differentiating ourselves by innovative, exclusive or singular expressions." The chapters by Saliou Dione, Abdoulaye Saine, and Fatuma Guyo in this book underscore the significance of Ghana as an insightful example to the respective cases of Senegal, Gambia, and Kenya.

Ghana's economic reforms: The three-decade experience

There are two significant points of note in Ghana's economic reform experience. First, the country's economic reform over the past generation has been dominated by neoliberal arrangements largely espoused through the Washington Consensus. Second, the consequential role of the leadership and legacy of Jerry Rawlings positions him as a crucial nexus in the complexity of factors that drove political and economic change in Ghana. Evidently, Ghana's economic reform experience offers a case that underscores the challenges of attempting economic reforms along with political institutional reforms in sub-Saharan Africa – one that offers different set of outcomes compared to examples from Asia and Latin America (Bienen & Herbst, 1996). Like most cases of political and economic transformation in Africa, Ghana's acquiescence to different approaches to domestic economic reform has been largely prompted by political change, and vice versa. Gyimah-Boadi and Jeffries (2000) show this association in a politico-historical approach that recounts and digests the pursuit for economic reforms within different political regimes from the Acheampong military regime to the ascendance of the Rawlings regime (from 1970 to 1996) – a crossover from military politics into democratic governance.

Assessing the efficacy and coverage of Robert Bates's (1981) arguments on urban bias in Ghana (especially during the Acheampong administration), Gyimah-Boadi and Jeffries (2000) show the importance of the urban electorate, linked to the above-mentioned points – the dominance of neoliberalism, and the Rawlings factor in economic reform. After economic decay and uncertainty in the 1970s and early 1980s, and a brief interlude of neo-Marxist agenda by Rawlings and his Armed Forces Revolutionary Council (AFRC) regime, the introduction of neoliberal policies highlighting deregulation, liberalization, and privatization, also happened under Rawlings the PNDC and NDC administrations.

To discuss the main phases and themes related to Ghana's reform experience over the past three decades, it is essential to reframe these rather broad and often chronologically analyzed stages in Ghana's economic reform evolution to capture both the dominant politics of the era as well as the changes to economic policy. Over the past generation, one of the transcending political denominators to the various attempts at economic growth and reform in Ghana has been the personality and politics of Jerry Rawlings. Thus, it is useful to catalog such reform experiences as pre-Rawlings (also referred to as the era of economic decline in Ghana), Rawlings, and post-Rawlings eras. Apart from the obvious reason of length of time in office, given the little over two-decade rule by Rawlings under both military and civilian rule, this frame is particularly notable for three important reasons. First and chiefly, Rawlings represents a confluence between dictatorship and democratic development – one that required some political commitment or pressure to crossover. Scholars like Ninsin (2015), and Shillington (1992), have expressed the reluctance of Rawlings and his PNDC administration to embark on the democratic reforms in the 1990s except for the pressure from foreign donor institutions that urged the administration to consider political reforms along with economic assistance. However, though a "reluctant democrat," Ninsin (2015) argues that Rawlings went through the stages of democratic development with his own intents and purposes until the trajectory of political reforms was irreversible in 1992. Thus, the move from a military dictator to democratic leadership was partly necessitated by a dreadful need for economic reform and development which required some external donor assistance, spurring Rawlings toward political change (see Handley, 2013).

Second, Rawlings's entry into Ghanaian politics illustrates Richard Sandbrook's "New Broom" hypothesis which recognizes that there is less incentive for economic reforms by corrupt networks who reap from prevailing statist arrangements though they will reluctantly agree to much needed loans and grants from IMF and World Bank with the intent to downplay the conditions attached to these loans (2000). However, the new broom offered to a new political dispensation may help sweep away the economically unproductive clientele networks and government-enabled rents unhindered by the entrenched groups (Sandbrook, p. 76). In both military interventions in 1979 and 1981, Rawlings rode a wave of mass popular support for his house-cleaning measures and draconian approach to punishing past government functionaries declared guilty of corruption by established administrative tribunals. Thus, handed the broom on two occasions, his administrations were empowered to 'clean the mess' of the previous administrations, with almost no checks and balances as the Rawlings-led military interventions had infused fear into any would-be opposition through firing squads, arrests, and detentions, and threatening some alleged corrupt opponents (see Oquaye, 2004).

Third, the initial economic reform efforts by Rawlings and his PNDC administration were crucial and foundational to subsequent outcomes with long-term effects on economic growth policy in Ghana. Most significant of these preparations was the ideological debate that set the tone for the adoption of particular economic reforms and adjustments policies in Ghana. Eboe Hutchful (2002) details the intense ideological arguments between the "monetarists" and the "structuralists" in the early attempts at economic reform by the PNDC administration – differences in approaches that shaped policies regarding currency devaluation and the institution of a national self-reliant macroeconomic framework – to set the basis for a sound negotiation with external actors like the IMF. Such evidence of political and technocratic deliberations offers the discourse of economic reforms in Ghana some ideological credibility from the start, and which subsequently shaped policy outcomes.

Pre-Rawlings era: economic decline in Ghana

Clearly, the necessity for economic reforms in Ghana comes from the combination of factors that negatively impacted the post-independent economy, largely among them, the instability of the political climate to allow for continuity of economic development policy and programs. The results of this political deficiency were both visible in microeconomic indicators, as well as the macroeconomic structure – abysmal and unstable GDP and income figures, a monoculture export economy, uncertain development agenda that switches between nationalization and liberalization, and a weak state perpetuating the colonial predatory and kleptocratic tendencies. Huq (1989) asserts that the failure of the economy to grow and the resultant fall in the living standard of average Ghanaians represented a major feature of post-independent Ghana. Figure 1.1 depicts the sluggish nature of GDP growth in the post-independent era. Between 1971 and 1983,

GDP per capita declined considerably at an average yearly rate of about 4%, and this impact was very evident into the early 1980s of the Rawlings years as per capita income stood at $350 by 1984 lowering Ghana's status from a leading developing country at independence to a low-income developing country (Huq, 1989).

The import and export sectors also showed significant underperformance with the value of exports that was as high as one-quarter of the GDP at the current rates during the later 1950s showing persistent decline to an abysmal 10% in the 1970s, as noted by Huq (1989). This poor sectoral performance could be mainly attributable to the continuous dependence on main raw material exports – cocoa, gold, and timber – often priced in financial hubs in Europe and North America, and a similar fate as industrially manufactured and foreign-priced goods were the predominant imports. Accordingly, this arrangement denotes a continuation of the colonial Gold Coast economy (Shillington, 1992). This balance-of-payments problem was often further deepened by the volatility of the world commodity market which further dwindled or destabilized the windfalls from the traditional exports intended to fund the typically ambitious post-independent projects of infrastructure and industrialization (Shillington, 1992).

After political independence, the development agenda was characterized by illogical pendulous shifts between nationalization and liberalization as Nkrumah and subsequent regimes attempted diverse economic agenda often shaped and directed by political imperatives. The centralization and use of state power and resources – the establishment of state companies and marketing boards packed with political cronies and party supporters of Nkrumah and the CPP, amid other excesses – culminated in the military takeover. In the late 1960s, the liberal Progress Party (PP) and Kofi Busia reverted to liberalization policies with a focus on the cocoa industry which boosted a good windfall, but inadequate economic and political controls led to massive devaluation of the cedi in the early 1970s (Kallick, 2010). According to Kelsall (2013), after the military overthrow of the PP government, Acheampong and the Supreme Military Council (SMC) denounced the liberalization arrangements of the Busia administration and returned to widespread economic controls which included the nationalization of the country's gold mines. Such inconsistent changes in economic agenda that came along with the successive irrational political alternations often pointed to the development of personal rule rather than a well-vetted ideologically sound economic development agenda with the chance of continuity in its pursuit.

Relatedly, with the economic development agenda essentially driven by the post-independent state, the state quickly became an instrument for patronage politics right from the start, as Nkrumah and the CPP used the state to reward their supporters. Job expansion in the civil service and public enterprise, as well as state-sponsored farms in parliamentary constituencies were pursued for political reasons rather than economic rationality (Kallick, 2010). With Nkrumah's statist agenda, national resources were invested in projects that sought to entrench his rule and ideals irrespective of their economic viability and sustainability, leading to a scatter of non-performing projects around the country (Berg,

1971). This approach to political economic development festered along with the decay of the state and its incipient institutions, and also the degeneration in the body politic manifested in economic behavior. Different scholars point to the emergence of the phenomenon of kalabule – a local term for black-marketeering – became excessive as workers in various economic sectors experienced hardships (Austin 1996; Sandbrook, 1985). Kelsall (2013, p. 77) states that at one point during the Acheampong administration, cocoa farmers were receiving only 10% of the world price, which then led to decreasing crop purchases and widespread smuggling of the crop. Consequently, the Acheampong regime's economic mismanagement and excessive misuse of state resources while the rest of the population faced harsh economic conditions led to its label as "one of the continent's worst kleptocracies" (Kelsall, 2013, p. 77).

In almost rapid succession, military takeovers often propelled by the economic hardships in the country, and deterioration of leadership, Lieutenant General Fred Akuffo deposed Acheampong in 1978, only to be ousted from office in the following year by Flight Lieutenant Jerry John Rawlings. Hutchful (2002, pp. 33–34) aptly captures the national mood that preceded the Rawlings military takeover with the assertion that the nature and character of the then political situation in Ghana included "a severe economic crisis and the debilitation and de-institutionalization of the state … and complete delegitimation of the regime … the extensive but shallow and uneven politicization of civil society as a result of this crisis." The overwhelming need for a change in the economic direction and strategies through reforms exists in the unique political economic situations that drove Ghana to the precipice of economic collapse.

Agreeably, Hutchful (2002, p. 34) concludes that "Rawlings' coup both reflected and propelled these proto-revolutionary movements, laying bare deep ideological cleavages within civil society as to how this crisis was to be resolved. This political scenario was to affect the overall political environment within which adjustment was to be approached." The Rawlings era initiated and shaped critical economic reforms that continue to influence the generation of economic development in Ghana.

Rawlings era: recovery and adjustment

The attempt to address Ghana's dire economic situation by the early 1980s was a matter of need as the abysmal economic decline of the post-independent era has been further exacerbated by ongoing changes in the international economic system. Problems like balance-of-payment deficits, fiscal and structural challenges, and lack of dependable socioeconomic infrastructure characterized most developing economies, and required some remedies. On the continent of Africa, Ghana was an example of this widespread economic disorder affecting the developing world.

Debates about the resolution of these economic issues mainly centered on the roles of the Bretton Woods institutions – IMF and World Bank – both driven by orthodoxy from the developed world and the imperatives of struggling developing economies like Ghana. So, the need to provide financial resources and technical expertise for stagnated economies (including Ghana) was undergirded by neoliberal ideals like deregulation, privatization, and liberalization, which required structural reforms. Like other countries in Africa and the developing world where statist arrangements have dominated most of the post-independent era, Ghana's structural reforms meant minimization of the role of the state to allow for the reframe of trade policy, deregulation to ease the business environment, and opening up the private sector for increased investment. Thus, Kahler (1990) avers that the initiation of structural adjustment by the IMF consisted of both the resurgent ideology of the developed industrialized world and the structuralist realities and demands of the developing world. Therefore, the combined policy-based lending with greater control over the framing of internal policies was adopted. From the World Bank's point of view, Ghana presented an exceptional example of policy-based lending, and with a compliant political administration, it also offered a good testing ground for the approaches of economic adjustment (Hutchful, 2002). Ghana's economic reform path from 1983 was a combination of the elements of the ERP by the Rawlings administration with the IMF-sponsored SAP. What was the ERP and SAP in Ghana, and how did these two significant economic reform programs impact the economy during Rawlings's era? From the perspective of Rawlings and the PNDC, the ERP was a necessity intended to weather the economic challenges that had worsened through the 1970s and early 1980s, and with the risk of economic collapse. The litany of political–economic crises includes: the 1983 famine brought on by the widespread bush fires that destroyed vast vegetation cover, farms, and plantations; the dry seasonal spell that led to a drop in water level in the Volta Lake affecting hydroelectric power production from the Akosombo dam necessitating electric power rationing; popular outcry against the effects of the 1983 budget of austerity; a cut in Nigerian oil supplies and subsequent deportation of over a million Ghanaian residents from Nigeria (see Rawlings, n.d.). Thus, the immediate intent of the ERP according to Hutchful (2002), was to generate a theoretical path through revision–renewal–preservation as epitomized by the threefold approach to economic recovery and reform.

The first phase (ERP I – 1983–1986) was directed at stabilization to reduce inflation and offer external equilibrium; promotion of economic growth by building a resilient export sector through a boost of incentives in productive sectors and restoration of the socioeconomic infrastructure (Rawlings, n.d.). First under this phase was exchange rate reform, which include series of currency devaluations were issued to bring the cedi to par with the international market rate, to help with debt-service payments, and licenses granted to foreign exchange bureaus to trade in foreign currencies. Second was the focus on the elimination of price and distribution controls which started with the reduction of goods and services subject to government price controls. Third emphasized fiscal and monetary discipline by setting credit limits to check expenditure, and contract budget deficit while reforming the tax structure to open up other streams of revenue collections. Fourth directed attention to the export sector rehabilitation which removed obstacles that deterred export producers and incentivized their work. For instance, the Cocoa Marketing Board (CMB) was reformed, and export earnings retention scheme introduced to permit withholding of foreign exchange proceeds such as 45% in the case of Ashanti Goldfields Corporation. Fifth effort with the ERP I phase was to ensure public sector investment through elimination of infrastructural limitations to ensure that economic growth is well supported.

The second phase (ERP II – 1987–1990) represented the adjustment stage with efforts to strengthen ongoing reforms while minimizing and correcting existing economic policy weaknesses. Since this phase followed the introduction of the Structural Adjustment Facility (SAF), targets included annual real GDP rate of 5% and the reduction of inflation to a double-digit 25% to 8% in 1990 (Frimpong-Ansah, 1992). Other structural and institutional reforms focused on the financial and education sectors, and also prevailing state enterprises. In this phase of the ERP, legislation was designed to regulate minerals and mining and further meant to control small-scale mining – an issue that has currently become a national nuisance with Chinese illegal artisanal gold mining dominating the headlines. Based on research, Richard Aidoo explores this particular issue in Chapter 8 of this volume. Other critical legislation introduced include the National Investment Code, establishment of the Ghana Stock Exchange, and a new Banking Law. Most significantly, since this era also witnessed the introduction of the SAF, a major attempt to formally address the socioeconomic impacts of adjustment and the recovery program led to the establishment of the Programme of Actions to Mitigate the Social Costs of Adjustment (PAMSCAD) in 1987. This was a pro-poor endeavor to deal with the social dimensions of adjustment (SDA), and the first of its kind in Africa supported by the World Bank (Hutchful, 2002). As a poverty-focused initiative, PAMSCAD aimed at four affected social groups – small farmers and hired labor; poor households with limited access to social services such as water, healthcare, and education; unemployed and those with meagre incomes; and households in the often-marginalized northern regions of Ghana.

The third phase (ERP III – after 1993) was meant to sustain and accelerate the achievements gained through the recovery and adjustment phases. Based on the Accelerated Growth Strategy (AGS), the efforts were directed at encouraging sustainable development and poverty reduction through private sector initiatives. With good projected targets for GDP, inflation and other microeconomic indices, and emphasis on inter-sectoral growth initiatives (Hutchful, 2002). Most notable was the introduction of a coordinated program of socioeconomic development – a blueprint commonly known as Ghana Vision 2020 – which characterized Ghana's intended economic policy as "open and liberal market economy" with the objective of maximizing the welfare and well-being of all Ghanaians. The most pertinent vision of Ghana Vision 2020 was the transformation of Ghana from a low-income to a middle-economy country within a generation – an objective Ghana realized in 2011 when the World Bank revised its classification of the Ghanaian economy (see Aryeetey and Baah-Boateng, 2016).

The ERP, which embodied the tenets of the SAPs in Ghana, was also geared toward the remedy of the long-term balance-of-payment problems developed in the 1970s, and like other African countries, this included external help with the existing or looming debt crisis. Assistance included more lending through loans and grants, and some debt forgiveness. A known feature of SAPs along with all the several objects contained in the ERP was the policy-based lending, which was a shift from project-based lending, and intended to provide sufficient motivation for borrowing countries to keep their national economies structurally sound and sustainable. Policy-based lending consists of two main instruments, namely Structural Adjustment Lending (SAL) and Sectoral Adjustment Lending (SECAL) – both envisioned as "quick disbursement loans supporting reform program which addressed the structural causes of macroeconomic imbalances and poor economic performance (World Bank, 1998, p. 2).

Chitonge (2015) notes that with such frame and aim, SAPs are both diagnostic and prescriptive as they are designed to provide reform recommendations and conditional resources to help restore the national economy. Generally, SAPs have had a disappointing record across Africa as most governments have often implemented SAPs reluctantly, partially, and only under external pressure. Reasons offered include the effects of devaluation and the impacts of austere measures on the socioeconomic well-being of populations, the misfit of the assumptions of the neoclassical models as African governments often maintain bigger roles in economic planning and institutions, and the inclusion of controversial post-Cold War political condition by western IFIs and states (particularly the US and the Washington-based institutions) requiring less corruption and greater democracy (Grosh, 2010). As many on the continent failed or were challenged in recovery and adjustment, Ghana's exceptionalism in achieving the accolade of possessing the most notable adjustment record in Africa may simply be due to a less extent on government willingness and to a greater degree on the nature of economic desperation with a paucity of options. This was particularly so as per capita GDP in Ghana had declined for nearly a decade before Ghana began structural adjustment (Grosh, 2010). Hence, government had to provide some sense of economic respite to counter the prolonged despair.

Post-Rawlings era: HIPC and the golden age of business

In 2000, the political tide switched to John Kufuor and the NPP after winning an election runoff with 56.6%. This new political era was the first time in over two decades that the power to frame and execute economic policy had changed hands, away from the original architect of Ghana's economic recovery and SAPs – Jerry Rawlings. In spite of the newness and hope in political change, the 1990s have generally been characterized by macroeconomic instability with high expenditure, fiscal deficits, unstable cedi, and high inflation. These led to a culmination of dramatic economic collapse during the last year and a half of the Rawlings administration, stemming from severe terms-of-trade shock (Opoku, 2010, p. 158). Consequently, on assumption of office by Kufuor and the NPP,

Ghana became an HIPC in 2001. This was an initiative introduced jointly by the World Bank and the IMF in 1996 with the objective of helping developing countries to reduce external debt burden. To enable countries like Ghana concentrate on a pro-growth and pro-poor economic agenda, HIPC was designed to offer debt-ridden countries a robust exit from the situation of debt crisis (Chitonge, 2015) with two iterations of the initiative – HIPC 1 and 2. HIPC 2 was hailed as an improvement over HIPC 1 as it guarantees broader, deeper, and faster debt relief, and this was demonstrated in 2005 as the HIPC 2 initiative was augmented by the Multilateral Debt Relief Initiative (MDRI) following the G8 meeting at Gleneagles, which promised 100% debt relief for poor countries by multilateral lenders like the EU (Chitonge, 2015, p. 98).

How did the post-independence economic hope turn so bleak at the start of the millennium? Opoku (2010, p. 158) ponders over "this reversal of fortune" despite the glimpses of achievements during the neoliberal economic reforms by Rawlings and the PNDC, and draws on the World Bank's assessment which perceives the problem facing the Ghanaian economy "as failure to pursue sound macro-economic policies." Grappling with the optics of Ghana becoming an HIPC and the underwhelming achievements after years of economic reform, Kufuor announced at his inauguration a new era in Ghana dubbed a "golden age of business" and proceeded to introduce institutions, policies, and initiatives that underscored the private sector as the engine of economic growth in Ghana. Evidence of these efforts include the creation of a Ministry of Private Sector Development, and a Private Sector Development Strategy, the establishment of Ghana Investment Fund, introduction of a farmer ownership scheme known as the Corporate Village Enterprise (COVE) and diverse Presidential Special Initiatives (PSI) intended to increase domestic production and manufacturing. Two of the known PSI lunched were the Integrated Action Programme for Cassava Starch Production and Export, and Export Action Programme for Garments and Textiles in Ghana – initiatives that were directed at opening up locally based production to a global market by taking advantage of the newly proclaimed economic dispensation in Ghana under the Kufuor administration.

Another consequential economic reform effort under the NPP administration was the Financial Sector Reform Programme (FINSAP) (2001–2008) which was directed at building on the gains, and dealing with the bottlenecks in the financial sector realized under the initial FINSAP (1988–1999). Some of the constraints that FINSAP under the Kufuor/NPP administration was to remedy include the cash-dominated payment system, large unbanked population, the absence of credit information system, a complex foreign exchange regime, a general lack of legislative frame that focused on the rights and responsibilities of borrowers and lenders, and also a legal structure that allows Ghana to be recognized as an international and regional financial hub (Bawumia, 2010, p. 111). These reform efforts were collectively placed under the Financial Sector Strategic Plan (FINSSP) aimed at making the financial sector preferable to domestic businesses, promote savings, ensure competitiveness, achieve rigorous regulatory regime as well as a diversified domestic financial sector (Bawumia, 2010,

p. 112). The comprehensive legal reforms that emerged out of these attempts under Kufuor comprise the Bank of Ghana Act 2002, the Banking Act 2004, Payment System Act 2003, Long-term Savings Act 2004, Venture Capital Trust Fund Act 2004, Foreign Exchange Act 2006, Home Mortgage Finance Act 2008, and Borrowers and Lenders Act 2008.

Towards the end of the two terms in office, the Kufuor/NPP administration had a major chance to test the efficacy and progressiveness of these instituted reforms. After years of despondent exploratory expeditions, commercial quantities of hydrocarbons reserves were discovered along Ghana's coastline in 2007 – a find that had until then eluded previous administrations. The oil which was discovered under the NPP administration began pumping in December 2010 under the administration of John Evans Atta-Mills and the NDC. This resource was projected to make a significant contribution to Ghana's development by opening up a crucial revenue source in addition to the regular gold and cocoa exports, and improve the economic well-being of Ghanaians. In Chapter 6, Antoinette Tsiboe-Darko's research evaluates the socioeconomic impacts of the oil industry on local communities, and Isaac Odoom looks at a transnational dynamic in the oil industry by Chinese companies (Chapter 7).

Indicative of the imperfections that arise from most reform attempts, the transfer of power to Atta-Mills and the NDC underscores some of the criticisms that were leveled against Kufuor and the NPP administration and its reform policies. Apart from the widespread effects of election-induced competitive clientelism, which often set back macroeconomic stability as governments ran large budget deficits in election years, the Kufuor/NPP administration was blamed for rampant cronyism among other corrupt activities (Killick 2010; Kelsall, 2013). Opoku (2010, p. 171) asserts that the Kufuor/NPP administration did adopt neoliberal reform arrangements and attempted a clean break from the previous PNDC and NDC administrations in many ways, however, "the promises of "total departure" from Rawlings era remained largely unfulfilled." As Kelsall (2013, p. 79) notes:

> An evaluation of the Private Sector Development Strategy (PSDS) [under Kufuor administration] remarked that the lack of demonstrable impact on "bread and butter" issues made it difficult to attract and sustain political commitment, and some programs had been stymied by personnel changes, both of which contributed to patchy implementation of reforms.

Along with other development resources from Asian countries like China, Ghana continues to embrace diverse forms of economic reform packages from the IMF and World Bank, amid domestic popular and political protests due to the inconsistent outcomes of these reforms. For instance, in April 2015, Ghana received approval for an Extended Credit Facility (ECF) with a three-year arrangement for Special Drawing Rights (SDR) of $918m. The ECF is aimed at restoring debt sustainability and macroeconomic stability in Ghana which will help promote a return to high growth and job creation, while protecting social spending (International Monetary Fund, 2017).

Structure of the book

With over three decades of various political and economic actors in pursuit of economic reforms, and a checkered report card for institutional reforms and economic growth, how have these domestic and international political actors, and varied reform approaches continuously shaped the outcomes of Ghana's economic development efforts? This stocktaking volume with knowledgeable contributors (both in academia and policy worlds) achieves the following objectives: First, it helps establish the uniqueness of Ghana as a case study in Africa, and the developing world in general. This book represents a collection of engaging research and arguments from different scholars who provide discussions highlighting the exceptionality or otherwise of Ghana as a known case for political and economic reforms, on the continent of Africa. Second, this volume offers a presentation of how global and domestic political or institutional actors have variedly contributed to shape Ghana's economic development course in the past three decades. Third, this work offers discussions that enable the reader to assess any changes that have occurred after these economic reforms, as diverse issues confronting Ghana's economic development are explored. Finally, the compilation also offers some reflective discussions offering local and subregional perspectives of the Ghanaian political economy, which is also strongly influenced by both private and state actors from the West and the East.

To achieve the set objectives, the book consists of three main parts: Part I represents a conceptual overview of economic reforms in Ghana. Part II highlights various global and local perspectives of Ghana's experiences at political–economic reforms, and Part III presents perspectives on issues that test the progress of political and economic reforms, as it reviews introspective research accounts of Ghana's stewardship over natural resources. Part III also offers reflective expositions of what other African countries can glean from Ghana's political and economic reform experiences. This introduction is followed by Part I in which Lord Mawuko-Yevugah uses Chapter 2 to set a conceptual background that introduces a framework to show how domestic and international political processes, and actors have shaped both Africa and Ghana's postcolonial economic development vision through economic reforms, particularly based on a neoliberal perspective.

In Part II, Ernest Opoku-Boateng (Chapter 3) offers a fresh take on the neoliberal agenda of the Washington Consensus – a unique Canadian perspective with a human-centered approach to economic and political reforms. With years of cooperation in Ghana, this quiet North American power has been a staunch supporter of political and economic reforms with emphasis on environmental and human rights justice. In Chapter 4, Mariam Dekanozishvili explores the challenges the European Union (EU) faces as a donor, development, and foreign policy actor and how this impact its relations with Ghana, and Africa in general. The subsequent chapter draws on two Asian examples – China and Japan – as Naaborle Sackeyfio contends that despite lucrative economic engagement with China, securing an upper-middle-income status will depend on how Ghana avoids donor state dependency; the lessons gleaned from Japan, and how it navigates externally directed reforms to protect and expand agency.

In Part III, there are three reflective research chapters on issues concerning the management of Ghana's resources: Antoinette Tsiboe-Darko (Chapter 6) brings a new dimension to the debate on social responsibility in the oil industry, which focuses on the role being played by community stakeholders to ensure that oil wealth has wide-ranging benefits for regions that lie close to the exploration. Next, Isaac Odoom (Chapter 7) investigates the role of Ghanaian agency in Ghana–China relations with a focus on Chinese engagement in Ghana's energy sector. He concludes by emphasizing the need for Ghanaian elites to balance their engagement with China and other western actors with a focus on prudent natural resource management. In Chapter 8, Richard Aidoo presents a case study from Ghana's Western Region that deals with a perennial problem in Ghana. Based on research, he shows the role of local actors in the increased Chinese involvement in illegal gold mining (locally known as galamsey), and captures some of the resentment directed toward the Chinese. The chapter reflects on the impacts this issue may have on Ghana–China diplomacy, especially growing economic engagements.

Part III also comprises three other reflective chapters that consider lessons from Ghana's reform experiences, from the perspectives of selected African countries. Saliou Dione's historical and cross-analytic exposition of Senegal's path toward economic self-determination alongside the case of Ghana draws pertinent shared experiences as well as dissimilarities between these two West African neighbors (Chapter 9). In Chapter 10, Abdoulaye Saine explores ways in which Gambia, emerging from 22 years of military and quasi-military dictatorship could potentially glean from Ghana's own democratic and economic successes to further reforms in all vital sectors of its economy and politics. He also contends that a renewed and reinforced Gambia–Ghana relationship, is a win–win proposition, and a worthy example of improved intra-Africa trade. Finally, Fatuma Boru Guyo (Chapter 11) analyzes issues of marginality and social exclusion within the context of socioeconomic and political development of Kenya, and further ponders whether Ghana's democratic reform experiences can offer any practical guidance to Kenya's political development. In the concluding chapter, Richard Aidoo draws on the various themes and discussions in the entire book to address the often-touted exceptionalism of Ghana's politically driven economic reform path.

References

African Development Bank. (2018). Africa Information Highway – GDP by country: Statistics from the World Bank, 1960–2017. Retrieved June 30, 2018, from opendataforafrica.org/mhrzolg/gdp-by-country-statistics-from-the-world-bank-1960-2017?country

Aryeetey, E., & Baah-Boateng, W. (2016). Understanding Ghana's growth success story and job creation challenges. In Bhorat, H. & Tarp, F. (Eds.), *Africa's lions: Growth traps and opportunities for six African economies* (pp. 77–108). Washington, DC: Brookings Institution Press.

Aryeetey, E., Harrigan, J., & Nissanke, M. (2000). *Economic reforms in Ghana: The miracle and the mirage*. Trenton, NJ: Africa World Press.

Austin, G. (1996). National poverty and the vampire state in Ghana: A review article. *Journal of International Development*, *8*(4) 553–573.

Bates, R. (1981). *Markets and states in tropical Africa: The political basis of agricultural policies*. Berkeley: University of California Press.

Bates, R. (1990). Macropolitical economy in the field of development. In James E. Alt & Kenneth A. Shepsle (Eds.), *Perspectives on positive political economy* (p. 48). Cambridge, UK: Cambridge University Press.

Bawumia, M. (2010). *Monetary policy and financial sector reform in Africa: Ghana's Experience*. Accra, Ghana: Combert Impressions.

Berg, E. J. (1971). Structural transformation versus gradualism: Recent economic development in Ghana and Cote d'Ivoire. In Foster P. & Zolberg A. R. (Eds.), *Ghana and Cote d'Ivoire: Perspectives on modernization* (pp. 185–230). Chicago, IL: University of Chicago Press.

Bienen, H., & Herbst, J. (1996). The relationship between political and economic reform in Africa. *Comparative Politics 29*(1) 23–42.

Broad, R. (2004). The Washington Consensus meets the global backlash: Shifting debates and policies. *Globalizations 1*(2) 129–154.

Broad, R., & Cavanagh, J. (1999). The death of the Washington Consensus? *World Policy Journal 16*(3) 79–88.

Buur, L., & Whitfield, L. (2011). Engaging in productive sector development: Comparisons between Mozambique and Ghana (Working Paper 2011: 22). Copenhagen: Danish Institute for International Studies.

Callinicos, A. (2007). Globalization, imperialism, and the capitalist world system. In A. McGrew & D. Held (Eds.), *Globalization theory: Approaches and controversies*. New York, NY: Polity.

Cardoso, H., & Faletto, E. (1979). *Dependency and development in Latin America*. (Marjory M. Urquidi, Trans.). Berkeley: University of California Press.

Chitonge, H. (2015). *Economic growth and development in Africa: Understanding trends and prospects*. Abingdon, UK: Routledge.

Ferguson, Y. H., & Mansbach, R. W. (2012). *Globalization: The return of border to a borderless world*? New York, NY: Routledge.

Frank, A. G. (1966). The development of underdevelopment. *Monthly Review 18*(4), 17–31.

Freedom House. (2018). Freedom in the world 2018: Ghana profile. Retrieved August 3, 2018, from https://freedomhouse.org/report/freedom-world/2018/ghana

Frimpong-Ansah, J. H. (1992). *The vampire state in Africa: The political economy of decline in Ghana*. Trenton, NJ: Africa World Press.

Grosh, B. (2010). Structural adjustment in Africa. In K. A. Appiah & H. L. Gates (Eds.), *Encyclopedia of Africa* (pp. 427–429). Oxford, UK: Oxford University Press.

Gyimah-Boadi, E., & Jeffries, R. (2000). Political economy of reform. In E. Aryeetey et al. (Eds.), *Economic reforms in Ghana: The miracle and the mirage* (pp. 32–50). Trenton, NJ: Africa World Press.

Handley, A. (2008). *Business and the state in Africa: Economic policy-making in the neoliberal era*. Cambridge, UK: Cambridge University Press.

Handley, A. (2013). Ghana: Democratic transition, presidential power, and the World Bank. In K. Stoner & M. McFaul (Eds.), *Transitions to democracy: A comparative perspective* (pp. 221–243). Baltimore, MD: Johns Hopkins University Press.

Harvey, D. (2005). *A brief history of neoliberalism*. Oxford, UK: Oxford University Press.

Hay, C., & Marsh, D. (1999). Introduction: Towards a new (international) political economy? *New Political Economy 4*(1) 5–22.

Higgot, R. (1985). Towards a nonhegemonic IPE: An Antipodean perspective. In C. N. Murphy & R. Tooze (Eds.), *The new international political economy* (pp. 7–21). London, UK: Palgrave.

Herbst, J. (1993). *The politics of reform in Ghana, 1982–1991*. Berkeley: University of California Press.

Huntington S. P. (2004). *Who are we? The challenges to America's national identity*. New York, NY: Simon & Schuster.

Huq, M. M. (1989). *The economy of Ghana: The first 25 years since independence*. London: Macmillan.

Hutchful, E. (2002). *Ghana's adjustment experience: The paradox of reform*. Geneva, Switzerland: United Nations Research Institute for Social Development.

International Monetary Fund (IMF). (2017). Ghana. IMF Country Report No. 17/262. Retrieved October 25, 2018, from www.imf.org

Jerven, M. (2015). *Africa: Why economists get it wrong*. New York, NY: Zed Books.

Kahler, M. (1990). Orthodoxy and its alternative: Explaining approaches to stabilization and adjustment. In J. M Nelson (Ed.), *Economic crisis and policy choice: The politics of adjustment in the third world*. Princeton, NJ: Princeton University Press.

Kelsall, T. (2013). *Business, politics, and the state in Africa: Challenging the orthodoxies on growth and transformation*. New York, NY: Zed Books.

Kennedy, P. (1980). *Ghanaian businessmen: From artisan to capitalist entrepreneur in a dependent economy*. Munich, Germany: Wettforum Verlag.

Keohane, R. O. (1989). Neoliberal institutionalism: A perspective on world politics. In R. O. Keohane (Ed.), *International institutions and state power: Essays in international relations theory* (pp. 3–4). Boulder, CO: Westview Press.

Killick, T. (2005). *The politics of Ghana's budgetary system* (CDD/ODI Policy Brief No. 2). Accra, Ghana: ODI/CDD.

Killick, T. (2010). *Development economics in action: A study of economic policies in Ghana*. Abingdon, UK: Routledge.

Lal, D., & Myint, H. (1996). *The political economy of poverty, equity, and growth: A comparative study*. Oxford, UK: Oxford University Press.

Lieber, R. J., & Weisberg, R. E. (2002). Globalization, culture, and identities in crisis. *International Journal of Politics Culture and Society*, *16*(2), 273–296.

Mohan, G., & Lampert, B. (2012). Negotiating China: Reinserting African agency into China–Africa relations. *African Affairs*, *112*(446) 92–110.

Ninsin K. A. (2015). Ghana. In S. Bitar & A. F. Lowenthal (Eds.), *Democratic transitions: Conversations with world leaders* (pp. 102–137). Baltimore, MD: Johns Hopkins University Press.

Nugent P. (1995). *Big men, small boys, and politics in Ghana. Power, ideology and the burden of history, 1982–1994*. Ann Arbor: University of Michigan Press.

Opoku, D. K. (2010). From a "success" story to a highly indebted poor country: Ghana and neoliberal reforms. *Journal of Contemporary African Studies 28*(2) 155–175.

Oquaye, M. (2004). *Politics in Ghana, 1982–1992: Rawlings, revolution, and populist democracy*. New Delhi, India: Thomson Press.

Overseas Development Institute (ODI). (2011). Mapping progress: evidence for new development outlook. London, UK: Overseas Development Institute.

Owusu, G. Y. (2017). *In pursuit of Jubilee: A true story of the first major oil discovery in Ghana*. USA: Avenue Lane Press.
Pieterse, J. N. (2004). *Globalization and culture*. Lanham, MD: Rowman & Littlefield.
Radelet, S. (2010). *Emerging Africa: How 17 countries are leading the way*. Washington, DC: Center for Global Development.
Rawlings, J. J. (n.d.). Profile – Towards economic recovery and growth. Retrieved September 15, 2018, from www.presidentrawlings.com
Risse, T. (2007). Social constructivism meets globalization. In A. McGrew & D. Held (Eds.), *Globalization theory: Approaches and controversies*. New York, NY: Polity.
Sandbrook, R. (1985). *The politics of Africa's economic stagnation*. Cambridge, UK: Cambridge University Press.
Sandbrook, R. (2000). *Closing the circle: Democratization and development in Africa*. New York, NY: Zed Books.
Scholte, J. A. (2005). Globalization: A critical introduction. New York, NY: Palgrave Macmillan.
Shillington, K. (1992). *Ghana and the Rawlings factor*. New York, NY: St. Martin's Press.
Taylor, S. D. (2007). *Business and the state in Southern Africa: The politics of economic reform*. Boulder, CO: Lynn Rienner.
White House. (2009). Remarks by the President to the Ghanaian Parliament. Retrieved September 20, 2018, from www.obamawhitehouse
Williamson, J. (1993). Democracy and the Washington Consensus. *World Development*, *21*(8) 1329–1336.
World Bank. (1998). Higher Impact Adjustment Lending (HIAL) in sub-Saharan Africa: An update. Retrieved September 30, 2018, from www.worldbank.org

Part I

Conceptual considerations

2 Politicizing economic reform in Africa

Ghana's political–economic framework

Lord Mawuko-Yevugah

Introduction

Since the attainment of political independence in the late 1950s and early 1960s, African countries have been preoccupied with the issue of socioeconomic development and transformation. This preoccupation has resulted in fierce debates among various stakeholders on the most suitable approaches and strategies for accelerated and sustained economic growth and development in the respective African countries. While the first few years of the post-independence era witnessed some modest results in terms of economic growth and infrastructural development, by the end of the first decade after independence, the continent had descended into what has been called the "African crisis" or the "African tragedy" (Arrighi, 2002; Leys 1994). This broadly refers to political instability and economic decay. Thus, by the mid to late 1980s, barely two decades after decolonization on much of the African continent, a new process of economic policy reform became a defining characteristic across the African continent mainly in response to the "crisis of development." What was the nature of policies implemented across the continent during the period of reform? What were the interplay of factors and actors driving these reforms? What have been the implications of the implementation of economic reform policies for the continent's postcolonial developmental and transformative agenda? In order to answer these questions, this chapter explores how an interplay of domestic and international political and economic processes and actors have influenced and shaped Africa's postcolonial developmental vision through the implementation of specific set of policy reforms. In doing so and in order to provide an intellectual context for the analysis throughout the rest of the book, this chapter provides a broad overview of competing theoretical approaches to policy reform historically, and showing how the current neoliberal policy agenda became a hegemonic construct in Africa's postcolonies from the 1980s.

Negotiating conceptual and theoretical issues

While there could be various ways of conceptualizing policy reform, a common thread which runs through every definition sees policy reform as a durable and significant policy change that improves aggregate socioeconomic welfare, consistent also with an objective function that recognizes distributional and environmental considerations. Thus, an underlying rationale for initiating a policy reform ought to be a concern for general welfare, the public interest, rather than particular vested interests. In that regard, for economists, policy reform would have been seen typically as measures that increase productivity and growth rates, but these goals could obviously be redefined to encompass a broader set of non-economic objectives. In addition to particular measures, reforms can also be about policymaking processes, for example greater transparency in policymaking such as when firms claiming special assistance have to submit to a process of public scrutiny and justification. Obviously, not all policy changes would meet this definition of reform. For example, a redistribution program would not unless it could be shown that this program resulted in increased productivity or met more widely accepted social objectives (e.g., social stability). Similarly, programs that are essentially window-dressing exercises such as anti-corruption campaigns introduced by a deeply corrupt regime or "one-stop-service" investment programs without significant bureaucratic reform would not meet this definition. It is important to emphasize durability in the sense that the reforms can be implemented and will not be quickly overturned by a successor administration. Reforms come in many forms, from the large to the incremental. The literature focuses on the "big bang" reforms that constitute a major change in policy direction and which, if durable, are sometimes referred to as "turning points" that lead to accelerated growth and improved living standards.

In terms of scholarship, a number of scholars and intellectual ideas have contributed significantly to influencing economic policy or development over the years. This section draws on earlier works by the World Bank (1984), Lin (2011), and Lin and Rosenblatt (2012) to give a chronology of the dominant ideas of economic development since the 1770s to the present era. To begin with, mention could be made of Adam Smith in 1776 with his popular literary piece *An Inquiry into the Nature and Causes of the Wealth of Nations*. Here, Adam Smith (1723–1790) emphasized two major themes, namely the invisible hand and market liberalism as very important economic ideas. Smith is of the view that humans are economic beings and may want to acquire property. As a result, individuals have self-interest that inspires them to do something that will ultimately lead to peace in their societies. Additionally, Smith further notes that the invisible hand should be allowed to regulate the market and that the role of government should be limited in the society.

Further, in the 1840s, dominant ideas of economic development included the problems of political economy, liberty of individual action in economic and political spheres, concept of "utilitarianism," economic growth as a function of factor accumulation with John Stuart Mill (1848) being one of the leading proponents of the above ideas. This era was followed by the 1940s to 1960s. During this period, a number of ideas were contributed to economic development which led to major reforms. The major ideas in this era of economic development began with the theory of "the big push," balanced growth, planning, investment programming, and a strong government role in industrialization; international aid theory and the goal of colonial emancipation. One of the leading thinkers here was Paul N. Rosenstein-Rodan, who headed the World Bank research department in 1947.

The next set of ideas in this era (1940s–1960s) consisted of the "structuralist" approach, stages of development – the takeoff; the two-gap model, emphasizing savings and investment, sectoral disaggregation; international aid policy stressed country leadership. Scholars that spearheaded these economic development reform ideas included Arthur Lewis (1954), Chang (1949), Myrdal (1957), Walt W. Rostow (1960), Simon Kuznets (1930, 1966), Hollis Chenery (1975) among others. Another set of ideas spearheaded by Hirschman (1958) consisted of unbalanced growth, "favouring industries with strong backward and forward linkages," suspicious of planning, sequential growth, the idea of "we cannot achieve all objectives at once"; "convert import to import substitutes." Not only the above but also, the next set of economic development ideas consisted of the dependency argument, "Capitalism and underdevelopment in Latin America," the center–periphery concept, "the decline in terms of trade against the export of primary commodities was secular and led to the transfer of income from resource-intensive developing countries to capital-intensive developed countries" – the strategy was to develop domestic manufacturing industries through a process known as import – substitution (Lin, 2011). Proponents of the above economic ideas included Andre Gunder Frank (1967), Cardoso and Faletto (1967), Prébisch (1950), Singer (1950), Amin (1976) among others.

In the 1970s, a couple of economic development ideas also emerged. These included the shift from physical capital to human capital, from capital-intensive to appropriate less capital-intensive technologies, from employment in large cities to SMEs, etc. with major thinkers like Jan Tinbergen (1956), Gary Becker (1964), T. W. Schultz (1968, 1971) among others backing these ideas. The 1980s followed this era with the end of the heyday of development economics, and a shift to market liberalism, structural adjustment, reaction to failures of structuralism, new focus on removal of government distortions, leading toward Washington Consensus. Also, there was the revival of institutional economics with major thinkers consisting of Douglas North (1981, 1990) and Anne Kruegar (1974).

Over the years, neoliberalism has been used to describe the theory and practice of unfettered economic liberalization policies. The World Bank and International Monetary Fund (IMF)'s policy prescriptions which came to represent neoliberalism in Africa and other regions of the developing world advocated a tight range of economic policy instruments. They included a strong emphasis on fiscal discipline, including prioritizing the control of inflation, restricting state spending and reducing balance-of-payment deficits. With roots in the classical liberal political economy of scholars such as Adam Smith, neoliberalism is based on a particular set of ideological assumptions about the relationship between the individual and the state. In classical liberal theory of the late eighteenth and early nineteenth centuries, the state's coercive power was interpreted as the primary threat to individual freedom. But as argued by Richard Peet (2003, p. 9), neoliberalism "is an entire structure of beliefs founded on right-wing but not conservative, ideas about individual freedom, political democracy, self-regulating markets and entrepreneurship."

Among key neoclassical economists, whose works have influenced the resurgence of neoliberal ideas are Frederick Hayek (1944) and Milton Friedman (1962). Among other things, these theorists contend (1) that the ideal society is composed of utility-maximizing individuals with perfect information who engage in free exchange in free market democracies; (2) that free markets, which they also call competitive or capitalist markets, need democratic governance to operate most efficiently; and (3) that the combination of a free market economy and a democratic government is not only more economically efficient but also socially desirable. They link personal individual freedom with progress and economic development, and privilege economics over politics as the primary organizing force in society. While democratic government is necessary for capitalist markets to function freely, free societies should limit the sphere of government. Hayek describes the purpose of democracy as "essentially a means, a utilitarian device for safeguarding internal peace and individual freedom" (Hayek, 1944, p. 70).

In his seminal work, *The Road to Serfdom*, written toward the end of the Second World War, western society is seen as, "above all, an individualist civilization." He contends that during the modern period of European history the general direction of social development was one of freeing the individual from the ties which had bound him to the customary or prescribed ways in the pursuit of his ordinary activities. This increasing economic freedom, he contends, led not only to rapid economic growth and the development of science and technology but also to "the undersigned and unforeseen by-product of political freedom." Hayek equates all forms of governmental planning with socialism and maintains that, through planning, government exerts a coercive power that poses the greatest single threat to individual freedom. He argues that even minimalist infringements of property rights present a step on the *Road to Serfdom*, the title of his widely cited book. Friedman in one of his key works, *Capitalism and Freedom* (1962), posits that competitive capitalism, "as a system of economic freedom and a necessary condition for political freedom" (p. 4), provides the only guarantee for a free society. As does Hayek, Friedman maintains that government regulations – whether limiting economic activities or requiring contributions to social security – deprive citizens of some "essential part" of this freedom. He defines political freedom as "the absence of coercion of a man by his fellow men" and suggests that "[b]y removing the organization of economic activity from the control of political authority, the market eliminates this source of coercive power." For Friedman, government should restrict its role to that of rule-maker and umpire of productive activities rather than that of participant. A market orientation serves not just to increase overall economic efficiency but also provides the more crucial function of limiting the scope of government action, thus reducing the chance that a majority can exercise tyranny over a minority. Put together, the ideas of Hayek and Friedman provide the intellectual foundations for the implementation of neoliberal market-led policies in the developed as well as in the developing world.

Aside from the influence of the two thinkers discussed above, the resurgence of the new liberal agenda is also attributed to key major developments within the international political economy. First, there was a crisis of the welfare state and Keynesianism in the developed western countries, which helped propel neoconservative political elites into power in the United States and the United Kingdom. Thus, the ascension to power of Britain's Margaret Thatcher and America's Ronald Reagan in 1979 and 1981 respectively helped to usher in free-market economic and liberal political reforms aimed at dismantling the welfare state in both countries. The second key event in the international political economy, which propelled the resurgence of the new liberal agenda, was the two significant oil price hikes by the Organization of Petroleum Exporting Countries (OPEC) in 1973–1974 and 1978–1979 (Smith et al., 2006). This had particularly deleterious effects on non-oil-exporting Third World countries, resulting in balance-of-payment difficulties and mounting international debt. The third key factor for the rise and dominance of neoliberalism was the collapse of state socialism in the former Soviet Union and Eastern Europe by the end of the 1980s and the consequent demands for economic perestroika and political glasnost (Peet, 2007).

Neoliberal policy reform in Africa

In 1981, the World Bank commissioned a study into what became known as the "Africa's postcolonial crisis." The publication of the report, christened the *Berg Report* also coincided with the crisis in the wider global economy and therefore provided an important basis for the introduction of the neoliberal policy reform agenda within the African context. The *Berg Report* concluded that the African crisis was self-inflicted resulting from the misguided policy choices and decisions by the first generation of African leaders who had overextended the role of the state and stifled the smooth operation of the market (World Bank, 1981; see also Bayart, 1993; Callaghy, 1987). To reverse this trend and resolve the crisis, the World Bank and the IMF proposed linking all future flows of western financial capital to the willingness of African leaders to sign and implement a set of market-based policy prescriptions.

The main policy instrument by which the findings and prescriptions of the *Berg Report* came to be articulated across Africa during the next decades was the Structural Adjustment Programs (SAPs). The SAPs promoted economic growth through a series of deregulation and privatization activities. It can be summarized in 10 points, including (a) fiscal discipline; (b) financial liberalization; (c) tax reform – including cutting marginal taxes; (d) unified and competitive exchange rates; (e) secure property rights; (f) deregulation; (g) trade liberalization; (h) privatization; (i) elimination of barriers to direct foreign investment; and (j) removal of government subvention and subsidies on health, education, and agriculture. These programs, which initially entailed economic shock therapy of macroeconomic stabilization came to be known as "the Washington Consensus," a term first used in 1989 by a World Bank economist, John Williamson (1990) in an attempt to

> distill which of the policy initiatives that had emanated from Washington during the years of conservative ideology that had won inclusion in the intellectual mainstream rather than being cast aside once Ronald Reagan was no longer on the public scene.
>
> (Willhelmson, 2000, p. 254)

A basic tenet of the Washington Consensus was that unhindered market exchanges would be the driving force of economic growth and development:

> It involved minimizing the role of government, through privatizing state-owned enterprises and eliminating government regulations and interventions in the economy. Government had a responsibility for macrostability, but that meant getting the inflation rate down, not getting the unemployment rate down.
>
> (Stiglitz, 2003, p. 230)

The structural adjustment policies also represented a form of policy conditionality whereby loans from the World Bank, IMF, and regional development banks, aid from bilateral donors and even private finance, became effectively conditional on the agreement by the recipient government to implement often far-reaching economic policy reforms. World Bank and IMF intervention through the conditionality associated with structural adjustment was thus to formally promote economic growth, but by imposing a very particular model of development and a narrow set of economic instruments. These external interventions significantly constrained the capacity of developing countries to experiment with their own models. As Green argues, the structural adjustment reforms were based on the assumption that the global economic integration through free trade is the effective route to promote growth, and that the benefits of growth will in the long term be beneficial to both the rich and the poor (Green, 1995).

Over time, the Washington Consensus was applied as a universal blueprint for development throughout the continent. Broadly, the key policy instruments in the implementation of the SAPs were privatization of state enterprises and downsizing of the public sector, trade and financial liberalization, fiscal austerity, and tight monetary policy to reduce inflation (Mohan et al., 2000). These measures, were aimed at stabilizing the domestic economy, making it attractive for private-sector-led development and attractive to foreign direct investment. As a result, across the board, the SAPs emphasized export-led growth, privatization and liberalization, and the efficiency of the free market (Hoogvelt, 2001). In terms of specific policies, the SAPs generally required countries to devalue their currencies against the US dollar, dismantle import and export restrictions, balance their budgets, and remove price controls and state subsidies (Armah &

Amoako-Tuffour, 2008). Justifications provided for the introduction of these policies by neoliberal theorists and commentators are plenty (Bhagwati, 2004; Friedman, 2005; Wolf, 2004). The introduction and implementation of these reform policies could be seen as an attempt by the West to govern Africa and the rest of the global South through the rationalities and discipline of the market (Gill, 1995). This new form of control over the former colonies in the post-colonial era unlike the colonial era is led by the IMF and World Bank, who through the transmission of neoliberal ideas and practice, and especially through the use of conditionality, are able to coerce developing countries to adopt neoliberal reforms (Mawuko-Yevugah, 2010; Taylor, 2004). The transfer of neoliberal ideas from core to periphery and the enactment of neoliberal policy initiatives at an international level have focused on open trade, freedom of investment, and the removal of regulations on capital movements. These have been difficult to distinguish from the broader processes of neoliberal globalization, which have characterized international political economy in the postwar period argues, neoliberalism has become hegemonic largely through the mechanisms of globalization and that neoliberal hegemony has been reproduced and secured through discourses of globalization, open trade, and market reform. Indeed, as Cox (1996, 2002), points out, these discourses have been central to World Bank and IMF rhetoric. Thus far, globalization has been inextricably linked with the neoliberal agenda pursued by the IFIs, the increasing power and influence of multinational corporations, the increasing mobility of capital in global markets, and the time–space compression, which results from technological advancement.

Political economy of policy reform in Ghana

In 1983, Ghana's Provisional National Defence Council (PNDC) military government of Flt Lt Jerry Rawlings introduced an economic recovery program (ERP) under the auspices of the World Bank and the International Monetary Fund (IMF) to kick-start what would become an enduring relationship between the country and the two Bretton Woods Institutions. The introduction of these reform policies marked a significant policy shift from the state-led policy framework that had been laid after the attainment of political independence in 1957. The reasons for the shift could be understood within the context of a wider crisis in the postcolonial African political economy, one that resulted in the publication of the World Bank's *Berg Report* (1981) as alluded to above. As noted earlier, the publication of this report effectively marked the introduction of the neoliberal restructuring agenda in Africa's postcolonies (see Green, 1998; Grosh, 1994; Kim, 2005; Smith, 2006). Thus, as noted, due to a combination of internal and external factors, much of the African continent had descended into a "crisis," which by the virtue of the World Bank's *Berg Report* could only be overcome through the implementation of specific market-led reforms. The Ghanaian political scientist, Boafo-Arthur appropriately sums up Ghana's deteriorating socioeconomic situation at the time: "by the early 1980s, Ghana had reached abysmal levels in its socioeconomic development. Only effective and sustainable measures could salvage the economy" (1999, pp. 46–47). It was against the backdrop of these dire economic indicators coupled with a severe drought and the expulsion of about two million Ghanaians from neighboring Nigeria that year that the ERP was launched in 1983. The recovery program, which was Ghana's version of the Structural Adjustment Programs already introduced in a number of African countries culminated in the implementation of rigorous and comprehensive market-led reform policies geared toward the resuscitation of the economy.

Ghana's reform policies were drafted in two major phases, each addressing a particular ailment identified in the economy. Phase one of the recovery program, dubbed "the stabilization phase," lasted between 1983 and 1986. This aspect of the recovery was aimed at halting economic decline, especially in the industrial and export commodity production sector. It involved macroeconomic stabilization measures comprising fiscal, monetary, and exchange rate policies; the liberalization of prices; and the restructuring of the public and financial sectors. The second phase, marking the period between 1987 and 1989, was the structural adjustment and development phase. This phase focused mainly on growth and development, but with a special emphasis on social services. The key elements of the strategy for implementing the ERP have been: (a) a realignment of relative prices to encourage productive activities and exports through the strengthening of economic incentives; (b) a progressive shift away from direct controls and intervention toward greater reliance on market forces; (c) the early restoration of monetary and fiscal discipline; (d) the rehabilitation of social and economic infrastructure; and (e) the undertaking of structural and institutional reforms to enhance the efficiency of the economy and encourage the expansion of private savings and investment (Boafo-Arthur, 1999, pp. 46–47; see also Hutchful, 2002).

The implementation of SAPs resulted in a major turnaround in Ghana's overall financial and economic performance, at least during the early years. In the first decade after the start of the reform policies, growth in real GDP recovered, allowing gains in per capita incomes; inflation declined, and the general position regarding balance of payments switched from deficits to surpluses, facilitating external payments and a build-up of exchange reserves. The recovery in output growth, combined with the gradual liberalization of exchange restrictions, boosted the expansion in the volume of imports to an average of 10% a year. The rising external financing requirements have been covered in part by modestly growing inflows of private capital, including direct investment, and by an increase in the inflows of official external assistance. The inflows of official grants and concessional loans rose from the equivalent of less than 1% of GDP in 1983 to about 10% of GDP by 1990 (Barwa, 1995, p. 4). During the ensuing decade, the country earned much praise from the World Bank and the IMF as well as from western donors, for being a good reformer and great economic performer (see Tsikata, 2001).

The World Bank, in its 1994 *Adjustment in Africa* report, argued that the structural adjustment policies made a huge impact in terms of bringing countries such as Ghana from near economic collapse to a semblance of stability and modest growth (World Bank, 1994, p. 40). In terms of microeconomic stability, the recovery efforts proved to be successful in terms of short-term growth. GDP in real terms increased by 5.3% in 1986. Per capita real income grew by 2.6%; agricultural output increased by 4.6 percent, and services expanded by 5.4% (see Government of Ghana, 1987). The country's infrastructure, which was almost nonexistent at the onset of the adjustment program in 1983, also witnessed an appreciable level of repair and development. In the view of Donald Rothschild (1991, pp. 10–11), the implementation of the SAPs in Ghana "reversed the decline of recent years." For his part, Peter Gibbon (1992) rated Ghana as being among Africa's most successful countries, a thesis to which the appreciable macroeconomic outrun as a result of the implementation of SAPs lends credence.

During the period described above, however, the focus of western donors was more toward economic liberalization with less focus on political reform. The nature of the state or the type of political system thus had no bearing on the implementation of these policies. The end of the Cold War toward the end of the 1980s and early 1990s however signaled a new era in the relations between Ghana and its international development partners. Unlike the preceding decade where aid relations were solely premised on the implementation of what came to be known as *economic conditionalities or the Washington Consensus* policies in the form of market-led policies referred to above, the post-Cold War era prioritized political reform and good governance as the basis for donor assistance (Abrahamsen, 2000; Gibbon, 1992; Gould, 2005; Grosh, 1994). So, as a result of this new imperative for political reform as well as pressures from domestic actors for democratic rule, Ghana had to negotiate the delicate process of transitioning from an authoritarian military regime to constitutional democracy (Mawuko-Yevugah, 2016; Tsikata, 2001). Such a process would need massive logistical support in the form of institutions, systems, and processes for democratic governance. Given the natural reluctance on part of such regimes to easily give up power, lack of such logistical support could become a convenient excuse for the Ghanaian military regime to stall the democratization agenda.

Financial support from external donors has therefore been very critical in sustaining the country's fledgling democracy. This has mostly taken the form of resources for the Electoral Commission to organize successful elections. The central role of a credible electoral system for democratic consolidation and in promoting peace and security makes it particularly important for the Electoral Commission to be given all the logistical support. Donor support has also been critical in helping to build effective institutions for democratic governance, including the legislature, judiciary, and other key constitutional bodies and institutions. After years of mutual suspicion and hatred, the Ghanaian political establishment and civil society coalesced around the idea of a return to multiparty democratic governance resulting in political settlement which culminated in the inauguration of the Fourth Republic in January 1993. With western donors and development partners keen to seize the discursive shift toward democratic reform and good governance in order to reinvent their own discredited neoliberal agenda played a key supportive toward a successful political transition in Ghana (Abrahamsen, 2000; Mawuko-Yevugah, 2010).

As the standard-bearer of Africa's liberal democratic renaissance, Ghana has been a beneficiary of both multilateral and bilateral aid reform policies (Whitfield, 2005). It is important to note that the nature of Ghana's politics and political system has historically been shaped either by the dictates of the internal political economy or the changing dynamics of the broader global political economy (Gyimah-Boadi and Jeffries, 2000). Thus, the preoccupation of the post-independence era with accelerated socioeconomic transformation, a centralized political system was deemed as the suitable vehicle for shepherding the state. Similarly, the geopolitics of the Cold War period of the 1980s coupled with the harshness of the economic liberalization policies meant the reliance on authoritarian, repressive, and centralized states, in the form of military dictatorship the most suitable system for implementing such policies. With the crisis of the neoliberal agenda by the early 1990s coinciding with the end of the Cold War and the mainstreaming of social development and poverty reduction on the global development agenda, ultimately resulted in political liberalization and good democratic governance as the basis for the implementation of the post-Washington development agenda (Abrahamsen, 2000). As the Ghanaian postcolonial state has thus undergone considerable evolution from the one-party centralized state and political system of the 1960s through the authoritarian military dictatorships of the 1970s and 1980s to the current neoliberal state and multiparty democratic political system, so has the types and nature of developmental and economic policies adopted and implemented undergone considerable change. Thus, like other countries within either the African continent or even the larger developing world, an interplay of domestic and international political and economic processes and actors have influenced and shaped Ghana's postcolonial developmental vision through the implementation of specific set of policy reforms.

Conclusion

This chapter sought to provide a broad theoretical and historical overview of political economy of policy reform from historical to contemporary times. Focusing on the implementation of a neoliberal policy agenda across the African continent from the 1980s, the chapter argues that an interplay of domestic and external political and economic factors, forces, and actors which have shaped and influenced economic policy choices and outcomes in the postcolonial era.

In particular, the chapter explored the interplay of political and economic dynamics in Ghana's implementation of neoliberal policy reforms since the beginning of the 1980s. It provided an overview of the country's postcolonial political economy and showed how as a result of a combination of internal and external factors, the country had no choice but to embrace the policy prescriptions of the World Bank and the IMF in the form of SAPs. These policies as shown included: (1) a realignment of relative prices to encourage productive activities and exports through strengthening of economic incentives; (2) a progressive shift away from direct controls and intervention toward greater reliance on market forces; (3) the early restoration of monetary and fiscal discipline; (4) the rehabilitation of social and economic infrastructure; (5) the undertaking of structural and institutional reforms to enhance the efficiency of the economy and encourage the expansion of private savings and investment; (6) good governance and democratic reform (added as part of the neoliberal policy reform agenda from the early 1990s). The chapter thus provides the conceptual context for examining the various aspects of the implementation of specific policies as part of the reform policies in subsequent chapters.

References

Abrahamsen, R. (2000). *Disciplining democracy: Development discourse and good governance in Africa*. New York, NY: Zed Books.

Amin, S. (1976). *Unequal development: An essay on the social formations of peripheral capitalism*. New York: Monthly Review Press.

Armah, B., & Amoako-Tuffour, J. (2008) *Poverty reduction strategies in action: Perspectives and lessons from Ghana*. Lanham, MD: Lexington Books.

Arrighi, G. (2002). The African crisis. *New Left Review* 15 (May–June). Retrieved February 20, 2019 from www.newleftreview.org/?view=2387

Barwa, S. D. (1995). *Structural adjustment programmes and the urban informal sector in Ghana*. Issues in Development, Discussion Paper, No. 3, International Labour Office.

Bayart, J. (1993) *The state in Africa: The politics of the belly*. London, UK: Orient Longman.

Becker, G. (1964). *Human capital: A theoretical and empirical analysis, with special reference to education*. Chicago, IL: University of Chicago Press.

Bhagwati, J. (2004). *In defense of globalization*. New York, NY: Oxford University Press.

Boafo-Arthur, K. (1999). Ghana: Structural adjustment, democratization and the politics of continuity. *African Studies Review 42*(2) 41–72.

Callagy T. (1988). The state and the development of capitalism in Africa: Theoretical, historical and comparative reflections. In Donald Rothchild et al. (Eds.), *The precarious balance: State and society in Africa*. Boulder, CO: Westview Press.

Cardoso, F. H., & Faletto, E. (1970). *Dependency and development in Latin America*. Berkeley: University of California Press.

Chenery, H. B. (1975). The structuralist approach to development policy. *American Economic Review 65*(2) 310–316.

Cox, R. (2002). *The political economy of a plural world: Critical reflections on power, morals and civilization*. New York, NY: Routledge.

Friedman, M. (1962). *Capitalism and freedom*. Chicago, IL: University of Chicago Press.

Friedman, T. (2005). *The world is flat: A brief history of the twenty-first century*. New York, NY: Farrar, Straus and Giroux.

Gibbon, P. (1992). Structural adjustment and the pressure toward multipartyism in sub-Saharan Africa. In P. Gibbon et al. (Eds)., *Authoritarianism, democracy and adjustment: The politics of economy reforms in Africa*. Uppsala, Sweden: Scandinavian Institute of African Studies.

Gill, S. (1995). Globalization, market civilisation, and disciplinary neoliberalism. *Millennium: Journal of International Studies 24*(3): 399–423.

Gould, J. (2005). *The new conditionality: The politics of poverty reduction strategies.* New York, NY: Zed Books.

Government of Ghana. (1987). *Budget statement.* Accra, Ghana: State Publishing Corporation.

Green, R. (1998). A cloth untrue: The evolution of structural adjustment in sub-Saharan Africa. *Journal of International Affairs 52*(1) 207–234.

Grosh, B. (1994). Through the structural adjustment minefield: Politics in an era of economic liberalization. In J. Widner (Ed.), *Economic change and political liberalization in sub-Saharan Africa.* Baltimore, MD: Johns Hopkins University Press.

Gyimah-Boadi, E., & Jeffries, R. (2000). Political economy of reform. In E. Aryeetey et al. (Eds.), *Economic reforms in Ghana: The miracle and the mirage* (pp. 32–50). Ghana, Africa: Africa World Press.

Hayek, F. (1944). *The road to serfdom.* Chicago, IL: University of Chicago Press.

Hirschman, A. (1958). *The strategy of economic development.* New Haven, CT: Yale University Press.

Hoogvelt, A. (2001). *Globalization and the postcolonial world: The new political economy of development.* New York, NY: Palgrave.

Hutchful, E. (2002). *Ghana's adjustment experience: The paradox of reform.* Geneva, Switzerland: United Nations Research Institute for Social Development.

Kim, K. (2005). Development crisis in sub-Saharan Africa: Globalization, adjustment and the roles of international institutions. In C. John-ren & S. David (Eds.), *Global development and poverty reduction.* Cheltenham, UK: Edward Elgar.

Krueger, A. O. (1974). The political economy of rent-seeking society. *American Economic Review 64*(3) 291–303.

Kuznets, S. (1930). *Secular movements in production and prices: Their nature and their bearing upon cyclical fluctuations.* New York, NY: Houghton Mifflin.

Kuznets, S. (1966). *Modern economic growth, rate, structure and spread.* New Haven, CT: Yale University Press.

Lewis, W. A. (1954). Economic development with unlimited supplies of labour. *Manchester School* 22(2): 139–191.

Leys, C. (1994). Confronting the African tragedy. *New Left Review 1*(204) 33–47.

Lin, J. Y. (2011). New structural economics: A framework for rethinking economic development. *World Bank Research Observer 26*(2) 193–221.

Lin, J. Y. (2012). *New structural economics.* Washington, DC: World Bank.

Lin, J. Y., & Li, Z. (2008). Policy burden, privatization and soft budget constraint. *Journal of Comparative Economics 36* 90–102.

Lin, J. Y., & Rosenblatt, D. (2012). Shifting patterns of economic growth and rethinking development. *Journal of Economic Policy Reform 15*(3) 171–194, doi: 10.1080/17487870.2012.700565.

Mawuko-Yevugah, L. (2010). *Governing through developmentality: The politics of international aid reform and the (re)production of power, neoliberalism and neocolonial interventions in Ghana.* Ph.D. dissertation, University of Alberta, Canada.

Mawuko-Yevugah, L. (2016). *Reinventing development: Aid reform and technologies of governance in Ghana.* New York, NY: Routledge.

North, D. (1981). *Structure and change in economic history.* New York, NY: Norton.

North, D. (1990). *Institutions, institutional change and economic performance.* Cambridge, UK: Cambridge University Press.

Peet, R. (2007). *Geography of power: The making of global economic policy*. New York, NY: Zed Books.

Peet, R. et al. (2003). *Unholy trinity: The IMF, World Bank and WTO*. New York, NY: Zed Books.

Rostow, W. W. (1960). *The stages of economic growth: A non-Communist manifesto*. Cambridge, UK: Cambridge University Press.

Rothchild, D. (1991). *Ghana: The political economy of recovery*. Boulder, CO: Lynne Rienner.

Sachs, J. D. (2005). *The end of poverty: Economic possibilities for our time*. New York, NY: Penguin.

Schultz, T. W. (1968). *Economic growth and agriculture*. New York, NY: McGraw-Hill.

Schultz, T. W. (1971). *Investment in human capital: The role of education and of research*. New York, NY: Free Press.

Singer, H. (1950). Gains and losses from trade and investment in under-developed countries. *American Economic Review* 40, Papers and Proceedings, 473–485.

Smith, M. (2006). Beyond the "African tragedy": Discourses on development and the global economy. Farnham, UK: Ashgate.

Stiglitz, J. (2003). *The roaring nineties: A new history of the world's most prosperous decade*. 1st ed. New York, NY: Norton.

Taylor, I. (2004). The "all-weather friend"? Sino-African in the twenty-first century. In I. Taylor et al. (Eds.), *Africa in international politics: External involvement on the continent*. New York, NY: Routledge.

Tinbergen, J. (1956). *Economic policy: Principles and design*. Amsterdam, the Netherlands: North-Holland Publishing.

Tsikata Y. (2001). Aid and reform in Ghana. In S. Devarajan et al. (Eds.), *Aid & reform in Africa*. Washington, DC: World Bank.

Whitfield, L. (2005). Trustees of development from conditionality to governance: Poverty reduction strategy papers in Ghana. *Journal of Modern African Studies 43*(4): 641–664.

Willhelmson, J. (2000). *The Washington Consensus*. Washington, DC: World Bank.

Williamson, J. (1990). What Washington means by policy reform. In J. Williamson, *Latin American adjustment: How much has happened* (pp. 5–20). Washington, DC: Institute of International Economics.

Wolf, M. (2004). *Why globalization works*. New Haven, CT: Yale University Press.

World Bank. (1981). *Accelerated development in sub-Saharan Africa: An agenda for action*. Washington, DC: World Bank.

World Bank. (1984). *World Development report*. New York, NY: Oxford University Press.

World Bank. (1994). *Adjustment in Africa: Reforms, results, and the road ahead*. Washington, DC: World Bank.

World Bank. (1998). *Assessing aid: What works, what doesn't, and why?* New York, NY: Oxford University Press.

Part II

A world of reforms

Diverse global perspectives

3 Is there a consensus from Ottawa?

Canada's role in Ghana's economic reforms

Ernest Opoku-Boateng

Introduction

The story of Ghana's experience with structural reform is often described as one of unfulfilled promises. For decades, Ghana was a poster child of neoliberal reform in the developing world. Starting in the 1980s, the country religiously liberalized trade, removed subsidies, and deregulated its economy. It opened its domestic markets to investors, privatized state-owned enterprises, and intensified exports, deepening its integration into the global financial system. Success has been observed in certain areas but the general observation is that the neoliberal agenda has not delivered as expected as the economy has been consistently unstable, and dependent on commodity exports and foreign aid (Azeem and Adamtey, 2004; Hutchful, 2002; Panford, 2001).

While assessments of Ghana's neoliberal experience are common, they do not always tell the entire story. This is because such assessments tend to focus on the dominant prescriptions of the Washington Consensus (WC) and the ideations and actions of dominant powers and institutions such as the United States (US) and International Monetary Fund (IMF) (Leith and Soderling, 2000). The perspectives, actions, and motives of middle powers such as Canada in the making and managing of development efforts in Africa are hardly discussed (Akuffo, 2012). Yet these actors by virtue of their unique history (e.g., non-imperialist history) and engagement approach (e.g., targeted, ethical, and soft power approach) with specific countries or organizations can exert influence beyond what their international pedigree or resource commitment indicates (Gilley and O'Neil, 2014). They can also mediate the effects of structural reforms by tackling other issues such as environmental and human rights justice that affect people's lives and economic sophistication. These observations suggest a need for change in the conceptualization and assessment of these economic reform programs.

This chapter attempts a new approach from this rather quiet North American polity along with an evaluation of the uniqueness of its development reform engagement in Ghana. A new approach, particularly one that considers the perspective of middle powers as well as actions taken in other arenas of engagement is needed to enhance current understanding, and inform future reforms.

Analyzing Canada's unique take on the WC as exemplified in its engagement with international financial institutions (IFIs) and Ghana over the last 60 years is an initial step in this direction. Reflective of the country's normative image as a humane internationalist, constructive multilateralist, and strong promoter of human rights and sustainable development (Black, 2014), this uniquely Canadian perspective emphasizes long-term engagement, inclusive growth centered around poverty reduction, gender equality, and environmental sustainability. The perspective also focuses on a new global development finance and delivery architecture that offers flexibility and leverages new partners and innovative financing mechanisms – a useful template for seeking change in the process and outcomes of development policies.

Washington Consensus and Canada: multi-conceptual and definitional issues

The WC and its neoliberal underpinnings emerged in the 1980s as a response to the failure of the Keynesian model to explain and address the economic disasters of the 1970s (Saad-Filho, 2010). As a development approach, WC encompasses a set of neoliberal ideas or policy prescriptions deemed desirable by the US Treasury and international financial institutions such as the World Bank and the IMF, first for Latin America (Williamson, 2004), and then as a "standard" or equally applicable reform package for developing countries including those in Africa to ensure economic stability and growth (Janvry & Sadoulet, 2016; Saad-Filho, 2010). Key elements of the WC include fiscal discipline; balanced budgets; reorientation of public expenditure priorities; tax reform; financial liberalization, including deregulation of the banking sector; openness to foreign direct investment (FDI); unified and competitive exchange rates; trade liberalization for goods and services; privatization of public enterprises; deregulation; and secure property rights.

As the dominant development paradigm of the 1980s and 1990s, the WC and the Structural Adjustment Programs (SAPs) it inspired had a profound effect on the economy of many African countries, including cuts in social services and subsidies, the divestiture of state enterprises, devaluation of national currencies, and the retrenchment of public sector workers (Konadu-Agyemang, 2000; Panford, 2001). Proponents have hailed its positive impacts including the restoration of internal and external equilibrium and the facilitation of global trade (Ostry et al., 2016) while critics, particularly of its one-size-fits-all approach and fixation on "getting the price right," have lamented the heavy cost that it has imposed on vulnerable populations and the environment.

Calls for reforms have been varied and widespread (Saad-Filho and Johnson, 2005). Post-WC reformers such as Stiglitz (1998) have called for changes to address not just the social cost of adjustment but also cater to the needs of private entrepreneurs in responding to the new economic conditions set in place by structural adjustment. Others have called for pro-poor policies that respond to the imperatives of sustainability, equity, democracy, and social justice, and fosters economic growth, mass employment, the satisfaction of basic needs, and the provision of welfare for the vast majority (Saad-Filho, 2010). In more recent times the focus has been on an inclusive growth agenda that puts people first (Saad-Filho, 2010). Common to these calls for reform is the centrality of addressing the needs of vulnerable populations, a return to the role of the state in economic development, and greater pragmatism in design and delivery of development strategies (Janvry & Sadoulet, 2016). The current discussion about Canada's perspective on the neoliberal agenda is situated within this inclusive growth and post-WC debate.

Washington Consensus: Canada's evolving domestic and global perspectives

Neoliberalism enjoys broad support among Canada's political establishment. Successive Canadian governments irrespective of ideology have used neoliberal strategies to address domestic challenges such as stagnating growth, mounting deficit, and unemployment. In response to the recession of the 1980s for instance, the Brian Mulroney government focused on market expansion and trade liberalization, especially with the US. Under this approach, exports to the US were prioritized (Pratt, 1994). The North American Free Trade Agreement (NAFTA) was signed in 1993. State intervention and expenditure were scaled backed while industrial policies proposed under the previous liberal government were shelved. In the 1990s, the Jean Chretien government, as part of its deficit reduction efforts, adopted austerity and cost-cutting measures that led to massive cuts in federal–provincial transfers and social spending. To ensure sustained expansion of output and employment, significant emphasis was placed on low inflation, fiscal adjustment, and labor market reforms. Changes were made to unemployment insurance and pension benefits to strengthen the federal government's fiscal position. Similar initiatives were followed by the Paul Martin and Stephen Harper governments, but this time accompanied by increased government spending.

Globally, Canada has championed neoliberalism particularly in Latin America, Asia, and Africa, leveraging its multilateral proclivities such as OECD and the IFIs. In doing so Canada has used different tools of economic and financial diplomacy including trade, investment support, targeted research, military, and disaster assistance. It has also advocated for and supported efforts to improve institutional effectiveness, reduce aid conditionalities, mainstream gender, human rights, and environmental considerations into programs. Specific actions have included channeling more than 60% of its official development assistance (ODA) through the World Bank group, harmonizing aid strategies and policies with other donor countries, and tying Canadian aid, including lines of credit to structural reforms (Department of Finance, 2017).

Canada's work on neoliberal reforms can be traced back to the 1950s when it provided support under the UN's Expanded Program of Technical Assistance and also served as a key architect of the Colombo Plan, which was designed to keep communism at bay by encouraging socioeconomic progress and political stability in South Asia. Like today's SAPs, assistance under the Colombo Plan was aimed at generating trade through market expansion and was tied to various conditions, including the purchase of machinery from donors and the implementation of agreeable reforms (Cavell, 1952).

The 1960s and 1970s saw the establishment of the Canadian International Development Agency (CIDA), which like its counterparts in the UK and the US was leveraged, alongside military aid and training programs to address the security and development needs of poor and newly independent African and Latin American countries to counter communist influence and foster a pro-West orientation in critical areas (Maloney, 2008). In the 1980s, Canada joined the rest of the developed world to promote SAPs for developing countries. Not only did it vote in favor of structural adjustment lending at the Bretton Woods institutions, but, by 1989, support for IMF/World Bank SAPs had become a major focus of CIDA, with the organization's projects becoming more conditional (Pratt, 1994).

Despite its strong initial support for structural reform, Canada was one of the first countries to call into question the efficacy of the dominant prescriptions of the WC. Working with UNICEF, Canada in the late 1980s called for SAPs with a "human face," and subsequently donated $8.4m in 1987 to support investment in nutritional programs under Ghana's Programme of Actions to Mitigate the Social Costs of Adjustment (PAMSCAD) (Hampson and Maule, 1992).

In the 1990s, Canada expressed concern about the debt-servicing burden of developing countries and called for debt forgiveness (Pratt, 1994). It noted that debt servicing did not only take away the ability of nations to address other pressing needs but also efforts to service unmanageable debt could lead to environmentally unsustainable export growth. To this end, Canada joined the Paris Club to write off the debt of the poorest countries through the Heavily Indebted Poor Countries (HIPC) Initiative and the Multilateral Debt Relief Initiative (MDRI). To date, Canada has cancelled roughly $1bn in debts owed by developing countries and committed to provide the IMF, World Bank, and African Development Bank with $2.5bn over the next 40 years (the lifespan of the MDRI) to compensate them for the debts they have cancelled (Department of Finance, 2017).

Canada–Ghana relations: Stability, benevolence, and mutual respect

Canada's engagement with Africa has generally been described as inconsistent, incoherent, often contradictory, and lacking understanding and a long-term vision (Hornsby, 2013; York, 2018). Particular mention has been made of erratic aid policies that benefit Canadians and reinforce inequities; security policies that fail to match normative advocacy of high-minded principles with sufficient resources to realistically support them; and large extractive industry investments that undermine local environments and human security (Black, 2015). Canada's failure to leverage diaspora and immigrant networks in its Africa policy has also been criticized (York, 2018). For most critics, Canada's lack of interest in Africa is based on the perception among policymakers that Africa is risky, poor, and offers no strategic, economic, or business opportunities (Akuffo, 2012).

Applying the whole-of-Africa lens to Canada–Ghana relations is problematic. For unlike other African countries, Ghana and Canada have a long and stable relationship based on common history and shared values around good governance, inclusiveness, tolerance, respect for human rights, and gender equality in a peaceful world. The two countries also have common membership of international organizations such as the UN, Commonwealth, and the International Organization of the Francophonie, as well as a favorable image of each other which allows them to collaborate on issues of common interest. Ghana has consistently been a priority country for Canadian assistance and investment, given its abundant mineral wealth, growth potential, peaceful business climate, and democratic credentials (GAC, 2012; Sevunts, 2017; Sheik, 2012). For these same reasons, the country is also rated low risk for engagement (CIDA, 2009). Finally, with a strategic location (near the Sahel where Canadian military and investment assets are deployed) and history of political leadership on the African continent, engagement with Ghana provides Canada with a number of strategic, security, and geopolitical advantages that few African countries can offer.

Canada's special relationship with Ghana dates back to 1906 when Quebec missionaries established a base in Navrongo. It was cemented in 1957 when Canada established diplomatic relations with Ghana's newly independent government in Accra, the second in Africa after Egypt, and made the country the first to receive Canadian aid. Since then the country has remained a core recipient of Canadian assistance, placing consistently among the top 20 and receiving an average of $20 to $30m a year in general and budgetary support (CIDA, 2009; CIDA, 2009). This is in addition to military assistance, which began in 1961 with the deployment of the 30-member Canadian Armed Forces Training Team Ghana (CAFTTG), the first Canadian military assistance mission in the world, to train and professionalize the Ghanaian army (Kilford, 2009).

Further exemplifying exceptionalism, Ghana was in 2002, selected as one of six African priority countries targeted for increased aid as part of Canada's commitment at the G8 Summit in Kananaskis to increase aid by 8% and to provide more funding to African countries through the $500m Canada Fund for Africa. In 2013, Ghana was declared a priority market for Canadian goods under the Global Markets Action Plan because of its human rights record, market potential, resource endowments, existing investment links, and the early-mover advantages it offered to Canadian business and trade interests (GAC, 2013; Sheik, 2015).

Ghana's stable business and political climate and history of strict adherence to economic and structural reform makes it an attractive place for Canadian investment, especially in the resource and mining sector (Sheik, 2012). As of 2016, merchandise trade between the two countries stood at $265.3m, making Ghana the fourth biggest market of Canada in sub-Saharan Africa (Canadian

High Commission, 2018). Also, more than 100 Canadian companies operate in Ghana, especially in the mining sector with over $2bn in investment.

Canada–Ghana relations are characterized by collaboration and mutual respect. Common membership of international organizations such as the UN and Commonwealth facilitates this process. At the UN, the two countries have worked closely to support peacekeeping activities. The same is true at the Commonwealth where cooperation has focused on democratic governance, electoral reform and sustainable development with Canada using the opportunity to initiate broader conversations on human rights and other values. Canada has collaborated with the Ghana Police Service on conflict prevention and as part of its broader West African security agenda supported the establishment of the Kofi Annan Peace Keeping Training Centre. By so doing, Canada seems to be taking advantage of Ghana's strategic location and political clout in West Africa, which makes it an important ally and a potential staging point in the promotion of global peace and security, especially in the fragile Sahel region.

Image continues to play an important role in Canada–Ghana relations. In Ghana, Canada deservedly or not, is seen as a benevolent, caring, good international polity as well as a humanitarian, moral actor, and a non-imperial power (Akuffo, 2012; Engler, 2017; Kilford, 2009). This allows Canada to shape policy in Ghana well beyond its resource commitment or international pedigree and to escape unnecessary scrutiny meted out to great and middle powers in global affairs. For instance, Canada has since 2015 been supporting gay rights in Ghana by financing organizations such as Solace Brothers in Ghana. It has also been accused of complicity in the overthrow of Ghana's first president (Engler, 2017; Kilford, 2009). Yet it has not received the same level of backlash as the UK and the US that have been championing the same course or accused of similar interventions. Meanwhile, many Canadians have a favorable view of Ghana, with CIDA (2009) identifying the country as low risk. This favorable perspective allows the Canadian government to support Ghana's efforts without fear of public backlash.

Canada–Ghana relations: Approach to economic and political reform

Canada has played an active but understated role in Ghana's development since 1957. It has informed the country's economic, social, and environmental agenda through sustained and integrated development assistance for research, policy, and private sector development; direct and targeted interventions that address the concerns of vulnerable sectors, people, and communities; military aid; as well as lobbying and support for changes in political, electoral, and sociocultural norms such as child marriage, and national capacity building that seek to lay a foundation for inclusive and transformational change (CIDA, 2009; GAC, 2017a). In doing so, Canada has focused on themes and geographical areas of need and leveraged accountability mechanisms such as the 2015 Mutual Accountability framework as well as the expertise and resources of local and international organizations such as the UN, the World Bank, Solace Brothers, and Abantu for

Development in program delivery and financing. In 2012, Ghana signed with Canada and 14 other donors the 2012–2022 Government of Ghana-Development Partners Compact on Leveraging Partnership for Shared Growth and Development which outlines commitments and the shared desire of Canada and Ghana for a sustainable improvement in the quality of life of all citizens of Ghana.

Canadian support has ebbed and flowed to reflect domestic and international priorities (Hornsby, 2013), but, overall, net aid flow to Ghana over the last 55 years has been steady, totaling about $1.5bn as of 2015 (CIDP, 2018; IndexMundi, 2018; Kilford, 2009). In 2017, Canada provided $88m in ODA (Canadian International Development Platform – CIDP, 2018) and pledged an additional $120m for the Ghanaian government's Planting for Food and Jobs (Tanko, 2017).

Unlike the World Bank and IMF, Canada's engagement in Ghana goes beyond economic and structural reforms (GAC, 2018b). It also includes lobbying and support for democracy and good governance, human rights, peace, and security, as well as changes in sociocultural practices such as child marriage, gender-based violence aimed at laying a broad and solid foundation for transformational change. In the lead-up to the 2008 general elections, for instance, Canada helped train journalists on human rights reporting, the police on conflict resolution and Ghana Electoral Commission officials on peaceful and transparent elections. It also supported Abantu for Development's efforts to bring women more fully into the election process, both as candidates and as voters through training women candidates and organizing media campaigns and media sensitization programs. In 2015, $1.2m in funding was provided to Solace Brothers Foundation to address violence against LGBT individuals through victim support services, including legal aid, education, and training of paralegals. Investments were also made in social infrastructure and sanitation projects for girls to restore their dignity (GAC, 2018b).

Though subtle and often presented as an instrument of Canadian generosity, Canada's engagement has not been devoid of political undertones. Canadian aid to Ghana for instance, increased significantly following the overthrow of Nkrumah's government, which according to Kilford (2009) was a delight to Ottawa and Washington as it kept communism at bay. According to Engler (2017), during the three years between 1966 and 1969 the National Liberation Council military regime, received as much Canadian aid as during Nkrumah's 10 years in office with $22m in grants and loans. Canadian support after the coup consisted of military, technical, and food aid, including $1.82m worth of flour to Ghana (Kilford, 2009). Canada also offered hundreds of Canadian University Students Overseas (CUSO) volunteers to fill skill gaps as teachers and agriculturalists. This was meant to maintain economic and political stability. For some, however, this also demonstrated tacit Canadian support for the 1966 coup makers, most of whom were Canadian-trained and were thought to be sympathetic to the West (Engler, 2015; Kilford, 2009).

The 1970s and 1980s were interesting times for Canada–Ghana relations (CIDA, 1975). For instance, the early 1970s saw a sharp decline in Canadian military assistance but a significant increase in other forms of support. Two-thirds of CIDA's ODA allocation in the 1970s for instance, went to 10 countries worldwide, including Ghana. This was in line with Prime Minister Pierre Trudeau's doctrine of prioritizing economic and technical aid over military assistance, which he considered to be wasteful, risky, and incompatible with Canada's benevolent image. In 1979, the year of Jerry Rawlings's first coup in Ghana, Canada provided \$15.4m in assistance (IndexMundi, 2018), a decline from the year before. This downward trend continued to the early 1980s, including 1983. The reason for such decline is not obvious but the socialist inclinations of the Armed Forces Revolutionary Council (AFRC) regime and the initial strong opposition expressed by key allies such as the US and the UK cannot be overlooked. In 1984, Canada provided about \$36m in aid, up from \$5.9m in 1983. This is not surprising given that Ghana was in the throes of a drought and a refugee crisis fueled by the deportation of millions of Ghanaians from Nigeria and had agreed to implement IMF and World Bank imposed economic reforms, which Canada supported.

Another area of cooperation where politics has informed policy is climate change. Canada has provided significant funding through the Green Climate Fund to support mitigation and adaptation in developing countries including Ghana (OECD, 2016). In 2011, however, Canada withdrew from the Kyoto Protocol (KP), citing costs, US and Chinese inaction, and Kyoto's misplaced focus on greenhouse gases (GHGs) instead of short-lived climate forcers which it believed were more potent and required immediate attention. To gain allies and legitimize this minority position, in 2012, Canada joined forces with the US (which did not ratify the KP), Ghana and Bangladesh (two poor and vulnerable countries) to establish the Climate and Clean Air Coalition to Reduce Short-Lived Climate Pollutants (CCAC) with the stated aim of catalyzing rapid reductions in short-lived climate pollutants to protect human health, agriculture, and the environment. Besides supporting the development of green businesses including waste recycling, this initiative may have succeeded in mitigating any reputational damage Canada's withdrawal may have caused.

A unique feature of Canada's work in Ghana is its thematic and geographic approach to program delivery. Thematically, Canada focuses on issues such as accelerated growth through climate-smart agriculture, gender equality, and environmental sustainability. Geographically, it concentrates on the Northern, Upper East, and Upper West Regions, where poverty is endemic (CIDA, 2009).

A thematic and geographic approach seeks to align Canadian initiatives with local priorities (e.g., the Ghana Poverty Reduction Strategy and Ghana's Shared Growth and Development Agenda II), Canada's G20 commitments and 2008 Official Development Assistance Act (ODAA) requirements and by so doing, foster national ownership, enhance policy coherence, and increase the effectiveness of Canadian support (CIDA, 2012). This approach also offers an opportunity to address regional and sectoral inequalities ignored and/or exacerbated by the Structural Adjustment Programs that Ghana has implemented over the years. Agriculture and women are great examples.

Though important contributors to the Ghanaian economy, both were neglected and negatively impacted by SAP's market and export-oriented policies (Konadu-Agyemang, 2000; Panford, 2001), which in the case of agriculture included reduction in food production and increased poverty among farmers. For women, the removal of subsidies, the imposition of user fees and the mass retrenchment of male public workers under SAP forced many to take up extra work in the informal sector to supplement household incomes. Cuts in educational and health spending also increased their social and reproductive burdens (Bawa, 2017). The same is true of the more rustic and relatively underdeveloped North, where historical vulnerabilities resulting from harsh climatic conditions, resource poverty, dependence on subsistence and rain-fed agriculture, and imbalanced government policies, including overconcentration of resources and infrastructure in the south, were ignored and compounded by SAP's one-size-fits-all approach and focus on export crops.

By promoting research, climate-smart agricultural practices, value-chain improvements; entrepreneurship and capacity building through farmer-based organizations (FBOs), especially in agro-food processing and the production of local staples such as sorghum and millet Canada is helping revamp this critical economic sector and laying a foundation for sustained and endogenous growth (Morris et al., 1999). Gender and spatially focused Canadian initiatives such as land title reforms, entrepreneurship training, micro-enterprise skills development in batik making, and investment in social infrastructure (GAC, 2018b) are supporting women's integration into the market and restoring their dignity. They are also helping address regional disparities in development.

Canada's engagement in Ghana has not been without controversy. For example, Canadian mining companies, which have a dominant presence in Ghana, including about $2bn in investment, have been accused of human rights and environmental abuses in their areas of operation and yet have not been held to account by the Canadian government, leading to accusations of complicity (Ellimah, 2015). Canada has worked with mining companies to improve Corporate Social Responsibility (CSR) (Kwakyewah & Idemudia, 2017). But a lot remains to be done as these initiatives are not just voluntary but also seen as subverting local communities' rights and helping mining companies avoid taking responsibility for environmental and social damage in areas of operations (Ellimah, 2015; Essex, 2012). In 2017, the Canadian government released its 2017 Enhanced CSR policy, aimed at improving the ethical and environmental conduct of Canadian companies abroad (GAC, 2017c). This will however require political will and enforceable instruments. This is even more urgent in light of recent accusations against mining companies in Ghana and Africa of engaging in illicit transfers and repatriation of profits and denying local communities of their fair share of revenues. The Ghana government's strong interest in this area as well as tax cooperation agreements with OECD countries provide an opportunity for Canada to show its commitment to sustainable and ethical mining practices.

An Ottawa consensus: (Re)conceptualization of neoliberalism with Canadian characteristics

Given Canada's intimate relationship with the IFIs and other key proponents of the neoliberal agenda, exonerating it completely from the legacy of the WC is challenging. In fact, some have argued that as an elite member of the World Bank with significant voting power, Canada has been complicit in the hegemonic actions of the West in imposing neoliberal policies on developing countries (Engler, 2015). However, a look at Canada's work in Ghana as well as its voting records, policy positions and official reports at these organizations reveals a distinctly Canadian perspective on some key elements of the WC such as the conceptualization of development, the measurement of progress, and the role of the state in economic reform. This distinct Canadian take on the Washington Consensus constitutes the "Ottawa consensus."

As a policy framework, the Ottawa consensus is situated within the inclusive growth spectrum of the post-Washington consensus debate. It is underpinned by a normative framework that emphasizes both negative and positive obligations to do good and no harm (Cameron, 2014; GAC, 2017b). The Ottawa perspective advocates for a multi-pronged approach to economic and social reforms, taking into account the multidimensionality of development, the complementarity of state, civil society, and market interventions as well as the importance of strong institutions and governance in driving change (CIDA, 2011). It calls for inclusive growth and development – that is, broad-based expansion of economic opportunity and prosperity that works for everyone (GAC, 2017b). It places emphasis on poverty reduction, gender equality, human rights, and environmental sustainability, and calls for a more nuanced approach to the measurement of progress that goes beyond GDP growth. Cognizant of the growing complexity of global challenges and the uniqueness of countries, the Ottawa consensus calls for national ownership, and tailored solutions informed by local priorities (GAC, 2016; Medhora, 2016). It also calls for the reform of global institutions such as the IMF and the World Bank to give greater representation to developing countries, integrate environmental and social concerns into development activities and leverage new and innovative financing options (Department of Finance, 2017).

Core elements

The Ottawa consensus consists of six key elements. The first is inclusive growth and development. Canadian policymakers posit that growing poverty and inequality poses a significant threat to global peace and security and that inclusive growth and development that is human-centered and addresses the needs of the most vulnerable, including women can address this risk (Department of Finance, 2017; G7, 2018). Central to Canada's plan for inclusive growth is strong and continued commitment to social inclusion and diversity; environmental sustainability, including strong climate action; inclusive economic models driven by labor, property, and human rights reforms, and small and medium enterprise (SME) development.

The second element of the Ottawa consensus is gender equality and empowerment (GAC, 2017a). Recent global efforts notwithstanding, the plight of women continues to be precarious (CIDA, 2011; UN, 2015). They constitute majority of the poor, do 75% of unpaid work, receive less pay than men, and bear the brunt of structural reforms, which also fail to consider their unique ability to transform economies, societies, and households (McKinsey Global Institute, 2015). Placing women at the center of development (instead of taking them into account as currently practiced) and empowering them economically will ensure that growth reaches the poorest and most vulnerable. It will also address the gender gaps fostered by traditional Structural Adjustment Programs that hold back growth and perpetuate poverty (GAC, 2017a; McKinsey Global Institute, 2015).

Canada has promoted gender equality by championing women's political participation (e.g., 50% of Canada's cabinet are women), channeling support to women's projects, advancing women's property and reproductive rights under the Muskoka initiative, and dedicating a significant proportion of its climate change funding under the Copenhagen and Paris Agreements to adaptation in developing countries, focusing on women-dominated sectors and activities such as agriculture (Department of Finance, 2015). In 2017 Canada released its new feminist international assistance policy (GAC, 2017a), which is expected to enhance gender empowerment efforts in countries such as Ghana, where socio-cultural norms and lack of access to basic services continue to hamper full integration into the economy. To be credible, however, Canada needs to genuinely resolve its own women's rights issues such as missing Indigenous women and pay equity gaps and alleged human rights abuses by Canadian mining companies in Latin America and Africa (Bawa, 2017).

The third element is the place of the developmental state in economic reform. The role of the state vis-à-vis the private sector is one of the most contentious aspects of the Washington consensus (Panford, 2001). Generally speaking, proponents of the Washington consensus see a limited role for the state and have sought to diminish state influence through privatization of services, cuts to government expenditure on essential services and divestment of state-owned enterprises (Alfredo Saad-Filho, 2010; Edelman & Haugerud, 2005: 113). The private sector is seen as more efficient and has been promoted often at the expense of the public sector (Hutchful, 2002; Panford, 2001). While Canada recognizes the private sector as driver of economic growth, it also sees a critical role for the state particularly one that is strong, capable, and committed. This includes providing leadership; restructuring the economy; addressing market externalities; cofinancing investments; and creating an economic environment that is conducive to the private sector, innovation, and competition as sources of long-term growth (G7, 2018).

Another important element of the Ottawa consensus is trade. Lopsided trade liberalization under structural adjustment has led to negative outcomes in many

African countries, including Ghana. In most cases, the expected benefits of trade have not materialized (Sundaram et al., 2011). Even where they have, such benefits have not been shared equally (Panford, 2001; World Economic Forum, 2016). To promote shared prosperity, the Ottawa consensus calls for a progressive trade agenda that puts people first – i.e., trade that contributes to broader economic, social, and environmental objectives; is compatible with climate change commitments; benefits the middle class and all who aspire to join it; and addresses inequalities at all levels that hold back the ability of women, minorities and the poor to participate fully in, and benefit from international trade (GAC, 2017b, 2018a).

Canada has promoted progressive trade by offering market access to developing countries, including human rights and gender provisions in trade agreements and by working with the World Trade Organization and OECD to promote high standards and regulations related to food safety, product safety, consumer protection, health, environment, or labor protection. Despite these efforts, very few developing countries have been able to enter the Canadian market because of distorting subsidies, supply chain restrictions and other technical barriers to trade (Biggs, 2016). As the new African Continental Free Trade Agreement takes shape, key partners such as the US take a second look at Africa's trade potential, and many African countries, including Ghana push for trade rather than aid, Canada's progressive trade agenda offers an opportunity for collaborative action, which may include permanent and comprehensive market access accompanied by simple, transparent rules of origin. Canada's already existing patchwork of foreign investment protection agreements with African countries such as Nigeria offers a basis for such action.

The final element of the Ottawa consensus is about development finance in a changing world. Financing economic reforms in developing countries currently relies on institutions, conditionalities and a global order that dates back to the Second World War. This approach is not only rigid and inadequate vis-à-vis the enormous finance challenge posed by global issues such as climate change, but it also fails to recognize the emergence of new global actors such as China that are offering flexible finance options with fewer constraints (Halper, 2010). To be responsive and relevant, Canada calls for a new global finance architecture that is coordinated across and among donors and policy fields, targets resources where needed most and leverages innovative financing mechanisms such as blended finance, repayable contributions, and incentive-based funding and monitors for results.

Canada has demonstrated support for this new architecture by endorsing the 2005 Paris Declaration on Aid Effectiveness (PD), the 2008 Accra Agenda for Action and the Addis Ababa Action Agenda on Financing for Development, which encourage developing country ownership, policy coherence, mutual accountability, and a broader spectrum of financial partnerships (Essex, 2012). Canada has also established the Development Finance Institute (FinDev Canada) to draw upon a range of financing instruments to support private sector investment in developing countries, and continues to host and fund Convergence, a platform to promote blended financing by public, private and philanthropic partners (OECD, 2016). For countries like Ghana with significant infrastructure and socioeconomic needs and yet constrained by World Bank and IMF conditionalities, Canada's proposed approach to development finance provides flexibility and potential access to additional funds. The increasing debt to GDP ratio of many countries, as they move away, post HIPC, from concessional sources of financing toward market-based domestic debt makes effective monitoring imperative.

An assessment of Canada–Ghana relations

Canada is one of many players seeking to shape Ghana's economic and political future. Isolating the effect of Canada's engagement on Ghana's economic and political progress is therefore challenging. A look at Canada specific initiatives, however, indicates that its focused, broad-based, and soft power approach to reforms has yielded some benefits. For instance, between 1979 and 1997 Canada supported the Ghana Grains Development Project, which built research capacity, led to discovery of quality maize varieties and increased food production and security (Morrison, 1999).

Coupled with recent education, training, and research initiatives such as the Systems Approach to Improving and Sustaining Food Security in West Africa, the country has helped increase agricultural productivity and adoption of climate-smart agriculture, especially for women farmers, across Ghana's three northern regions (CIDA 2009). These actions have also helped increase the availability and consumption of safe and nutritious food staples among Ghana's poorest households. In 2015 and 2016, 375,000 households were trained on improved nutrition practices, 10,514 children were treated for acute malnutrition using therapeutic foods while 22,000 female and 8,000 male farmers improved their agricultural production through climate-smart practices and technologies. About 21,000 farmers were able to move across the poverty line, contributing to a significant reduction in the depth of extreme poverty in the three northern regions (GAC, 2018).

Another tangible outcome of Canada's intervention in Ghana is increased access to water, sanitation and hygiene infrastructure and adoption of good sanitation and hygiene practices across northern Ghana. As a result of recent interventions 315,000 people now live in open defecation-free communities, which represents a critical stride towards reducing the incidence of sanitation-related diseases. About 200,000 people living in dry and underserved communities across northern Ghana also gained access to safe drinking water while 23,000 girls in the same area now have access to appropriate sanitation facilities such as latrines and tippy taps at school, ensuring they are able to attend school during their menstrual cycle (GAC, 2017e).

In 2010, more than 3,000 people were trained in micro-enterprise skills development, engineering batik making. About 1879 farmers from 370 farmer-based organizations were also trained in extension services and information sharing

(GAC, 2017e). In 2015 Canada provided support for Land Tenure Reform project, resulting in over 7,000 landholders registering their properties under one project alone (GAC, 2018b). Other interventions include investment in basic sanitation and infrastructure; the training of midwives and pediatric nurses as well as the provision of nutritional programs and sanitation projects for girls (AidData, 2018).

Canada's support for broad-based reforms, including free and fair elections has helped create a peaceful and business-friendly environment for people and investors and cemented Ghana's democratic credentials (Freedom House, 2018). Training and support for media and civil society has contributed to a vibrant media landscape (Reporters Without Borders, 2018) while work with the Ghana Revenue Authority, Parliamentary Accounts Committee (PAC), and Audit Service has enhanced accountability and financial management. Its thematic and geographic focus has also helped to highlight and address the regional and historical inequalities that were neglected and, in some cases, exacerbated by structural adjustment programming.

Despite its relative success, the Ottawa perspective as operationalized in Ghana has limitations, which if addressed would successfully move Ghana towards its sustainable development goals and serve as a template for others. First, it needs to shift from the current aid-based model and recognize the enormous opportunities that Ghana presents as a trading and investment partner (du Toit, 2018). According to CIDA (2009) development assistance is at the heart of Canada's bilateral relationship with Ghana. While recent focus on commercial interests signals a shift, it has not been substantial. Canada still focuses on providing financial assistance instead of strengthening the country's ability to trade or create wealth. For example, while two-way trade between Ghana and Canada stood at $256m in 2015, Canada offered $130m in ODA. This is in sharp contrast to Ghana China relations (du Toit, 2018). For instance, in 2017 the volume of trade between Ghana and China stood at $6bn, making Ghana the 7th largest trading partner of China in Africa. During that same period China's non-financial direct investment inflows into Ghana was estimated at $123m and the volume of China's newly signed contracts in Ghana reached $2.9bn (Africa Footprint, 2018).

Second, it needs to remove conditionalities and leverage new actors and financing options to provide flexibility (Brown et al., 2014). While Canadian policy has long prioritized few conditionalities (Essex, 2012), and much of the country's aid is untied, Canada continues to take cues from general neoliberal trends (e.g., HIPC) proffered by the IMF and World Bank and to harmonize aid strategies and policies with other donor partners such as the UK and the US, leading to the preservation of certain conditions. This has been criticized as constraining and neo-imperialist, and in some cases, detrimental to the well-being of the vulnerable populations such as women, that they are intended to help (Bawa, 2017; Essex, 2012). Collaborating with traditional donor partners such as IMF and the World Bank is important but Canada should find ways to assert its independence. It should also work with new actors such as China and other entrepreneurs to deploy new finance options and deepen understanding and use of blended finance models to complement traditional sources of finance.

An area where Canada needs to match rhetoric with real action is human rights. Canada is a strong advocate of human rights and environmental justice. In Ghana, it has advanced human rights by supporting the work of agencies such as Solace Brothers and Equitas. At the same time however, it seems to have turned a blind eye to environmental and human rights abuses allegedly committed by Canadian mining companies, leading to accusations of complicity (Ellimah, 2015; Kwakyewah & Idemudia, 2017). Failure to hold companies to account, coupled with its inability to address domestic human rights cases such as the missing and unsolved murders of aboriginal and gender equity gaps has led many to question the genuineness of Canada's commitment to human rights (Bawa, 2017).

To address this perception, Canada needs to hold companies to a higher standard. It should also promote transparency by addressing the tension and contradictions between its humanitarian, commercial, and geopolitical objectives. Current corporate social responsibility guidelines including the *2014 Enhanced Corporate Social Responsibility (CSR) Strategy, Doing Business the Canadian Way: A Strategy to Advance Corporate Social Responsibility in Canada's Extractive Sector Abroad* (GAC, 2014) and OECD (2008), are positive steps but are not enough. They are voluntary and lack enforceability. Potential actions could include: giving the Office of the Extractive Sector CSR Counsellor established under the CSR Strategy prosecutorial powers in addition to its review and advisory role; forcing Canadian mining companies in Ghana to pay their fair share of taxes; stopping illicit transfers, if any; articulating Canada's commercial and humanitarian interests in projects sponsored; holding Canadian companies abroad to the same environmental standards at home; and permitting legal challenges for noncompliance through Canadian courts.

To a large extent, Canada's engagement with Ghana has been influenced more by global development paradigms than domestic politics. However, recent shifts toward commercial and private interests as well as actions and pronouncements under the erstwhile Harper conservative administration (Ibittson, 2013), particularly in relation to women's reproductive rights and social practices deemed "barbaric" by the Canadian government indicate that this could change. To isolate the inclusive growth and progressive trade agenda from ideological influences as well as prevent their appropriation by elites to reinforce development choices that perpetuate poverty and inequality, Canada needs to develop a coherent African strategy that articulates the political, operational, and discursive use of these concepts in the African context. Coupled with operationalizing principles and a review mechanism, such as an approach should also permit regular review and reporting to reflect changing needs, which in this case may involve not just focusing on gender rights but also youth unemployment, which is seen by many African countries, including Ghana as equally critical to inclusive development.

Concluding remarks

Debates about the Washington Consensus will continue. In the unfolding drama of complex global problems such as climate change, growing inequality, and financial uncertainty, however, a business-as-usual approach to the neoliberal agenda is no longer tenable. As this chapter has illustrated, focusing on the actions of dominant players could forestall a fulsome understanding of the true impacts of the Structural Adjustment Programs in countries such as Ghana. Assessments of results and recommendations for changes should look to different perspectives and implementation strategies. Canada's approach to the neoliberal agenda as exemplified in its dealings with the IFIs and Ghana offers a fresh perspective. Though not perfect, and extending it to other contexts should be done with caution, it offers lessons that can be useful for a nuanced approach. These include engaging for the long term while taking into account context and exceptionalism; providing sustained, adequate and theme rather than sector-focused support, while taking into account local needs and priorities; complementing economic and structural reforms with culturally and context-appropriate changes in other areas of engagement to deliver transformational change; making women the reason for rather than a consideration in reform; and leveraging partnerships and new finance mechanisms to support coherence, innovation, and flexibility in delivery while being cognizant of the power differentials strongly institutionalized in the international and state-financing systems.

References

Akuffo, E. A. (2012). *Canadian foreign policy in Africa: Regional approaches to peace, security, and development*. Farnham, UK: Ashgate.

Azeem, V., & Adamtey, N. (2004). Lessons from experiences with ex-ante poverty impact assessments of macroeconomic adjustment policies: The case of the Ghana. Retrieved May 4, 2018, from www.new-rules.org/storage/documents/epiam/ghana.pdf

Bawa, S. (2017). Assessing universalism and the rhetoric of development assistance in human rights research: Canadian–Ghanaian human rights engagements. *The Transnational Human Rights Review* 4. http://digitalcommons.osgoode.yorku.ca/thr/vol.4/iss1/3

Biggs, M. (2016). Inclusive trade, inclusive development: Opportunities for Canadian leadership. Retrieved March 22, 2018, from http://irpp.org/research-studies/aots6-biggs

Black, D. R. (2004). Canada and Africa: Activist aspirations in straitened circumstances. In I. Taylor and P. Williams (Eds.), *Africa and international politics*. New York, NY: Routledge.

Black, D. R. (2014). Humane internationalism and the malaise of Canadian aid policy. In S. Brown, M. Den Heyer, & D. R. Black (Eds.), *Rethinking Canadian aid* (pp. 17–34). Ottawa, Canada: University of Ottawa Press.

Black, D. R. (2015). *Canada and Africa in the new millennium: The politics of consistent inconsistency*. Waterloo, Canada: Wilfrid Laurier University Press.

Cameron, J. D. (2014). Revisiting the ethical foundations of aid and development policy from a cosmopolitan perspective. In S. Brown, M. Den Heyer, & D. R. Black (Eds.), *Rethinking Canadian aid* (pp. 51–66). Ottawa, Canada: University of Ottawa Press.

Canadian High Commission. (2018). Canada–Ghana relations. Retrieved March 12, 2018, from www.canadainternational.gc.ca/ghana/bilateral_relations_bilaterales/canada_ghana.aspx?lang=eng

Canadian International Development Agency (CIDA). (1975). *Canada: Strategy for international development cooperation, 1975–1980*. Ottawa, Canada: CIDA.

CIDA. (2002). *Canada making a difference in the world: A policy statement on strengthening aid effectiveness*. Ottawa, Canada: CIDA.

CIDA. (2009). *Ghana country study 2009*. Ottawa, Canada: CIDA.

CIDA. (2011). *Report to Parliament on the government of Canada's official development assistance – 2010–2011*. Retrieved March 20, 2018, from http://publications.gc.ca/collections/collection_2012/acdi-cida/CD2-6-2011-eng.pdf

CIDA. (2012). *Report to Parliament on the government of Canada's official development assistance – 2011–2012*. Retrieved March 20, 2018, from http://publications.gc.ca/collections/collection_2012/acdi-cida/CD2-6-2012-eng.pdf

Canadian International Development Platform (CIDP). (2018). Retrieved February 11, 2018, from http://cidpnsi.ca/canadas-foreign-aid-2012-2

Cavell, Nik. (1952). Canada and the Colombo Plan: The Empire Club of Canada Addresses. Toronto, Canada, pp. 112–128. Retrieved March 22, 2018, from http://speeches.empireclub.org/60071/data?n=7

Department of Finance. (2014). *Canada at the IMF and World Bank Group 2013–2014: Report on operations under the Bretton Woods and Related Agreements Act*. Retrieved December 1, 2018, from www.fin.gc.ca/purl/bretwd-eng.asp

Department of Finance. (2015). *Canada at the IMF and World Bank Group 2014–2015: Report on operations under the Bretton Woods and Related Agreements Act*. Retrieved December 24, 2017, from www.fin.gc.ca/bretwood/bretwd14_1-eng.asp

Department of Finance. (2017). *Canada at the IMF and World Bank Group 2016–2017: Report on operations under the Bretton Woods and Related Agreements Act*. Retrieved December 1, 2018, from www.fin.gc.ca/bretwood/pdf/bretwd17-eng.pdf

du Toit, H. (2018). Global investors should follow China's lead in Africa: The world needs to shift from an aid-based narrative on Africa to one of investment. *Financial Times*, June 14. Retrieved June 13, 2018, from www.ft.com/content/0c1f0a24-6ef8-11e8-92d3-6c13e5c92914

Edelman, M., & Haugerud, A. (2005). Part II: What is development? 20th century debates. In M. Edelman & A. Haugerud (Eds.), *The anthropology of development and globalization: From classical political economy to contemporary neoliberalism* (pp. 105–154). Malden, MA: Blackwell.

Ellimah, R. (2015). Stained gold: A story of human rights violations in Ghana's mining industry. *Amphibious accounts: Human rights stories from the Global South*. Retrieved April 10, 2018, from www.amphibiousaccounts.org/#!/publicacion/27

Engler, Y. (2015). *Canada in Africa: 300 years of aid and exploitation*. Black Point, Canada: Fernwood Publishing.

Engler, Y. (2017). Canada's role in the overthrow of Ghana President Kwame Nkrumah. Retrieved May 5, 2018, from http://rabble.ca/blogs/bloggers/2017-02-24t000000/canadas-role-overthrow-ghana-president-kwame-nkrumah

Essex, J. (2012). The politics of effectiveness in Canada's international development assistance. *Canadian Journal of Development Studies 33*(3) 338–355.

Freedom House. (2018). Freedom in the world 2018: Democracy in crisis. Retrieved June 14, 2018, from https://freedomhouse.org/report/freedom-world/2018/ghana

Gilley, B., & O'Neil, A. (2014). *Middle powers and the rise of China*. Washington, DC: Georgetown University Press.

Global Affairs Canada (GAC). (2013). Global markets action plan. Retrieved April 5, 2018, from http://international.gc.ca/global-markets-marches-mondiaux/assets/pdfs/plan-eng.pdf

GAC. (2014a). 2014 Official Development Assistance (ODA) report. Retrieved April 4, 2018, from http://international.gc.ca/gac-amc/assets/pdfs/publications/2014-15oda_report.pdf

GAC. (2014b). Enhanced corporate social responsibility (CSR) strategy, doing business the Canadian way: A strategy to advance corporate social responsibility in Canada's extractive sector abroad. Retrieved May 1, 2018, from www.international.gc.ca/trade-agreements-accordscommerciaux/assets/pdfs/Enhanced_CS_Strategy_ENG.pdf

GAC. (2015). *Report to Parliament on the government of Canada's official development assistance – 2014–2015*. Retrieved April 12, 2018, from http://international.gc.ca/gac-amc/publications/odaaa-lrmado/daaa-lrmado_1516.aspx?lang=eng

GAC. (2016). *Report to Parliament on the government of Canada's official development assistance – 2015–2016*. Retrieved March 2, 2018, from http://international.gc.ca/gac-amc/assets/pdfs/publications/daaa-lrmado_1516_report.pdf

GAC. (2017a). *Report to Parliament on the government of Canada's official development assistance – 2016–2017*. Retrieved March 28, 2018, from http://international.gc.ca/gac-amc/assets/pdfs/publications/odaaa-16-17-eng.pdf

GAC. (2017b). Canada's feminist international assistance policy. Retrieved March 28, 2018, from http://international.gc.ca/world-monde/assets/pdfs/iap2-eng.pdf

GAC. (2017c). Canada's state of trade: Trade and investment update – 2017. Retrieved March 28, 2018, from www.international.gc.ca/economist-economiste/performance/state-point/state_2017_point/index.aspx?lang=eng

GAC. (2017d). *Report to Parliament on the government of Canada's official development assistance – 2016–2017*. Retrieved March 13, 2018, from http://international.gc.ca/gac-amc/assets/pdfs/publications/odaaa-16-17-eng.pdf

GAC. (2017e). Canadian international assistance in Ghana. Retrieved March 24, 2018, from www.international.gc.ca/world-monde/issues_development-enjeux_developpement/priorities-priorites/where-ou/ghana.aspx?lang=eng

GAC. (2018a). Joint Declaration on Fostering Progressive and Inclusive Trade. Retrieved March 22, 2018, from www.international.gc.ca/trade-commerce/trade-agreements-accords-commerciaux/agr-acc/cptpp-ptpgp/declaration_fpit-pcpi.aspx?lang=eng

GAC. (2018b). Canada and the World Project browser. Retrieved May 4, 2018, from http://w05.international.gc.ca/projectbrowser-banqueprojets/filter-filtre#charts

Government of Canada. (2018). International climate finance. Retrieved June 2, 2018, from https://climate-change.canada.ca/finance/https://climate-change.canada.ca/finance

G7. (2018). Charlevoix commitment on equality and economic growth. Retrieved June 11, 2018, from https://g7.gc.ca/en/official-documents/charlevoix-commitment-equality-economic-growth

Halper, S. (2010). *The Beijing Consensus: How China's authoritarian model will dominate the twenty-first century*. New York, NY: Basic Books.

Hampson, F. O., & Maude, C. J. (1992) (Eds.). *Canada among nations, 1992–93: A new world order?* Ottawa, Canada: Carleton University Press.

Hornsby, D. (2013). Turning perception into reality: Canada in Africa. Retrieved April 3, 2018, from www.opencanada.org/features/turning-perception-into-reality-canada-in-africa

Hutchful, E. (2002). *Ghana's adjustment experience: The paradox of reform*. Geneva, Switzerland: United Nations Research Institute for Social Development.

Ibbitson, J. (2013). Tories' new foreign-affairs vision shifts focus to "economic diplomacy." *The Globe and Mail*, November 27. Retrieved May 1, 2018, from www.theglobeandmail.com/news/politics/tories-new-foreign-affairs-vision-shifts-focus-to-economic-diplomacy/article15624653

IndexMundi. (2018). Ghana – Net bilateral aid flows from DAC donors, Canada. Retrieved April 4, 2018, from www.indexmundi.com/facts/ghana/indicator/DC.DAC.CANL.CD

Industry Canada. (2018). Trade data online. Ottawa, Canada: Industry Canada. Retrieved April 1, 2018, from www.ic.gc.ca/eic/site/tdo-dcd.nsf/eng/Home

Ismi, A. (2003). Canadian mining companies set to destroy Ghana's forest reserves. Ottawa, Canada: Canadian Centre for Policy Alternatives (October 1). Retrieved March 12, 2018, from www.policyalternatives.ca/publications/monitor/october-2003-canadian-mining-companies-set-destroy-ghanas-forest-reserves

Janvry, A. D., & Sadoulet, E. (2016). *Development economics: Theory and practice*. New York, NY: Routledge.

Kilford, C. R. (2009). *The other cold war: Canada's military assistance to the developing world 1945–1975*. Ontario, Canada: Canadian Defence Academy Press.

Konadu-Agyemang, K. (2000). The best of times and worst of times: Structural adjustment program and uneven development in Africa: The case of Ghana. *Professional Geographer 52*(3) 469–483.

Kwakyewah, C., & Idemudia, U. (2017). Canada–Ghana engagements in the mining sector: Protecting human rights or business as usual? *Transnational Human Rights Review 4*. Retrieved March 3, 2018, from http://digitalcommons.osgoode.yorku.ca/thr/vol. 4/iss1/8

Leith, J. C., & Soderling, L. (2000). *Ghana: Long term growth, atrophy, and recovery. A report for the OECD Development Centre Project Emerging Africa*. Paris, France: OECD. Retrieved April 2, 2018, from www.oecd.org/countries/ghana/2674846.pdf

McKinsey Global Institute. (2015). The power of parity: How advancing women's equality can add $12 trillion to global growth. Retrieved April 3, 2018, from www.mckinsey.com/~/media/McKinsey/Global%20Themes/Employment%20and%20Growth/How%20advancing%20womens%20equality%20can%20add%2012%20trillion%20to%20global%20growth/MGI%20Power%20of%20parity_Full%20report_September%202015.ashx

Maloney, S. (2008). Time to reassess Canada's foreign aid. *Policy Options* (September ed.). Ottawa, Canada: Institute for Research on Public Policy. Retrieved April 2, 2018, from http://policyoptions.irpp.org/magazines/canadas-working-poor/time-to-reassess-canadas-foreign-aid

Medhora, R. P. (2016). Follow the smart money: Canada's Foreign aid footprint in a changing world. *Policy Magazine* (June–August). Retrieved April 10, 2018, from www.policymagazine.ca/pdf/20/PolicyMagazineJulyAugust-2016-Medhora.pdf

Ministry of Food and Agriculture (MOFA). (2017). Planting for food and jobs strategic plan for implementation (2017–2020). Accra, Ghana: MOFA. Retrieved April 4, 2018, from http://mofa.gov.gh/site/wp-content/uploads/2018/03/PFJ%20document%20New%20New.pdf

Morris, M. L., Tripp, R., & Dankyi, A. A. (1999). Adoption and impacts of improved maize production technology: A case study of the Ghana Grains Development Project (Economics Program Paper 99-01). Mexico City, Mexico: International Maize and

Wheat Improvement Center. Retrieved March 5, 2018, from www.ispc.cgiar.org/sites/default/files/pdf/276.pdf

OECD. (2008). *OECD guidelines for multinational enterprises*. Paris, France: OECD.

Ostry, J. D., Loungani, P., & Furceri, D. (2016). *Neoliberalism oversold?* Washington, DC: International Monetary Fund. Retrieved December 8, 2018, from www.imf.org/external/pubs/ft/fandd/2016/06/pdf/ostry.pdf

Pratt, C. (Ed.). (1994). *Canadian international development assistance policies: An appraisal*. Montreal, Canada: McGill-Queen's University Press.

Pratt, D. (2007). Is there a grand strategy in Canadian foreign policy? (Lecture 2: Historical and theoretical considerations. The 2007 Ross Ellis Memorial Lectures in Military and Strategic Studies). *Journal of Military and Strategic Studies 10*(2).

Reporters Without Borders. (2018). Ghana country profile. Retrieved May 5, 2018, from https://rsf.org/en/ghana

Saad-Filho, A. (2010). Growth, poverty and inequality: From Washington Consensus to inclusive growth (DESA Working Paper No. 100). Washington: United Nations Department of Economic and Social Affairs. Retrieved March 5, 2018, from www.un.org/esa/desa/papers/2010/wp100_2010.pdf

Saad-Filho, A., & Johnson, D. (Eds.). (2005). *Neoliberalism: A critical reader*. London, UK: Pluto.

Sevunts, L. (2017). Canada's development aid in Africa driven by compassion and self-interest. Radio Canada International, July 10, 2017. Retrieved March 1, 2018, from www.rcinet.ca/en/2017/07/10/canadas-development-aid-in-africa-driven-by-compassion-and-self-interest-minister

Sheik, F. (2012). Canada eyes resources in Nigeria and Ghana as aid shrinks. *Guardian*, November 16. Retrieved May 1, 2018, from www.theguardian.com/global-development/2012/nov/16/canada-resources-nigeria-ghana-aid

Stiglitz, J. (1998). More instruments and broader goals: Moving toward the post-Washington Consensus (United Nations University, World Institute for Development Economics Research, Annual Lectures 2, Helsinki, Finland).

Sundaram, J. K., Schwank, O., & Von Arnim, R. (2011). Globalization and development in sub-Saharan Africa (DESA Working Paper No. 102). New York, NY: United Nations Department of Economic and Social Affairs. Retrieved May 5, 2018, from www.un.org/esa/desa/papers/2011/wp102_2011.pdf

Tanko, B. (2017). Canadian government supports planting for food and jobs programme. Accra, Ghana: Information Services Division, Government of Ghana.

Panford, K. (2001). *IMF – World Bank and labor's burdens in Africa: Ghana's experience*. Westport, CT: Praeger.

United Nations. (2015). *The Millennium Development Goals Report 2015*. Retrieved April 2, 2018, from www.un.org/millenniumgoals/2015_MDG_Report/pdf/MDG%202015%20rev%20(July%2 01).pdf

Williamson, J. (2004). The strange history of the Washington Consensus. *Journal of Post Keynesian Economics 27*(2) 195–206.

York, G. (2018). In Trudeau government's Africa strategy, the continent does not come first. *Globe and Mail*, April 10. Retrieved April 12, 2018, from www.theglobeandmail.com/world/article-in-trudeau-governments-africa-strategy-the-continent-does-not-come

4 EU as a democratic and development partner in Ghana

Credibility, coherence, and consistency in reforms

Mariam Dekanozishvili

Introduction

The European Union (EU) has been one of the various political and economic actors that Ghana has encountered on its road to sustainable democratization and economic growth. The EU has allocated €323m in support of the National Indicative Program for Ghana from the current eleventh European Development Fund (EDF), the primary source of EU funding for African Caribbean and Pacific countries (ACP), for the period of 2014–2020 (European External Action Service, 2016). The EU remains Ghana's biggest trade partner with over €2.3bn of exports in 2016 (European Commission, 2018). The Recently launched Ghana–EU interim Economic Partnership Agreement (EPA) promises improved access for Ghana's exports to the EU market, including value-added products.

The EU's engagement with Ghana has featured changing shades of aid, trade, and development policies shaped by internal developments in the EU, as well as the international context. From being an important trading partner and aid donor, the EU has increasingly asserted itself as a shaper of global development norms and promoter of these norms in the developing world. The new discourse on "democratic adjustment" could already be discerned in the programming process for Lomé IV that placed human rights and democratization at the forefront of the agenda (Crawford, 2005; Mailafia, 1997). The subsequent Cotonou Agreement of 2000 that marked the end of the EU's nonreciprocal preferences for ACP countries and paved the way for Economic Partnership Agreements signified a shift in the EU's approach to development. The EU bases the programming process for each ACP country, including Ghana, on the assessment of the conditions related to democracy, human rights, and good governance. Within the European political system, a consensus formed around a more political approach to development focusing on democratic governance with democracy, human rights, and the rule of law at its core. This new vision was outlined in the Joint Declaration on the EU's new Development Policy known as "European Consensus" (Council of the European Union, 2005; Orbie et al., 2017).

The EU's new approach emphasized the principles of "ownership" and "partnership." The EU envisioned itself not as a donor of development aid only, but also as a political partner holding political dialogues on areas of mutual interest (energy, transport, environment, migration, etc.) with recipient governments and jointly agreeing on key reform objectives (Koch et al., 2017). The new approach also entailed new aid modalities, as well as revision of the EU's conditionality instrument. From its traditional project approach which was criticized for lack of ownership, the EU has switched to a program-based approach aimed at supporting recipient countries' strategies and programs by channeling aid through the state budgets of recipient countries (Grimm, 2006). The new aid modality was accompanied by a new "performance-based conditionality" aimed at enhancing ownership, and effectively linking performance to disbursement. A key innovation of the reformed EU conditionality was the introduction of variable tranches that could be adjusted per recipient countries' performance (Adam et al., 2004).

Since then, the EU has taken a more politically oriented, incentive-based, and qualitative approach to governance in contrast to a more technocratic and economic approach of international financial institutions (Orbie et al., 2017). The EU's shift to a more comprehensive approach to development and democratic assistance has been reflected in its declared commitment to support Ghana's recently homegrown *beyond aid strategy* launched by President Nana Akufo-Addo and the New Patriotic Party (NPP) administration. The same spirit is maintained in the most recent EU–Ghana Joint Cooperation Strategy 2017–2020 that aims at consolidating Ghana's middle-income status and democratic governance, and strengthening partnership on shared values and political dialogue on a variety of areas including trade, competitiveness, migration, and climate change (European Union Delegation to Ghana, 2017).

Ghana, with its significant and stable democratic progress, despite unsteady economic performance over the last few decades, has been an exemplary norm-embracer in Africa and one of the few success stories for the EU's democracy promotion efforts beyond the EU's borders. Given the favorable context for democracy assistance, Ghana can be considered a test case for the EU's democracy promotion rhetoric in Africa. "If the reality of democracy promotion does not live up to the policy rhetoric in Ghana, then it is unlikely to do so elsewhere in Africa" (Crawford, 2005, p. 574). However, the stocktaking of political and economic reforms in Ghana lies in understanding political and administrative constraints and opportunities not only in the recipient country, but also regarding the donor actors. The EU with its complex bureaucratic apparatus and multilevel governance certainly deserves attention in this regard. Therefore, this chapter aims to focus on the challenges the EU faces as a donor, development and foreign policy actor, and how these challenges impact its relations with Ghana, and entire Africa.

The European Union's credibility challenge: Coordination, coherence, and consistency

Some scholars have argued that the EU's supranational development policy is distinctive as it transcends postcolonialism dynamics, promotes an incentive-based approach to democratic governance, and upholds virtues of regional integration (Carbone, 2010; Orbie, 2012, cited in Carbone, 2013). Others have challenged the EU's distinctiveness and asserted that the EU had used aid conditionality and development policy to promote trade liberalization commensurate with the existing trends and establish itself as a global actor. They have even questioned the existence of a supranational development policy (Farrell, 2008, cited in Carbone, 2013; Hadfield, 2007). This chapter does not intend to further this debate. It rather aims to unveil political and bureaucratic hurdles the EU has to cope with internally that, in turn, shape EU policies towards Africa and African partners' perceptions of the EU. When the EU's performance is perceived as ineffective, the credibility of the EU as a development and/or foreign policy actor gets undermined, reducing the EU's ability to influence the reform process in the partner countries. To be a credible actor, the EU's aspirations, as well as means by which it tries to achieve those aspirations, have to be perceived as legitimate and consistent by outsiders (Elgström, 2007; Fioramonti, 2009; Lucarelli, 2014). Thus, the EU's credibility is defined by its ability to formulate and articulate coherent political preferences and act consistently to fulfill them. This is, however, not an easy task for such a complex bureaucratic structure.

It can be argued that in its relations with Africa, the EU is constrained in terms of its capability to coordinate among member states and various institutions comprising the EU, particularly when mobilizing resources and expertise necessary to implement policies in African countries effectively. The EU often lacks coherence between development, trade, and other external policies. This incoherence places constraints on the EU as a development actor, which in turn affects the recipients' perceptions and strategies. Finally, inconsistency between the EU's objectives and instruments, between the EU's rhetoric and actions, or inconsistent application of values, norms, and conditionality instruments undermines the credibility of the EU in the eyes of its African partners.

Lack of coordination: Divergence of preferences

Development policy is a shared competence with the subsidiary division of labor between member states and the EU institutions, particularly the European Commission. The EU's ability to act autonomously and cohesively is contingent on the degree of convergence between member states' and EU institutions' preferences. Even though member states have gradually transferred some development policy competences and resources to the supranational level, they have also asserted the right to conduct their bilateral policies and programs, resisting any attempted interference by the European Commission (Carbone, 2017). Member state preferences often diverge over policies and procedures regarding how to achieve development objectives, and sometimes even over the long-term development goals (Koch et al., 2017).

In addition to divergent strategic interests of member states in relation to African recipients, several reasons have been discussed in the literature to explain the absence, or a limited will, of member states to coordinate their development and aid policies at the EU level. According to Molenaers (2012), varying internalization of development and aid effectiveness norms in member states inhibits coordination at the EU level. Delputte and Orbie (2014) suggest that member states often prefer to remain visible with their bilateral aid programs and are reluctant to dilute this visibility through collective EU action. Some EU member states, particularly Nordic countries, prefer to coordinate with all DAC donors beyond the EU (Delputte & Orbie, 2014).

Heterogeneity of member state preferences and varying degrees of interest in EU-level coordination, often determined by domestic political, economic, and bureaucratic context in member states, constrains EU's collective and consistent action in Africa (Bodenstein et al., 2017; Faust & Koch, 2014). After all, the EU is confined to using resources contributed by member states to the EDF, which falls outside of the EU budget. To the European Commission's disappointment, member states have repeatedly failed to increase their contributions to the EDF, despite their rhetorical commitment to more aid funding. Furthermore, several member states (the UK, Spain, and Ireland) have resisted an attempt to incorporate the EDF into the Community budget, a move that would make member states' contributions mandatory (Mackie et al., 2004). With the transformation of the EDF into a rolling fund, the European Commission has often been burdened with assuring timely commitment and disbursement of funds.

Experience with once very promising budget support programs for recipient countries has clearly demonstrated EU's coordination challenge. The support for this aid modality has been dwindling among EU member states. By 2015, only a handful of developing countries (Ghana excluded) remained recipients of this program. EU member states actively lobbied the European Commission to be more selective when providing budget support with a stronger focus on political governance criteria. Some member states have even abandoned provision of this aid modality in all partner countries despite reported positive results of the program in recipients' public financial management systems (Koch & Molenaers, 2015). Resistance often came from the national aid bureaucracies of the member states, mainly from those with right-leaning governments that prefer to have control over their aid activities. Their constituencies generally have more skeptical attitudes toward aid and perceive aid as direct support for corrupt recipient governments (Faust & Koch, 2014; Koch et al., 2017).

EU efforts to resolve coordination problems and improve aid effectiveness through joint programming once again encountered member state resistance. Joint programming aimed at stronger alignment with recipients' development plans, and more integrated responses by the EU delegations and member states. Those actions were expected to increase the EU's political and development impact in recipient countries (Carbone, 2017). However, most EU member states either adopted specific guidelines on joint programming or committed to it selectively.

The divergence of preferences and lack of coordination in the EU can subvert the value-added impact of the EU as a development actor in African countries. Competing objectives and duplication of efforts lead to ineffective use of scarce resources, as well as overburdening recipient governments with excessive administration (Orbie & Versluys, 2008). The EU's image of an autonomous coherent actor may also be undermined in the perceptions of African partners (Carbone, 2013). Lack of coordination constrains the EU's bargaining power and provides recipient governments with leverage for extracting concessions by playing off different donors (Carbone, 2008). While the coordination problems in the EU may increase recipient ownership over development process – the so-called coordination paradox – and can be evaluated in a favorable light (Carbone, 2010, 2017), they certainly have a negative impact on the credibility of the EU as a development actor in Africa. The EU strategies and policies can only be successful if collective action challenges are addressed (Bodenstein & Kemmerling, 2017). Yet, in the shadow of the 2008 financial crisis and ongoing migration hurdles, the EU's coordination challenge is far from disappearing.

Lack of coherence

The EU development policy sits at the intersection of various EU policy domains (trade, foreign and security, immigration, agriculture, etc.) governed by different rules with varying degrees of integration and driven by different policy actors (Gänzle et al., 2012). EU development policy cannot be conducted without identification of trade-offs and synergies across interacting policy domains. Coherence challenge can result from conflicts between development cooperation and other policy fields.

As Young and Peterson (2013) argue, the EU's partnership with ACP countries is a nexus of development partnership and trade policy which is designed to benefit the EU asymmetrically. Olsen (2009) has shown discrepancies between DG Trade and DG Development and Cooperation (DEVCO) during EPA negotiations between the EU and ACP countries, explaining how EU external policies are fragmented into patchy policy subsectors and lack coherence. Similarly, the nexus between EU security and development policies is beset by coherence problems (Furness & Gänzle, 2017). Different bureaucratic actors have managed different areas of the security–development nexus (e.g., civilian crisis response, humanitarian affairs) with different mandates and objectives catering to specific constituencies (Furness & Gänzle, 2017). The EU is often perceived to be employing its development policy to promote its foreign policy objectives in its relations with Africa and improve its image as a relevant foreign policy actor (Crawford, 2007). Citing democracy promotion as both part of the EU's CFSP and the development cooperation has been a signal of fragmentation of the policy field regarding organization, content, and programming from early on (Schmidt, 1999). At the practical level, bureaucratic hurdles and incoherence related to the division of labor between DG Development and Cooperation (known as EuropeAid) and European External Action Service (EEAS) may have a significant impact on the EU's position as a donor and tarnish the EU's reputation as being a capable, legitimate, and cohesive development and/or foreign policy actor. Furness and Gänzle (2017) ascribe this intra-EU incoherence to the EU's lack of strategic direction and clear priorities that is symptomatic of a system with no clear hierarchy.

The EU's various policy initiatives, including the European Consensus (2005), Division of Labor (2007), Policy Coherence for Development (2009), the Operational Framework on Aid Effectiveness (2011), and the most recent 2030 Agenda for Sustainable Development have sought to address coordination and coherence problems in the EU. The success of these proposals has often been questioned. At least, the gap between policies elaborated in Brussels and implementation outcomes in African countries remains (Carbone, 2013, 2017; Delputte & Orbie, 2014). The EU's new Global Strategy on Foreign and Security Policy (2016) also acknowledges the need for more flexible development policy better aligned with strategic priorities. In pursuance of its new approach of "principled pragmatism," the EU plans to adopt a joined-up approach to its humanitarian, development, trade, migration, etc. policies to enhance coherence in the EU.

Lack of consistency

Consistency problems in EU development and democracy promotion efforts in Africa can emerge due to a gap between the EU's proclaimed values, principles, and objectives, and its practices on the ground. Inconsistencies can arise within different facets of development policy itself, such as between poverty eradication and democratic governance, or ownership and asymmetric conditionality. Inconsistency in the EU's objectives and priorities, as well as in the application of EU policy instruments e.g., conditionality may raise questions regarding the EU's commitment to development and democratization objectives in Africa.

EU protectionist tendencies, despite being recognized as a global trading power, often lead to inconsistent behavior on the part of the EU which may undermine its credibility and influence in the transformation process in African partners (Lucarelli, 2014). Similarly, the credibility of the EU's proclaimed objective of sustainable development in Africa has been undermined by highly unequal sets of relationships between the EU and African countries, most notably with the EU's systems of subsidies in the Common Agricultural Policy (Taylor, 2016). Perception of the EU in Ghana as a credible and committed partner can play a crucial role for the successful implementation of the EU–Ghana interim EPA and prospective adoption of regional EPA within West Africa. Indeed, the suspicion that the EPA is perpetuating Ghana's status as a supplier of low-margin commodities for processing elsewhere and could impede the regional integration process in West Africa, e.g., introduction of different tariff-reduction rules, is lingering (Ntasano, 2010).

The lack of consistency between EU trade policy priorities, foreign aid policy, and democracy promotion objectives is often negatively viewed beyond EU borders, including African countries (Bodenstein & Kemmerling, 2017). The EU's twin goals of development cooperation – poverty eradication and democratic development – as pronounced in the Cotonou Agreement, more recent EU development policy strategies and documents, and the Treaty on the Functioning of the EU (Lisbon Treaty) often confronts the EU with a dilemma in African countries that make progress in poverty reduction but have rather poor democratic records (Del Biondo, 2011). The EU might turn a blind eye to certain countries that tend to make progress in eradicating poverty while stagnating or worsening politically. The EU has been criticized for letting particular interests take precedence over values and principles that it is supposed to uphold. By focusing on building state capacities, the EU has often compromised on democratic reforms in African countries. Short-term strategic or economic interests related to energy, migration, terrorism, and other issues have come to trump the pursuit of pronounced objectives of promoting democracy, the rule of law, and human rights. In this context, Crawford's (2007) argument in his study of EU democracy promotion in Ghana is particularly compelling. According to Crawford (2007), against the ongoing trend of "securitization" of development policies, EU democracy promotion has been limited in Ghana because the EU has few direct security interests in the country (p. 84). The absence of specific provisions on human rights or sustainable development – actively used concepts in EU rhetoric – in the EU–Ghana interim EPA could serve to reinforce the above argument.

It may be legitimate for the EU to balance its short-term interests against its long-term and more diffused objectives in African countries, but this often comes at the price of losing legitimacy and credibility in the eyes of the local populations in Africa. As Carbone (2017) demonstrates on the example of the EU joint programming initiative (the EU's response to address aid fragmentation) the translation of the EU's political commitments into concrete actions on the ground in Africa (and Ghana in this case) remains a problem. The disconnect between policy decisions in Brussels and implementation in target countries is a reminder of the EU's consistency challenge.

A credible actor is expected to show consistency in its application of policy instruments used to promote its values and objectives. The partners have to be certain that they will receive promised rewards upon fulfilling EU's requirements. If the EU communicates inconsistently regarding its norms, for instance by using diverging normative standards for different countries, it undermines its credibility. Conditionality instrument has long been a feature of EU's development policy and an essential tool of democracy promotion. Since the Cotonou Agreement, the economic concept of conditionality aimed at economic reforms (like the Structural Adjustment Programs) have gradually been replaced by so-called second-generation political conditionality – allocation and use of financial resources to sanction or reward recipients to promote democratic governance and human rights – linking the EU's development cooperation to political considerations (Fierro, 2003). Since the 2000s, progress on democratic reforms has become an important criterion for the EU to decide upon the allocation of aid funds provided through the EDF. Political conditionality was broadened to some extent by making good governance a fundamental element, making it possible for the EU to use sanctions in cases of severe corruption and bribery (Hadfield, 2007, pp. 43–44). Moreover, aid modalities such as budget support allow the EU to engage in dialog on political reforms (Koch & Molenaers, 2015).

The EU has not always shown consistency in its application of conditionality instruments. Earlier studies have shown that the EU only invoked sanctions in the cases of a coup d'état and flawed elections while neglecting human rights violations or deterioration of the democratic process (Del Biondo, 2011). Such inconsistency resonates with the argument that donors "tend to focus on minimalist, the electoral conception of democracy" (Diamond, 1999, cited in Del Biondo, 2011, p. 381) and that the EU utilizes political conditionality instruments and democracy promotion as a means to advance its economic liberalization agenda (Taylor, 2016). Donors, including the EU, have been perceived as applying sanctions against weaker states with less relevance for economic and security interests (Del Biondo, 2015; Sorensen, 1995). In a more recent study, Koch et al. (2017) contend that around the year 2008, when political problems started to mount in a number of budget support recipient countries in Africa, including corruption cases, human rights violations, and restrictions on political freedoms, European donors failed to send consistent signals to the recipient governments by treating some of them with considerable leniency. Such practice might incentivize some governments that are unwilling to reform their policies to look for ways to evade political conditionality, e.g., by pretending progress, or discourage reform efforts in more motivated ones.

Lack of commitment to the pronounced norms and principles outlined in various policy documents, strategies, and programs, and the resulting gap between the EU's rhetoric and action on the ground can hurt EU legitimacy and credibility as a development actor in Africa. Since the Cotonou Agreement, "ownership" and "partnership" have become buzzwords in the EU's development policy and programs. These principles implied more alignment to the recipient governments' priorities and strategies and jointly agreed on development targets and reforms to allow more recipient ownership. Ownership of reforms was considered indispensable for accountability and legitimacy of the recipient governments and effective implementation of economic reform programs (Adam et al., 2004). It was to this end that the EU reformed its traditional conditionality instrument based on policy measures and replaced it with performance-based conditionality underpinning EU's budgetary support scheme to ACP countries. Disbursement of aid was no longer tied to specific policy measures but rather to outcomes in key economic and social domains with choice of instruments left to the recipient government (Adam et al., 2004). However, the EU has often been criticized for not living up to its pronounced principles. In the context of Ghana, the EU has been observed to bring ready-made programs to the government of Ghana which played a minor role in shaping those programs. The government has been reluctant to decline aid proposals even when those were not in line with government's preferences, highlighting government constraints imposed by aid dependence and perpetuating an asymmetric donor–recipient relationship. Whitfield and Jones (2007) argue that Ghana has focused on pleasing donors rather than exerting ownership and control over its national strategies. The problem of ownership and partnership has emerged concerning the more recent EU Emergency Trust Fund for Africa (EUTF) for Africa. The EUTF that comes from the

EDF features a lack of formal oversight and loss of formal control and ownership by partners on how these funds are spent. Projects are often selected in disregard for local needs, based on the effectiveness of member states in lobbying for funds (Castillejo, 2016).

The unequal power balance and the manner in which the EPA was negotiated between the EU and Ghana seems to question the EU's commitment to put partnership and ownership principles to practice. By including services, investment, and procurement against Ghana's position trying to protect some sectors from EU competition, the EU denied Ghana, and other ACP countries, the right of ownership (Flint, 2008). These EU practices undermine EU credibility and may serve to reinforce the suspicion that the EU is predetermining and imposing democratic principles on African countries while lacking consistency in applying those same principles due to strategic or economic interests.

The increased priority of migration issues on the EU agenda that can only be effectively managed through efforts with African countries of origin or transit opens up more scope for a more balanced relationship and more real partnership. Unlike development aid and trade policies, the extent of African partners' dependence on the EU is far less pronounced, and the EU's need to cooperate with them to stem migratory flows far more obvious. This might lead to a better level playing field for African countries and more consistent commitment to the partnership on the side of the EU.

Broadly speaking, EU's development and democratization efforts in Africa feature two dimensions: internal dimension aimed at coordination of member states' development policies and external dimension aimed at reforms and transformation of African countries. Lack of coordination and coherence in the former and lack of consistency in the latter threaten to undermine EU credibility in the eyes of African partners and reduce the EU's impact and influence on political and economic reforms.

EU repeated efforts to reform its development aid policies and conditionality instrument can be perceived as an attempt to address the credibility challenge. However, institutional solutions to credibility problems are subject to further problems of credible commitment. Indeed, the more the EU is perceived as incapable, incoherent, and inconsistent in translating policy rhetoric into impactful actions, the more likely the partner countries are to lower their expectations of the EU and be more open to better alternatives. The increasing presence of China with its no strings and conditionality attached and noninterference approach might seem an appealing option for African governments as an alternative source of funding, as well as for improving their leverage when negotiating aid conditions and trade agreements with the EU (Aidoo & Hess, 2015; Fioramonti, 2009).

Whether Chinese presence provides an incentive for the EU to address its credibility challenge or exerts pressure on the EU to become more lenient with regard to democracy, good governance, and human rights in its relations with African countries is open to debate (see Grimm & Hackenesch, 2017).

Ghana's prospects in EU development and democracy promotion efforts in Africa

The EU's development policy in Africa has been defined by the nexus of strategic and economic interests and norm-based policies (democracy, human rights, good governance) and underpinned by the EU's credibility challenge. Looking at the EU's new Global Security and Foreign Policy Strategy, which is intended to guide all EU external actions, it is obvious that, in the future, the EU's development policy will have a broader scope and be more closely linked to the EU's strategic priorities, such as migration and security. In such a context, what can be Ghana's unique place in EU development policy?

The EU's attempt to legitimize its role as a development and foreign policy actor in Africa might offer some prospects for Ghana to position itself and convince the EU of its stature as a special "success story" for EU endeavors, given Ghana's good track record in political and economic reforms. Indeed, the EU's Strategy for Africa (2005) acknowledged that Ghana as a stable country plays an essential role in setting an example of what can be achieved in a favorable political climate. "In West Africa, Ghana is the prime example of a well-governed and stable country which has been able to convert economic growth into tangible development achievements" (European Commission, 2005, p. 10). Ghana's success allows the EU to point out its development and foreign policy successes to the increasingly Euroskeptic public at home and strengthen EU credibility in the eyes of other African partners. The EU can also use the successful outcome of its previous policies to have a selling point for further integration of development policy at the EU level, and overcome coordination and collective action problems However, the EU should be vigilant not to be trapped into a tendency of overlooking certain underachievements in Ghana for the sake of maintaining the label of "success story" as a rhetorical note. This can only add to the manifestations of the EU's credibility challenge.

Real success in developing countries is defined not only by social and economic development, but also by reducing undue influences and vulnerability to external actors. Even if current policies of the EU and other development actors realize the former, they rarely achieve the latter. What are Ghana's prospects in this regard?

Given the EU's increasing migration challenge and a realization that migration can only be addressed through joint efforts with countries of origin and transit, Ghana could arguably be strategically placed in the migration debate and negotiations. Ghana is an exporter of mostly high and medium-skilled human capital (*Ghana Business News*, 2015). EU's primary interest, however, in establishing joint migration management frameworks with origin countries focuses on migration control of mostly irregular and low-skilled migrants. In this respect, Ghana is less likely to have strategic relevance. Yet, Ghana is actively involved in EU migration management efforts, e.g., participation in the Valletta Action Plan, and benefits from the EU's Emergency Trust Fund since 2016. What complicates equal, partnership-based cooperation on migration issues between the EU and African countries, including Ghana, is the persistent tension between the

EU's supranational and intergovernmental levels of policymaking and implementation. Often, separate national policy agendas restrict effective solutions at the EU level. Lack of coordination within the EU restricts its ability to effectively engage on migration issues with African countries. Given the EU's complex institutional setup, addressing these challenges will require strategic decisions in the highest political venues of the EU. Whether member states manage to benefit from the multiplier effect of political cooperation and the EU's credible image will undoubtedly impact EU relations with Ghana and the entire continent for years to come.

Concluding remarks

This chapter uncovers the political and bureaucratic constraints that the EU faces as a development actor in Ghana, and with other African partners. The chapter suggests that the EU has to overcome a tripartite credibility challenge in order to effectively influence the reform process in the recipient countries: First, the EU needs better coordination among member states and various EU institutions when mobilizing resources and implementing policies in African partners. Second, the EU needs more coherence between development, trade, and other external policies. Third, the European regional bloc needs to ensure consistency between its objectives and instruments, and its rhetoric and actions to retain the image of a credible development and foreign policy actor in the eyes of the African partners. Against the backdrop of the EU's credibility challenge, Ghana may be uniquely positioned due to its relatively successful reforms: Ghana's "success story" provides the EU with a positive point of reference to legitimize its role as a development and foreign policy actor and push for more integrated development policy at the EU level.

The multiple crises (such as Brexit and EU immigration) that are hounding the EU only make it ever more challenging to find the right balance between strategic and economic interests, and norm-based policies in Ghana and its other African recipient countries. The EU's new Global Security and Foreign Policy Strategy that claims to guide the bloc's future external actions signals a strategic shift in EU development policy. Strategic priorities, such as migration and security, are likely to underpin EU development policy and its relations with African partners. In such a context, Ghana's challenge is to find a right niche as to how it could contribute to the EU's pressing priorities while maintaining the appeal of a successful reformer for the EU.

References

Adam, C., Chambas, P., Guillaumont, P., Jeanneney, S. G., & Gunning, J. W. (2004). Performance-based conditionality: A European perspective. *World Development 32*(6) 1059–1070.

Aidoo, R., & Hess, S. (2015). Non-interference 2.0: China's evolving foreign policy towards a changing Africa. *Journal of Current Chinese Affairs 44*(1) 107–139.

Bodenstein, T., Faust, J., & Furness, M. (2017). EU development policy: Collective action in times of global transformation and domestic crisis. *Development Policy Review 35*(4) 441–453.

Bodenstein, T., & Kemmerling, A. (2017). The European Union as a collective actor: Aid and trade in African public opinion. *Development Policy Review 35*(4) 567–586.

Carbone, M. (2008). Better aid, less ownership: Multi-annual programming and the EU's development strategies in Africa. *Journal of International Development 20*(2) 218–229.

Carbone, M. (2010). The European Union, good governance, and aid coordination. *Third World Quarterly 31*(1) 13–29.

Carbone, M. (2013). Between EU actorness and aid effectiveness: The logic of EU aid to sub-Saharan Africa. *International Relations 27*(3) 341–355.

Carbone, M. (2017). Make Europe happen on the ground? Enabling and constraining factors for European Union aid coordination in Africa. *Development Policy Review 35*(4) 531–548.

Castillejo, C. (2016). The European Union Trust Fund for Africa: A glimpse of the future for EU development cooperation (Discussion Paper 22, Bonn, Germany: German Development Institute).

Council of the European Union. (2005). Joint declaration by the Council and the representatives of the governments of the Member States meeting within the Council, the European Parliament and the Commission on the development policy of the European Union entitled "The European Consensus" [Official Journal C 46 of 24.2.2006].

Crawford, G. (2005). The European Union and democracy promotion in Africa: The case of Ghana. *European Journal of Development Research 17*(4) 571–600.

Crawford, G. (2007). The EU and democracy promotion in Africa: High on rhetoric, low on delivery? In A. Mold (Ed.), *EU development policy in a changing world: Challenges for the 21st century* (pp. 169–198). Amsterdam, the Netherlands: Amsterdam University Press.

Del Biondo, K. (2011). EU aid conditionality in ACP countries: Explaining inconsistency in EU sanctions practice. *Journal of Contemporary European Research 7*(3) 380–395.

Del Biondo, K. (2015). Donor interests or developmental performance? Explaining sanctions in EU democracy promotion in sub-Saharan Africa. *World Development 75* 74–84.

Delputte, S., & Orbie, J. (2014) The EU and donor coordination on the ground: Perspectives from Tanzania and Zambia. *European Journal of Development Research 26*(5) 676–691.

Elgström, O. (2007). Outsiders' perceptions of the European Union in international trade negotiations. *Journal of Common Market Studies 45*(4), 949–967.

European Commission. (2005). EU strategy for Africa: Towards a Euro-African pact to accelerate Africa's development, COM (2005)489 final, Brussels.

European Commission. (2018). Ghana – Trade statistics, European Commission Directorate General for Trade. Retrieved February 20, 2019, from trade.ec.europa.eu/doclib/html/122461.htm

European External Action Service. (2016). 2014–2020 National Indicative Programme – Ghana. Retrieved February 20, 2019, from https://eeas.europa.eu/sites/eeas/files/2014-2020_national-indicative-programme_ghana_en.pdf

European Union Delegation to Ghana. (2017). European partners working together. Joint co-operation strategy 2017–2020. Retrieved February 20, 2019, from https://eeas.europa.eu/sites/eeas/files/european_partners_working_together_in_ghana_2 017-2020_final_26_09_2017.pdf

Farrell, M. (2008). Internationalising EU development policy. *Perspectives on European Politics and Society* *9*(2) 225–240.

Faust, J., & Koch, S. (2014). Foreign aid and the domestic politics of European budget support (Discussion Paper 21, Bonn, Germany: German Development Institute.

Fierro, E. (2003). *The EU's approach to human rights conditionality in practice.* The Hague, the Netherlands: Martinus Nijhoff.

Fioramonti, L. (2009). African perceptions of the European Union: Assessing the work of the EU in the field of democracy promotion and peacekeeping. Report commissioned by the International Institute for Democracy and Electoral Assistance. Stockholm, Sweden: IDEA.

Flint, A. (2008). *Trade, poverty and the environment. The EU, Cotonou and the African–Caribbean–Pacific bloc.* New York, NY: Palgrave Macmillan.

Furness, M., & Gänzle, S. (2017). The security–development nexus in EU foreign relations after Lisbon: Policy coherence at last? *Development Policy Review* *35*(4) 475–492.

Gänzle, S, Grimm, S., & Makhan, D. (2012). *The European Union and global development: An "enlightened superpower" in the making?* New York, NY: Palgrave Macmillan.

Ghana Business News. (2015). Ghana has highest emigration rates for skilled workers. Retrieved June 15, 2018, from www.ghanabusinessnews.com/2015/05/13/ghana-has-highest-emigration-rates-for-skilled-workers

Grimm, S. (2006). *EU development cooperation: Rebuilding a tanker at sea.* Berlin, Germany: Friedrich Ebert Stiftung.

Grimm, S. & Hackenesch, C. (2017). China in Africa: What challenges for a reforming European Union development policy? Illustrations from country cases. *Development Policy Review* *35*(4) 549–566.

Hadfield, A. (2007). Janus advances? An analysis of EC development policy and the 2005 amended Cotonou Partnership Agreement. *European Foreign Affairs Review* *12*(1) 39–66.

Koch, S., Leiderer, S., Faust, J., & Molenaer, N. (2017). The rise and demise of European budget support: Political economy of collective European Union donor action. *Development Policy Review* *35*(4) 455–473.

Koch, S., & Molenaers, N. (2015). The Europeanisation of budget support: Do government capacity and autonomy matter? *European Politics and Society* *17*(1) 90–104.

Lucarelli, S. (2014). Seen from the outside: The state-of-the-art on the external image of the EU. *Journal of European Integration* *39*(1) 1–16.

Mackie, J., Frederiksen, J., & Rossini, C. (2004). Improving ACP–EU cooperation: Is "budgetising" the EDF the answer? (ECDPM Discussion Paper 51, Maastricht, the Netherlands: ECDPM).

Mailafia, O. (1997). *Europe and economic reform in Africa. Structural adjustment and economic diplomacy.* New York, NY: Routledge.

Molenaers, N. (2012). The great divide? Donor perceptions of budget support, eligibility and policy dialogue. *Third World Quarterly* *33*(5) 791–806.

Orbie, J. (2012). The EU's role in development: A full-fledged development actor or eclipsed by superpower temptations? In S. Grimm, S. Gänzle, & D. Makhan (Eds.), *The European Union: An "enlightened superpower" in the making?* (pp. 17–36) New York, NY: Palgrave Macmillan.

Orbie, J., Delputte, S., Bossuyt, F., Debusscher, P., Del Biondo, K., & Reynaert, V., et al. (2017). The normative distinctiveness of the European Union in international development: Stepping out of the shadow of the World Bank? *Development Policy Review* *35*(4) 493–511.

Orbie, J., & Versluys, H. (2008). The European Union's international development policy: Leading and benevolent? In J. Orbie (Ed.), *Europe's global role: External policies of the European Union* (pp. 67–90). Farnham, UK: Ashgate.
Olsen, G. R. (2009). The missing link: EPAs, security and development interventions in Africa. In J. Orbie & G. Faber (Eds.), *Beyond market access for economic development: EU–Africa relations in transition* (pp. 342–357). New York, NY: Routledge.
Schmidt, S. (1999). Die Demokratie- und Menschenrechtsförderung der Europäischen Union unter besonderer Berücksichtigung Afrikas. *Arbeitspapiere zu Problemen der Internationalen Politik und der Entwicklungsländerforschung*, no. 28/1999 (pp. 1–40). Forschungsstelle Dritte Welt.
Sorensen, G. (1995). Conditionality, democracy and development. In O. Stokke (Ed.), *Aid and political conditionality* (pp. 392–409). New York, NY: Routledge.
Taylor, I. (2016). Bait and switch: The European Union's incoherency towards Africa. *Insight on Africa 8*(2) 96–111.
Whitfield, L., & Jones, E. (2007). Ghana: The pollical dimensions of aid dependence (Working Paper No. 32, Global Economic Governance Programme, Managing Aid Dependency Project, Oxford, UK).
Young, A., & Peterson, J. (2013). We care about you, but...: The politics of EU trade policy and development. *Cambridge Review of International Affairs 26*(3) 497–518.

5 Ghana–Asian partnerships

The scramble for markets, power, and agency

Naaborle Sackeyfio

Introduction

Amid divergent models of political and economic development including reform, are fierce competition for markets and power by China, and, to a lesser extent, Japan. China's geopolitical interests are hotly contested, but palpably resource driven; while Japan, whose postwar success catapulted the country to the much-heralded "East Asian miracle" aims to flex its economic muscle on the continent. Frequently touted for its stellar credentials of stable democratic governance and robust track record of development, Ghana courts its growing status as one of the fastest, and site of foreign direct investment, petro-economy, and record development over the past decade. This chapter argues that despite lucrative economic engagement with China, securing an upper-middle-income status will depend on how well Ghana eschews donor state dependency; what lessons it learns from Japan, and how it navigates externally directed reforms to protect and expand agency. Doing so will augur well for a country whose promise in the 21st century is nonetheless imperiled by runaway development in a heightened resource-rich economy.

A framework

The first section briefly delineates the country's political history from independence to the current period. The second section examines the country's development strategies in the 21st century including donor-led and resource-reliant development. The third section explores Japan's development path after establishing the country as the first East Asian miracle to identify historical and institutional patterns that offer a stratagem for Ghana. The fourth section examines China's pivot to Ghana and the use of infrastructure as currency for leverage and power to argue that a Ghanaian renaissance on its terms requires what Mazrui (1967) referred to as continental jurisdiction – in matters of economic governance. The emphasis on infrastructure here stems from the observation that "Ghana's deficient infrastructure has been identified as one of the key obstacles hampering economic development objectives" (Odoom, 2017, p. 603). The author recognizes that the increasing array of multilateral platforms, trade alliances, in short globalization complicate the possibility of full continental jurisdiction, but argues for it, nonetheless. Additionally, an exploration of small-scale sector growth, development of an entrepreneurial class, and the connection to agency follows. A concluding section offers suggestions for how Ghana can triumphantly emerge, as a scramble for markets and power by Japan and China quickens.

Both China and Japan's contemporary relationship with Ghana is rooted in the 1955 Bandung conference at which Asian states sought closer and more fruitful connections to African states for political support at international organizations like the United Nations. While both states are uniquely positioned to forge meaningful economic alliances with African countries given a non-western trajectory, as they played no role in the continent's colonization. Ghana's engagement with both states and the wider Asian arc stems from its early involvement in international trade unions. The resultant activism of the early post-independent period belies what Sackeyfio-Lenoch (2017, p. 192) describes as a "narrative of African labor interests succumbing to the impulses and politics of international labor." Trade union alliances during the early independence period offer a purview of promising agency. For instance, in 1957, Ghanaian trade unions looked abroad for solidarity and embraced a global perspective within the context of nationalist struggle – but reversed course by adopting an inward-oriented perspective that focused on developing an African labor movement on African terms (Sackeyfio-Lenoch, 2017, p. 199). Despite a post-independent thrust toward industrial development and ultimately calamitous struggle between Kwame Nkrumah's regime, the Ghana Trades Union Congress (GTUC), International Federation of Christian Trade Unions (IFCTU) and the latter's own conflictual relationships with international labor organizations (Sackeyfio-Lenoch, 2017) attest to the difficult and ongoing process of development and agency.

Although China marshalled greater support among African states than Japan whose stereotypical views of Africa (see Adem, 2010) produced an initially at-arm's-length diplomacy, the need for raw materials and mineral resources required that it heighten its strategies for economic engagement. As Adem (2010, p. 885) observes, "Africa's potentially significant vote in the UN General Assembly in support of Japan's permanent membership in a reformed Security Council is a significant factor in the prime Minister Yoshiro Mori's decision to visit Africa two decades ago." Since that historic visit, one key detail has escaped notice – that Japan's emphasis on an impetus of "self-help" is reflected in Ghana's economic outlook – in terms of its electrification initiatives that began in the 1990s and in conjunction with political decentralization of power which aimed to empower ordinary individuals and local governance structures (see Sackeyfio, 2017). It is notable, then, that Ghana managed over the course of almost 30 years to inculcate the notion of self-help into a key aspect of energy development. These development plans however are not without flaws (Sackeyfio, 2017), but are nonetheless a positive development that requires a larger application across the country's economic spheres to produce fresh perspectives for revitalization.

Political–historical development and the promise of industrialization in the 20th century

Ghana's emergence as a pivotal regional and continental actor was buoyed by its pan-African credentials and largely spurred the country's first post-independent and nationalist leader, Kwame Nkrumah. With promises of industrialization that came on the heels of the completion of the country's first and largest human-made dam on the continent – the Akosombo dam, in the late 1960s and Volta River project, the euphoria of this period can hardly be overstated. Designed to produce aluminum smelting which would be used to produce bauxite and in turn electric power, a key input for industrialization, the dreams of the Volta River Project in 1966 despite fits and starts seemingly propelled the country into a new era – one that Nkrumah assured Ghanaians would be marked by self-sufficiency, not unlike his larger continental vision/brand of pan-Africanism. However, Cold War politics and the sobering realities of governance under great power conflict proved formidable for shedding the yoke of dependency. Ultimately, Nkrumah, despite a laudable legacy of pan-Africanism that appears resurgent succumbed to dictatorship and a political pogrom against erstwhile opponents, both real and perceived. After his ouster in 1972, Ghana vacillated between coup d'états and civilian rule. The early 1980s were marked by a brief revolutionary zeal and socialist tinge in the bloodless coup that installed former flight lieutenant J.J. Rawlings to power. Oil crises in the preceding decade produced shocks and a global recession that pummeled developing countries into a downward spiral. Debt crises and an economy on the brink left Rawlings little choice but to capitulate to international financial institutions as lenders of last resort. By the end of the 1980s, the country began to recover, but joined a large number of African states as highly indebted and thus beholden to the World Bank and International Monetary Fund (IMF). The agency and self-sufficient impetus that had so galvanized Nkrumah in his bulwark approach to dismantling or at least reducing dependency appeared insolvent. The end of the Cold War produced the Washington Consensus and reimagined landscape for core and developing states largely viewed as part of the global "periphery." No longer needed for proxy support, new limits on agency appeared with the creation of reification of conditionality agreements that stipulated "good governance" in exchange for aid and loan compliance. African leaders fell in line and the newly reinvented Rawlings emerged in the cloak of democracy largely woven from the invisible thread of necessity and political survival beginning in 1992. The mid 1990s were cause for triumph as international observers and financial institutions declared Ghana a "star pupil" to use Hutchful's (2002) phrase. Since the start of the 21st century, the embrace of market-oriented reforms including a widened scope for privatization and shrinkage of the state have more to do with the shrewd calculation of the Rawlings regime in the form of strategic noncompliance, political patronage, and rural bias as critical vectors (see Akonor, 2013). By the turn of the 21st century, the country's first peaceful transition to civilian rule with President J. A. Kufuor at the helm was equally extolled as a milestone for good governance.

Almost two decades later and several peaceful turnovers, many point to Ghana as a beacon for democracy in a region that is rife with conflict tropes and instability. On its economic front, primary export commodities like cocoa, gold, and other minerals have performed relatively well. Increased FDI, development partners like India, Brazil, and other states have expanded the country's investor portfolio, yet for all its advances in capacity-building efforts, a robust local entrepreneurial class is largely ephemeral, a disproportionate rural–urban ratio of development continues to exacerbate inequality and a substantial number of Ghanaians languish from rural neglect. Consequentially, the discovery of oil in 2007 and the spoils from a now petro-rich economy appear unevenly distributed between the country's economic strata – particularly those who need it. All the while, the benefits from a heightened scramble for markets and power by China and Japan are elusive for many Ghanaians. Although parliament houses, railways for commercial transport, and the country's ports are a vital locus for economic growth and expansion, the country could benefit from an institutional "reset" to expand the distributional gains to all. Emerging from the highly indebted poor country (HIPC) status into a lower-middle income developing state is significant, however a retooling of Ghana's trajectory is necessary for rethinking the country's scope of agency to chart a new course that privileges self-help locus akin to Nkrumah's pan-African call to action articulated several decades ago.

Donor-led development?

Can the growing prominence of model states like Ghana promote a new model of growth departing from the usual equation rooted in donor-led development?

A changing narrative suggest so, after all high growth rates are not exclusive to Ghana but the continent overall (see Lopes, 2010, p. 72). The notion of an emergence of "African lions" akin to the "Asian Tigers" suggests as much (see Lopes, 2010, p. 73) and almost a decade after Lopes's article, Ghana is ostensibly part of the club. Yet, negotiating new terms for debt burdens that offer a widened scope for local agency in executing these obligations that "bring capital back in" is necessary. As a developmental state, chartering a new course that harnesses technological innovations both within the country and elsewhere on the continent is critical. Telecommunications and technological expertise in the country show encouraging signs of renewal with an impetus fueled by demand.

However, there is much to suggest that the country's anchor for development in the 21st century is one that remains path-dependent. That is to say it pulses with neoliberal machinations and donor-led discourse despite appeals for self-help framework of governance – which is to suggest a policy devoid of dependence on aid for development (see Lumumba-Kasongo, 2010).

Decades after independence, little has changed: cocoa, gold, and other minerals remain a primary locus for exports. In the past two decades, mining activities have drawn considerable interest by eager investors. Yet as Bond (2008, p. 363) observes "ongoing struggles in Africa highlight the need for improved returns from foreign direct investment to state finances." A new language for transparency of international and local mining operation efforts have been underway since the turn of the 21st century, but the mechanisms for local perusal, particularly for district assembly actors who represent decentralized vehicles for governance are inexact. While Ghana has so far escaped the resource curse or conundrum that other states have fallen victim to, opportunities for spatial and sectoral development in the way of greater synergies between resource and non-resource-rich areas are a work in progress (see Bush, 2008), rural livelihoods, energy sources, and the backward as well as forward linkages required for bringing these areas into sharper focus are rather marginal at best (see Sackeyfio, 2017). To this end, Bush notes that across the continent and in resource-rich economies in particular, increases in oil and metals prices are not always matched by world market prices for other African commodities … and questions the notion of optimism in the largesse for commodities from African states given elite capture and what he calls "unprecedented benefits for mining companies" (2008, p. 362). He rightfully observes that "ongoing struggles in Africa highlight the need for improved returns from foreign direct investment to state finances" from which Ghana is certainly not excluded, after all. The manner of utilization of the country's natural resources imperil institutional reforms that would otherwise promote commodity diversification, and limit or even avoid the resource curse altogether (see Sachs et al., 1995; Sachs & Warner, 2001). Thus, developing indigenous technology not just within Ghana, but the wider continent offers the possibility of lesser dependence on donors for technical aid as well as expertise. Such progress, however, requires a united regional organization via the Economic Community of West African States (ECOWAS) or the African Union. Supporting local technological efforts in ways that divest agency and power to the recipients and innovators without the institutional bottlenecks is a critical step. Combining local technological expertise with foreign technological aid and innovation from China and Japan in ways that invite oversight from local stakeholders is also worthwhile. The next section juxtaposes Japan's institutional and development trajectory in brief to considers instruments that are potentially useful for Ghana's economic advancement.

Japan

Japan began its trajectory as a developmentalist state and novel case study for developing countries two decades after World War II ended. As a beneficiary of the German Marshall Fund, one cannot underscore the extent to which US aid via the fund rebuilt the country's infrastructure after the devastation of war, which included firebombing and two nuclear bombs. It is certainly no accident that the country emerged as a model for East Asian states in the region. A disciplined bureaucracy, technological innovation, inward-oriented development that rejected the neoclassical model for economic growth accounts for the miracle that resulted in a remarkably resilient Japanese state. Reflecting a curious blend of industrial policy via the then Ministry for International Trade and Industry

(MITI) – now the Ministry of Economy, Trade and Industry (METI) or, the country, much to the chagrin of IFIs embraced a policy which privileged the supply of capital to nascent industries which were only allowed to compete in world markets once they were ready. In contrast, much of the developing world in Africa found itself in the throes of economic crisis during this period as a consequence of path-dependent circumstances. These included the vestiges of colonial rule, inchoate institutions, artificially created boundaries cobbled together from the apparatus of violence. In short, Ghana and the rest of the continent faced the monumental task of developing nascent economies that were rudimentary and out of sync with juridical statehood and the machinery to develop technology and infrastructure. As corruption, economic malaise, oil crises, and inept leadership dotted the landscape of much of the continent, the prescription for these maladies was to simply reduce the role of the state in the economy. Thus, Japan's adoption of state-led development ran afoul of conventional wisdom, which by the 1970s suggested that an interventionist state in the economy would simply yield a distorted one.

A critical feature informs the East Asian miracle: the long trajectory of statehood, a relatively homogeneous makeup and principle of "Sakoku" or chained country and isolationist if not outright refusal to engage with other countries from the mid-16th century to 1868 when the country was forced to open up, allowed it to develop on its own terms. Developing a space for commodity specialization, following the global observations of state officials who traveled the world produced a state that in prescient terms recognized the importance of preserving its institutions both cultural and beyond from conquest. Avoiding the perils of cultural and political dilution it seemed were a key goal as was unification of the country. Africa of course had no such luxury, given that power often broadcast away from the center owing to absent population density in most instances (Herbst, 2000). Thus, with a relatively short history of centralized state power and for a confluence of reasons, this became a path-dependent feature with considerable institutional consequences for Ghana and the rest of the continent including the animus for colonial conquest.

Despite an ongoing Sino-Japanese rivalry (see Dreyer, 2006), the success of Japan's novel policies and economic strategy of selective capitalism and protection of nascent industry spread as other East Asian countries like Taiwan sought emulation. However, the Asian miracle halted during the 1990s or during what many refer to as a "lost decade" when shifting global conditions produced low-skilled labor shortages, demographic changes that include an aging population, deflation and the country has struggled since the 2000s to regain its posture, important lessons are evident, nonetheless. Dreyer (2006, p. 539) notes that,

> China's growth contrasts sharply with 15 straight years of stagnation in Japan … and the former's ascendant power is illustrated in Japan's slide from the mountain top of international prestige in 2003 when China became the world's second largest consumer of oil.
>
> (p. 539)

As a country whose industrial and technological advances dominated the globe for several decades, its descent from the second largest economy in the world to the third attests to the impact of globalization, commodities, and an oversupply of cheap labor that arguably informs China's rise. Despite a plethora of factors attributed to Japan's decline, its unique trajectory offers potent lessons for middle-income developing countries like Ghana whose economy has nonetheless experienced fits and starts that are institutionally rooted – and, in short, a consequence of governance and a deficit in agency.

It was only after Japan first hosted the Tokyo International Conference on African Development (TICAD) that the country began to strategize South–South cooperation. As a conference held every five years, some of the core principles emphasize South–South cooperation and African ownership – it is designed to reflect African leaders' own priorities for development (Ampiah, 2005, 2011; Burgschweiger, 2008, p. 416). The role of Japanese overseas development assistance to countries like Ghana is not accidental (see Ampiah, 2005, 2011; Eyinla, 2000; Lehman, 2008). The country's stability and one imagines – a shared articulation of a self-help (see Lumumba-Kasongo, 2011) policy orientation offers a unique synergy. As Lehman (2008, p. 6) observed, "Japan has watched as Ghana outlined a coherent development strategy that emphasizes growth factors, poverty reduction strategies, and attempts to increase transparency, aid effectiveness and harmonization." Burgschweiger (2008, p. 419) notes that "Japan has remained one of the largest aid donors globally with development assistance to Africa overall which some 12 years ago represented 34.2 percent of Japan's aid disbursements," however investment in Ghana is comparatively less than China. This is unsurprising, given that Ghana's exports to Japan are primarily agricultural, e.g., cocoa beans. Some 60% of cocoa beans destined for Japan come from Ghana (Lehman, 2008, p. 421). African engagement with the conference years later offers a glimmer of hope. It appears that a radical transformation that includes a local entrepreneurial class, technocrats, and incentives to promote infrastructural development linkages with technological innovation is emergent.

China's pivot to Ghana using the currency of infrastructural development

In 2014, bilateral trade between Ghana and China reached $4bn while China's foreign direct investment amounted to $1.1bn in the same year (Ghanaweb, 2018; cf. Odoom, 2017). The same, however, cannot be said of Ghana's trade volume with the red dragon. Its share of exports to China is historically low and the Ghana Trade promotion council reported less than 2% between 2000 and 2006 (see Tsikata et al., 2008). Notably, commodities from Ghana to China are primarily mineral and resource driven. Over the past decade, some scholarly perspectives have decried China's role in Africa as solely extractive. With well over $1bn in investments that are primarily resource driven, the seeming no conditionalities attached policy of the

Chinese has drawn surprise and concern. For instance, Odoom (2017, p. 603) asserts that

> Chinese aid and economic cooperation programs have emphasized infrastructure development at a time when traditional donors, including Washington and other Western countries and organizations have downplayed these arrangements.... Chinese assistance for infrastructure is not without strings, however, as many loans and grants are tied to Chinese input.

Agreeably, he also notes that Chinese infrastructural investments are a vital component. Offers to provide development aid picked up during the 1990s as China sought Africa's political support for votes at the United Nations which functioned as an important fulcrum if not olive branch for African states. As a country with a population of 1.3 billion that is short of raw materials, but boasts of unlimited human capital, the draw of the African continent looms large. Illustrative of China's draw as a preferred development partner over say, Japan or even India is the extent to which infrastructural development projects inform Ghana's landscape. From highways, to railways, parliament buildings, hydroelectric projects such as the Bui Dam, China offers a lucrative economic framework along with FDI that few states can match. McCormick (2008, p. 86) found that "China gives grants and loans for infrastructure, plants, and equipment."

Rethinking the principal–agent relationship between one of the continent's premier democracies and an economic giant is critical to capturing jurisdictional sovereignty that remains central to an African renaissance, self-directed development, as well as capacity building for technological expertise for local production and consumption. Thus far, the principle appears to apply as noted elsewhere to the energy resources. Ghana's trajectory is arguably imperiled by the allure of Sino-African partnerships which potentially involve sovereign wealth "giveaways" in the form of land, mining rights, and more in exchange for infrastructural development and decidedly deserves more public scrutiny.

Ideally, China's infrastructural imprint in Ghana will bear the kind of fruit that allows it and other recipients of this kind of development aid to utilize transportation, telecommunication, and technological developments to deepen economic partnerships within the continent. Avoiding externally driven infrastructural aid which fosters dependency is essential since the Sino-Ghanaian relationship remains asymmetrical. This dynamic is also reflected in Nigeria and South Africa, both regional hegemons. Indeed, well over a decade ago, a journal of the South African Institute of International Affairs warned that a "passive policy that looks no further than feeding China's appetite for raw materials contains grave dangers" (see eAfrica, accessed – from Dreyer, 2006, p. 551). Lingering questions about individual country agency in an era where virtually all African states on the continent have bilateral trading relationships with China despite a supposed win–win scenario is one reason the argument for adopting a policy of inward-looking development and growth is ideal.

Small-scale sector growth and the development of an entrepreneurial class

It is typically expected that after governments take office they will reformulate and implement policies that improve the living standards of their citizens; industrialization then is considered one means of doing so (Arthur, 2005, pp. 428–429). A series of economic reforms undertaken in the 1980s and beyond produced minimal emphasis on small-scale enterprises despite initial attention as a useful prospect for job creation (Arthur, 2005, p. 428). It is little wonder, that despite a rhetoric of development and accompanying plans to target rural populations, for instance, a retreat of the state substantially reduced public sector employment while procuring little evidence of industrial development. Donor conditions admittedly limited the kind of reset that was perhaps possible in the return to civilian rule during the early 1990s as structural adjustment policies and neoliberal reach changed the equation. Ninsin's (1992, p. 278) assertion that "only management training courses could provide the kind of training by such institutions which are well oriented and equipped could offer solutions to the acute problem of industrial development in Ghana" is instructive (cited in Arthur, 2005, p. 443). EMPRETEC Ghana or Empresariou Technologica (stems from a Spanish phrase for development-based enterprises) which emerged in 1988, is notable for its assistance to small-scale entrepreneurs in Ghana (Arthur, 2005, p. 439). Though it supports entrepreneurial skills and as Arthur (p. 439) notes, is regarded as an important anchor for industrial base in Ghana, the organization is donor reliant and utilizes micro-finance, the latter of which is far from the panacea it is often touted to be (see Adjei et al., 2009). While the organization contributes to local entrepreneurs, and other private capital nongovernmental organizations offer an important sphere for agency, state-led initiatives must play a critical role too. As Wisdom John Tettey noted,

> the task of helping the industrial sector is not only with non-state development organizations but also with the government since evidence from around the world illustrates how the state has played a catalytical role in the process of economic and industrial development.
>
> (2000, p. 331)

Accordingly, small and medium enterprises especially require backward and forward linkages, for instance in skills, innovation, capital; indeed (see Oyelaran-Oyeyinka et al., 1996).

The focus on entrepreneurs whose prospects for economic mobility lay with small or medium enterprise is deliberate; a growing body of research suggests that the entrepreneur rather than solely the private firm is a key unit of analysis

(Marcati et al., 2008). To secure and utilize adequate technological instruments requires understanding the local markets that either support or inhibit innovation. For instance, Robson et al. (2012, p. 604) find that resource barriers to innovation may be more pronounced in regional contexts associated with low levels of resource munificence which is widespread in developing countries. EMPRETEC and other organizations fill an important gap, but more is needed. The utility, then, of firmer Japanese–Ghanaian relations is to capitalize on technical assistance aid as part of the former's ODA assistance. The Japanese International Cooperation Agency, Japan Bank for International Cooperation (JBIC), and Japan External Trade Organizations (JETRO) are key agencies and institutional players for aid (see Lehman, 2008, p. 10). But Ghanaian institutions should seek greater ownership over policy instruments that fulfill merely donor goals.

Conclusion

In sum, an enduring challenge for Ghana as well as the wider continent remains economic integration (see Boafo-Arthur, 2000). The newly created African Continental Free Trade Area also referred to as a Common African Trade Agreement promises to integrate and indeed raise the percentage of trade between African countries. With future membership of two of Africa's largest economies – Nigeria and South Africa – the agreement may potentially reset a narrative of aid, dependency, and lack of ownership, despite an emerging landscape of stronger economies. Viable continental jurisdiction in economic affairs may well require the adoption of political and economic protectionism or continental arrangement through regional organizations that restrict access to mineral resources as well as sovereign wealth funds – that divvy up land, mining rights, etc. to multinational corporations and states. The current condition of the continent obliges its leaders to reconceptualize African problems, re-theorize and operationalize the solutions; reconstruct state power within the parameters of an African economic community; and reformulate strategies to resist or contain the negative aspects of globalization (Boafo-Arthur, 2000, p. 140).

The political and economic stability of Ghana is a good primer for beginning the necessary conceptualization of a pan-African future that rests on technological advances, intellectual property rights, and infrastructural development that is directed from within. Asian partnerships, though critical in the 21st century, can contribute only to the extent that Ghana utilizes technological expertise and aid as a fulcrum to develop its own. This is likely where the greatest potential exists for harnessing productive engagements with both states to propel Ghana's promise on its own terms, a strategic and challenging feat no less. It may be well worthwhile for future governments to incrementalize globalization and redirect natural and mineral resources in ways that reflect "ownership" and agency of internal as well as regional development. Just as trade union diplomacy during Ghana's early post-independent period illustrated the fractious nature of state building including establishing industrial development as well as labor, the country would do well to revisit a pivotal moment in which trade unionists managed to "actively engage in the shifting and competing policies of local, regional, and global trade unionism to obtain resources before and after independence" (Sackeyfio-Lenoch, 2017, p. 211). An unbridled scramble for market power in Ghana may yet raise the economic profiles of many of its citizens, but at a significant cost and ensuing unchecked development that is purely extractive in nature. Thus, technological progress, a robust entrepreneurial class and infrastructural development on African terms is critical to building a new tomorrow today.

References

Adem, S. (2010). Africa in Japanese diplomatic thought: An African perspective. *Journal of Black Studies 40*(5) 871–896.

Adjei, J., Thankom, A., & Hossain, F. (2009). Asset building and poverty reduction in Ghana: The case of microfinance. *Savings and Development* 3.

Akonor, K. (2013). *Ghana and IMF conditionality: The unevenness of compliance, 1983–2000*. New York, NY: Routledge.

Ampiah, K. (2011). Japan–Africa relations. *Journal of Japanese Studies 37*(2) 502–507.

Ampiah, K. (2005). Japan and the development of Africa: A preliminary evaluation of the Tokyo International Conference on African Development. *African Affairs 104*(414) 97–115.

Arthur, P. (2005). Promoting a local entrepreneurial class in Ghana: The issues and problems. *Canadian Journal of African Studies/La Revue canadienne des études africaines 39*(3) 427–459.

Boafo-Arthur, K. (2000). Trapped in development crisis and Balkanisation: Africa versus globalisation. *African Journal of Political Science/Revue africaine de science politique 5*(1) 124–145.

Bond, P. (2008). Accumulation by dispossession in Africa. In *Neoliberalism and globalization in Africa* (pp. 17–31). New York, NY: Palgrave Macmillan.

Burgschweiger, N. (2008). "Towards a vibrant Africa": The beginning of a new era of Japanese–African partnership? *Africa Spectrum 43*(3) 415–428.

Bush, R. (2008). Scrambling to the bottom? Mining, resources & underdevelopment. *Review of African Political Economy 35*(117) 361–366.

Dreyer, J. T. (2006). Sino-Japanese rivalry and its implications for developing nations. *Asian Survey 46*(4) 538–557.

Eyinla, B. M. (2000). The Tokyo agenda for action: A review of Japan's new strategy on African development. *Africa Spectrum 35*(2) 217–229.

Ghanaweb. (2014). China–Ghana trade yields US 4 billion. December 24. Retrieved August 27, 2018, from www.ghanaweb.com/GhanaHomePage/business/China-Ghana-trade-yields-US-4-billion-340278

Government of Japan. (1997). *Japan's Country Assistance Program for Republic of Ghana*. Tokyo, Japan: Government of Japan.

Herbst, J. (2000). *States and power in Africa: Comparative lessons in authority and control*. Princeton, NJ: Princeton University Press.

Lehman, H. P. (2008). The Asian economic model in Africa: Japanese development lessons for Africa. In *Bridging multiple divides* (pp. 26–29), Annual Meeting of the International Studies Association, 49th Annual Convention, San Francisco, CA, March.

Lopes, C. (2010). New fractures, old wounds: Africa and the renewal of south agency. *Africa Spectrum 3* 69–85.

Lumumba-Kasongo, T. (2010). *Japan–Africa relations*. New York, NY: Springer.

McCormick, D. (2008). China & India as Africa's new donors: The impact of aid on development. *Review of African Political Economy 35*(115) 73–92.

Marcati, A., Guido, G., & Peluso, A. M. (2008). The role of SME entrepreneurs' innovativeness and personality in the adoption of innovations. *Research Policy 37*(9) 1579–1590.

Mazrui, A. A. (1967). *Towards a Pax Africana: A study in ideology and ambition*. Chicago, IL: University of Chicago Press.

Odoom, I. (2017). Dam in, cocoa out; pipes in, oil out: China's engagement in Ghana's energy sector. *Journal of Asian and African studies 52*(5) 598–620.

Oyelaran-Oyeyinka, B., Laditan, G. O. A., & Esubiyi, A. O. (1996). Industrial innovation in sub-Saharan Africa: The manufacturing sector in Nigeria. *Research Policy 25*(7) 1081–1096.

Power, R. (2008). What does the rise of China do for industrialisation in sub-Saharan Africa? *Review of African Political Economy 35*(115) 7–22.

Robson, P. J., Akuetteh, C. K., Westhead, P., & Wright, M. (2012). Innovative opportunity pursuit, human capital and business ownership experience in an emerging region: Evidence from Ghana. *Small Business Economics 39*(3) 603–625.

Sachs, J. D., & Warner, A. M. (2001). The curse of natural resources. *European Economic Review 45*(4–6) 827–838.

Sachs, J. D., Warner, A., Åslund, A., & Fischer, S. (1995). Economic reform and the process of global integration. *Brookings Papers on Economic Activity 1995*(1) 1–118.

Sackeyfio, N. (2017). *Energy politics and rural development in sub-Saharan Africa: The case of Ghana*. New York, NY: Springer.

Sackeyfio-Lenoch, N. (2017). The Ghana Trades Union Congress and the politics of international labor alliances, 1957–1971. *International Review of Social History 62*(2) 191–213.

Tettey, W. J. (2000). Computerization, institutional maturation, and qualitative change: Analysis of a Ghanaian public corporation. *Information Technology for Development 9*(2) 59–76.

Tsikata, D., Fenny, A. P., & Aryeetey, E. (2008). *China–Africa relations: A case study of Ghana*. Ghana: Institute of Statistical, Social and Economic Research, University of Ghana. Retrieved March 6, 2019, from file:///C:/Users/owner/Downloads/Ghana.pdf

Part III

Lessons from Ghana

Reflections on resource management and reform experiences

6 Oil and social responsibility in Ghana

Antoinette Tsiboe-Darko

Introduction

In the wake of Ghana's discovery of oil in commercial quantities, the Western Region of Ghana which lies close to oil-producing areas has undergone socio-economic changes (Obeng-Odoom, 2014a; Yalley et al., 2012). The capital of the region, Sekondi-Takoradi, labeled "the oil city" is said to have the potential of becoming the hub of a booming oil industry in the country, and in the West African region (Obeng-Odoom, 2012). Many local dwellers have expressed sentiments on increased rents and the high costs of land in the region. The price of a plot of land is said to have doubled in Sekondi-Takoradi and its environs since oil discovery. The heightened demand for land for warehouse construction for storage of oil infrastructure, workshop facilities, and accommodation for both oil rig and office workers accounts partly for the hike in land prices (Yalley et al., 2012).

Studies on the social effects are also currently available. One such work by Boohene and Peprah (2011) soon after discovery indicated that there has been a gradual decrease in fish catch which has resulted in lower incomes, especially earned by women in surrounding communities. In addition, most of these women lack the requisite skills to find jobs in the oil sector and hence they are more likely to be impacted by any worsening economic and social burdens. Darkwah (2013), also mentions the unlikely event that the benefits of oil will significantly impact women.

Perhaps the earliest attempt at linking aspects of social responsibility to Ghana's oil sector can be traced to a forum held in 2009 soon after oil discovery by the corporate social responsibility movement (CSRM), in partnership with the Friedrich-Ebert-Stiftung (FES), a nongovernmental organization. This forum which was held at the national level discussed among other issues the impact of oil exploration activities on the fishing sector. It brought together various stakeholders including the government, international oil companies, traditional authorities, fisher folk, and some civil society organizations. At the forum, some of the major socioeconomic effects expected from the impact of the oil activities that came to the fore, were loss of livelihoods, especially in fishing, flooding by migrants for jobs thus increasing the unemployment rate in the region, inflation, that is increasing prices of items such as accommodation, food, leisure, increasing social vices such as commercial sex work, drug abuse, crime, and the health implications from pollution.

Several studies show that the petroleum and mining sectors of most African countries tend to neglect the development of the communities that lie closest to the resource. In Nigeria, the exploitation of oil in the Niger Delta region has resulted in social and political problems in the region (Ikelegbe, 2005; Mahler, 2010), and in Angola oil exploitation has severely marginalized the Ovimbindu populations (Le Billon, 2001). On the contrary, Canada's Alberta region has attained tremendous benefits in the education and social welfare of its people (Arku & Arku, 2011). This is indication that oil exploration can positively impact communities surrounding the resource. In Ghana, for instance, many studies conclude that mining has a dismal track record in poverty alleviation and contribution to positive socioeconomic change in resourced regions because institutions have failed to deliver gains at the local levels. Authorities at national levels are hence often overburdened with requests and responsibilities (Heuty & Aristi, 2009). Additionally, while communities recognize the benefits offered by multinational corporations, they still perceive that many do not live up to their full responsibility in the communities they work in (Garvin et al., 2009). Thus, there is a growing vigorous debate on the role of corporate social responsibility (CSR) in the development of natural resources in Africa (Campbell, 2011; Hilson, 2012; Jenkins & Yakovleva, 2006).

In the 1980s, some multinational companies surprisingly began embracing the idea that CSR was important (Hilson, 2012). Prior to that development, several heads of businesses had expressed indifference to the concept of CSR. They embodied the view that businesses were established mainly to produce profits and hence had no reason to go beyond what was asked of them by regulators. There was not any specific reason for the shift in ideology, but gradually CSR began to be recognized as a corporate strategy (Hilson, 2012).

Some of the arguments in support of CSR is premised on the idea that it was an alternative means of ensuring that economic and social development as well as environmental concerns were addressed as a necessary part of mining activities in resource-endowed countries (Campbell, 2011). CSR strategies could therefore become an avenue used in covering the gaps left by mineral exploitation in contribution to development and poverty reduction in resource-rich regions. Most of the disappointing impacts from extractive activities that had taken place in several mineral-rich countries in Africa could have been eschewed by strategically incorporating CSR activities (Campbell, 2011). Concurrently, there is the belief that even when there had been failures in initial development strategies or economic reform agenda, weaknesses could be overcome with proper engagements in affected communities and hence CSR still has advantageous parts to play in the economic well-being of communities (Gilberthorpe & Banks, 2011). Furthermore, Hilson and Yakovleva (2007) purport that the desire to ensure the sustainability of natural resource development by various businesses makes the concept of CSR very important. Again, they mention that mining companies especially need to have CSR as activity to improve their image to the public and to reduce the incidence of them being targeted by pressure groups in resourced regions of the world.

As Gilberthorpe and Banks (2011) note, this strong emphasis on CSR in the extractive sector represents a formal attempt aimed at correcting decades of environmental disasters and neglect of the rights of persons who live close to the resourced regions. This is particularly significant in countries like Ghana here economic reforms are driven by imperatives that are not often sensitive to resource and environmental concern. This chapter discusses how communities close to Ghana's oil-producing region in the wake of the distribution of oil wealth have become socially aware and responsible. There is a focus on community relations, perceptions of households in the communities and their responses to the perceived changes CSR will bring to them.

This chapter is especially beneficial as it takes a new dimension to the debate on social responsibility. Most studies on the CSR debate focus more on the roles assumed by governments and corporations, and not on the recipients of CSR activities. The chapter places more importance on the role being played by community stakeholders. It looks at how in communities close to Ghana's oil-producing region people have become more socially responsible and are demanding that they get a share of the oil wealth. The research work concludes that perhaps this high level of awareness and demand for social responsibility is the condiment needed for Ghana to ensure that oil wealth factors in the well-being of regions that lie close to the exploration.

Data sources

Secondary information for this work was obtained online from the reports of the government and nongovernmental agencies including Public Interest & Accountability Committee (PIAC), Petroleum Commission of Ghana, Ministry of Energy, Ghana National Petroleum Corporation (GNPC), Africa Centre for Energy Policy (ACEP), web pages and reports of international oil companies (IOCs) and from media reports. Extensive scholarly research works were also sourced to enrich the discussions and conclusions. Primary data was acquired from a mixed-method survey of community perceptions of oil activity conducted in 2014. Two out of six coastal districts were sampled for this survey. Perceptions of 420 households was obtained quantitatively from a mix of household heads engaged in fishing, farming, trading, and the provision of various services. Key informants' interviews with traditional authorities and focus group discussions with community opinion leaders was also conducted to better explain some of the findings of the quantitative survey.

A brief history of oil activity in Ghana

Oil activity in Ghana began when initial deposits was seen decades ago in the Western Region of Ghana in the 19th century. It is documented that the colonial administration did not do any explorative activity and was more engaged in the exploration of minerals such as gold, diamond, and bauxite (Panford, 2017). Several attempts are known to have been made by some companies including the West Africa Oil Company Limited and Société Française de Pétrole which is currently known as Total. Somehow these attempts were still not very successful (Asamoah, 2013). Eventually oil exploration and production commenced off the coast of Saltpond in 1970 but in small quantities. It was estimated that the field had a potential of up to 45 million barrels. Even though several other fields were discovered after Saltpond, none of these discoveries was viable or in commercial quantities (Ghana National Petroleum Corporation, 2013).

There was still strong belief that Ghana had great oil potential and in 1983, when the Ghana National Petroleum Corporation (GNPC) was established through PNDC Law 64. The corporation was mandated to undertake exploration, development, production, and disposal of petroleum in Ghana. Through GNPC the government then committed more resources to search for petroleum. An Exploration and Production Law (PNDCL 64) was enacted in 1984 and the Petroleum Income Tax Law (PNDCL 188) in 1987. The new laws added an increased intensity in petroleum activity and separated it from the mining sector whose laws at the time was being used for petroleum activity.

It was therefore very rewarding, and the expectations of Ghanaians heightened when in 2007 oil was discovered in commercial quantities along the coast of Cape Three Points in the Western Region of the country. The discovery was made by a consortium comprising GNPC, Kosmos Energy, Tullow Oil, Anadarko, Sabre Oil, and the E. O. Group. Significant quantities of oil first in the Mahogany-1 well in June 2007 then later in the same year in the Hyedua-1 well was discovered. Afterwards, more discoveries have been made. The first commercial production field which unitizes several of the discoveries is known as the Jubilee and is jointly owned by the consortium who made the discovery. The field has potential production totaling almost 800 million barrels of oil (PIAC, 2012).

Ghana began earning revenue from its oil resource soon after discovery. Initial estimates from the International Monetary Fund (IMF) predicted that by 2030, the country would have earned $20bn from oil exploitation (International Monetary Fund, 2008). Production and exploration laws, revenue management laws and local content laws were established to guide oil activities in Ghana and provide an enabling environment to attract the necessary investments. Some scholars have debated if these laws were enough for Ghana to avoid the occurrence of a natural resource curse in its oil sector development (Ackah-Baidoo, 2013).

Barely three years after production, oil overtook cocoa as the commodity and came second in export earnings for Ghana. To better understand the dynamics of key players in petroleum industry in Ghana, one has to have an overview of the activities in the sector. The petroleum sector in Ghana as is practiced in most parts of the world is characterized by a division of activities in the value chain referred to as streams. From the exploration phase to the development and production of petroleum, activities undertaken belong to the upstream sector. The upstream sector is highly intensive in capital accumulation and has restrictions for potential investors. These include stated minimum capital investments, well-established organizational structure and more emphatically local content and environmental plans and standards, which the operating company has to adhere to.

Notable among investors in Ghana's upstream petroleum sector are IOCs that also operate in other oil-producing countries. Tullow Oil PLC (Tullow Ghana) has operations in Kenya and Uganda. In Ghana, the national oil company, GNPC partners several (IOCs) including Tullow Oil, Kosmos Energy, Anadarko Petroleum, Hess Petroleum, and Vitol Energy. There are also some independent license holders who have blocks pending exploration activity. These include others like Springfield E&P.

Petroleum activities between the wellhead and refinery to transportation and storage are referred to as midstream. This sector is also limited and the only notable company involved, is the Bulk Oil Storage and Transportation Company Limited (BOST). At the end of the ladder in the oil sector are the downstream companies. These are the separately operated businesses that deal with the sale of finished petroleum products to the consumer. They include Allied Oil, Total Ghana limited, Star Oil, and GOIL. The discussion in this chapter focuses on activities related to the upstream sector alone. This is because the direct exploitative relationship and the ensuing environmental and social costs are a result of the actions and inactions undertaken by actors in the upstream sector. Other studies which also discuss corporate community relationships tend to focus on upstream activities (Akpan, 2006; Idemudia, 2010).

Theoretical perspectives on corporate social activities

Aguilera, Rupp, Williams, and Ganapathi (2007), propose a theoretical model to explain why CSR initiatives are beneficial to the creation of positive change, globally. Such initiatives they propose include methods of production which are more environmentally friendly, improved working conditions within the firm and between the firm and other stakeholders and social investments which support the provision of infrastructure in local communities in the firm's area of operation. So, despite the ongoing contestation that firms should not go beyond their core business of profit generation as discussed by Friedman (1970), businesses will continuously be pressured to engage in socially responsible initiatives to fulfil a wider array of social goals.

Friedman's argument is that the social responsibility of a business is to maximize profits within the bounds of the law. Hence the continued insistence on CSR creates a problem within the organization. Accountability within organizations was exclusively for shareholders and thus CSR would encourage the entry of other stakeholders, and hence the need for enough evidence to close the arguments on the necessity for a firm to engage in CSR. Accordingly, Godfrey and Hatch (2007) further argue that the concept of CSR is being misused as the various definitions have led to puzzlements in operationalizing the concept. They still concede that the concept has gained a lot of academic recognition and hence has increasingly become a common practice among businesses.

Nevertheless, Aguilera et al. (2007) argue that with several other studies indicating this positive effect of corporate social and environmental performance on the growth of the firm what the firm should do is to make its CSR activities robust and wholesome such that it still affords it a lot more room for improvements in all aspects of its activities. They propose then that theoretically a multi-level analysis of CSR activities needs to look at the micro, meso, macro, and supra levels of actors engaged in the sector using a combination of multidisciplinary theories including that from psychology, sociology, and legal studies. The approach they present is one which embraces all actors from employees to consumers, mangers, governmental and nongovernmental organizations and how they influence and motivate the occurrence of socially responsible operations in an organization. They also discuss how these actors across the various levels, within various national and institutional environments will influence and have effects on CSR efforts. At each level of analysis, they argue that the pressure and motivation for firms to engage in CSR is either instrumental, relational, or moral (Aguilera et al., 2007).

The model's emphasis on the role of social actors is still a very necessary part of the reasons why corporations engage in social activities. Even if corporations are established for the purpose of creating profits, they are still social actors. Thus, they will act in ways that are more likely to be shaped by their social orientations (Lee, 2008).

The model has its own limitations, and the proponents of the theory do recognize this. The analysis of the various actors is still not fully comprehensive (Aguilera et al., 2007). A more theoretical fleshing out of each specific issue such as that on employee reactions also gives a more elaborate analysis even though this could also be an even narrower analysis (Min-Dong, 2008; Rupp et al., 2006). Such analysis gives a lot more focus on voluntary firm actions whereas sometimes prevailing market conditions which influence the cash flow of the firm is what determines their ability to pursue socially responsible activities (Mackey et al., 2007).

Ghana's oil and CSR

Social responsibility to a large extent is influenced by setting up the right institutions. Despite the theoretical perspective that no matter the regulations, a firm will engage in CSR activities because it has mutual benefits which are all encompassing (Aguilera et al.), and examples from Norway suggests that aside from setting up the right institutions, petroleum licenses were tied indirectly to safe environmental, social, and other CSR practices. Ghana has therefore done very right to set up a comprehensive institutional framework and assigned roles and responsibilities to various government agencies and organizations, and accommodate the diverse roles of other non-state actors. Though the establishment of institutions alone are not the prescribed antidote to evading the resource curse, the success stories of resource-endowed countries such as Botswana that had strong institutional set ups (Acemoglu et al., 2002) present good justifications for Ghana to chart a similar course. The Petroleum Exploration and Productions Act (2016) is being fully implemented. Prior to this, the 1987 version enacted under the PNDC administration (along with the ongoing economic reforms) was used as a guideline for exploration and production. Rather unfortunately, this was a law with lapses that implied the Environmental Protection Agency (EPA) could not sanction polluters of the oil sector (Panford, 2017). Otherwise, the laws indicate that the peak of social responsibility is seen in the environmental rules that players have to abide by. Environmental impact assessments have to be rigorously undertaken by all potential investors as a part of their overall assessment before a block is assigned to them. However, the information contained in such reports is yet to ever be shared with any of the community stakeholders.

Another powerful level of institutional development though aimed more at ensuring transparency and accountability is the Petroleum Revenue Management Act – ACT 815. The Act covers the value chain of the collection procedures to the utilization of oil revenue created in line with the best international practice and in compliance with the principles for sovereign wealth funds or the Santiago Principles. Larsen (2005) notes that though Norway has escaped the curse, it is not only proper revenue management, and the establishment of common wealth funds that guarantees that oil wealth becomes the proverbial blessing. There is a multiplicity of other factors from good exploration and production practices to responsible environmental and social laws.

In July 2011, the Petroleum Commission Law established the Petroleum Commission (PC) for the regulation, management and utilization of petroleum resources and related purposes. The PC was set up as a corporate body just as the GNPC with perpetual succession and specific objectives. Petroleum commission provides guidelines for all operators in the upstream oil sector. The PC has a community relations department assigned with the responsibility of ensuring that relationship between the oil companies and the communities bearing or close to the resources is mutually beneficial. The department therefore provides a platform for oil companies to undertake corporate social responsibility activities. They also provide the platform for communities to report and discuss any issues they have about activities in the oil sector.

Communities in regions close to oil production are concentrated in six coastal districts of the Western Region of Ghana. From traditional rulers to individuals at the household level, there has developed a keen interest for oil activity. In 2011, shortly after oil production began, the chiefs and traditional authorities of the Western Region petitioned the government of Ghana to secede 10% of the oil revenue for the region. During the key informant interviews, traditional authorities commented that despite the fact that a great share of the Ghana's natural resources especially come from this region, it still remains poor in terms of infrastructural provisions, and many of its people are underemployed.

This demand can also be linked to the knowledge that there is a similar practice of revenue sharing in the mining sector. By law 80% of payments from royalties and corporate taxes from mining companies belong to the central government. The remaining 20% is then put in a Minerals Development fund. From this fund, the Mining Agencies receiving 10% and the administrator of Stool Lands gets the remaining 10%. From the portion of the latter authority, the District Assemblies receive a percentage, the traditional authorities also receive a share and the stools in mining areas receive the final share (Akabzaa, 2001).

Most people in these communities recognize issues of social responsibility to be about the environmental effects of oil exploration, opportunities for employment in the oil sector, support for the growth of basic economic activities, and social investments in infrastructure at the community level. Perceptions at the household, community and individual levels are being influenced by certain factors. Communication and technology has improved and covers all remote areas which were previously inaccessible. News spreads very fast. Community radio stations abound in the coastal districts. Civil society organizations and NGOs at the local level attest to and are carrying out a lot of research on the changes in livelihoods since oil discovery. All this has triggered a fast flow of information and diffusion of knowledge on the potential advantages to be obtained from natural resource development.

Data gathered from communities in the Western Region as far back as January 2014 indicates that knowledge on the environmental and social effects of oil activity was sufficient and widespread among respondents. Knowledge is a condition of being aware of something. It results in familiarity and understanding of phenomena or situations either through experience or by association. Respondents at the time spoke passionately about how oil activity had destroyed livelihoods dependent on farming and fishing in Nigeria. This was a situation they feared was going to happen in Ghana. They spoke about having heard discussions on radio, which had convinced them they had to be prepared for the negative effects oil activity.

There is evidence from some recent events that this kind of common knowledge at times feeds into a chain reaction involving people who now share it. In order to avoid the situation where actions of people then become unpredictable, special consideration has to be given to the source of information of the knowledge, the interpretation, and the external conditions which may affect it (Knight, 1992). Protesters clad in red outfits held a demonstration against oil activity on land occurred in April, 2018 in the Volta Region of Ghana. Newspapers and radio reports indicated that the protestors consistently mentioned that events that had occurred in the Delta region of Nigeria was a lesson for them. They were demanding that they wanted proof of assurance of environmentally safe operations otherwise they did not support any occurrence of oil activity in the region.

Officials of the metropolitan and district assemblies confirmed that the PC, IOCs, and sometimes representatives of CSOs in the coastal districts have held forums with the main aim of creating awareness of activities in the oil sector. There is however poor and inconsistent attendance to these discussions since most people will have to travel to attend these forums. In most cases some allowance is given to cover transportation costs. Communities assert that the awareness forums lay more emphasis on the restricted areas for fishing whilst oil activities are ongoing. They are not informed about any social and environmental issues and hence they rely on the media as their main source of information.

The poor attendance at forums, aside being a result of the frequent organization in fishing communities, is a reflection of the reluctance of most people to travel from their community to another community. AWD has a higher number of fishing communities than the STMA. The remaining communities engaged in farming and trade service had hardly heard of such an event being organized in their community.

For the traditional authorities, the forums have played a major role in enlightening them and those who have participated in ongoing oil activity. They have also discussed the needs of the communities with them through these forums and other meetings. The forthcoming implication on the fishing activity has also been a central issue discussed at these forums but a lot remains undone. The chief fisherman indicated that they have discussed with the key stakeholders the need for a wharf, a cold store, and an ice factory as a form of compensation for their loss of livelihoods. This is because they assert that there is an even lower "fish catch" since oil activity began. They are yet to see the results of these requests.

The oil companies currently operating the Jubilee Project are emphatic that these forums provide the platform for dialogue between them and the communities in affected districts. It is the major channel for disseminating information to the communities. It has also been useful in helping them identify the necessary help they could give to the communities in affected districts and in the provision of several amenities in their CSR initiatives. IOCs confirm that the forums are beneficial. There are still issues of concern which the forums seek to address. They are not as effective as they are meant to be in the dissemination of the relevant information and the feedback and these complaints are mainly from the district officials. "When you call for meetings and there is no promise of either allowance or refreshment very few people show up. Others also say they think we have nothing better to do" (key informant interview, district 2).

Other opinion leaders think if the forums are organized for only disseminating knowledge information, then it is not the problem. Positive results are often achieved. It is the act of reaching a consensus on what social infrastructure the community needs most final decisions that deters people from attending forums.

> The arguments are too much. Everyone wants to be heard to show they know better than the other. Thus, if there should be attempts to improve the livelihoods of those affected by the activity, then they are of the view that the wrong people are benefitting. As far as they are concerned, the stakeholders listen but do not respond or are responding in the wrong direction to their requests.
>
> (male participant, FGD district 2)

The communities in the regions close to oil activity have high expectations from oil. This expectation drives their demand for social investments in their communities. There is expectation that there will be more opportunities for employment and individuals indicated their preparedness to undergo any necessary training to enhance their skills to help them get jobs in the oil sector. To better explain how expectations molds the decisions of individuals and groups, we could consider a scenario where a rule is enforced to make a group of people "A" make a choice "B." The probability of "A" choosing "B," however, is influenced by another group "D" choosing "R." This is because "A's" choice is predetermined by the expected returns they hope to get from the range of choices available. This expected return is further based in part on the actions of the others with whom A interacts (Knight, 1992).

The scenario summarizes the importance of how expectations are shaped and why they should be managed. Some argue that the initial interaction with oil companies heightens the expectations in communities. The IOCs make lots of promises to help them obtain social license to begin their activities. Good and bad experiences in other countries have shaped the expectations of communities. It has instilled in them the desire not to be marginalized and that oil exploration does and could benefit their communities. Employment opportunities is one key benefit Ghana's mining sector has given to the resourced regions. Gold is estimated to employ between 300,000 to 500,000 people in the small-scale extractive sector (Tschakert & Singh, 2007).

Respondents confirmed that they were aware that most of them had no proper work skills or qualifications for oil sector employment as a result of low or no education. However, there are some individuals who have returned to school to obtain a basic certificate to enable them to have a better chance at being employed in the oil sector. The reality however is that oil sector jobs are highly technical and hence this is more about giving false hope (Darkwah, 2013). A simple online search of the available jobs in the oil sector gives an idea of some opportunities available. These include rig electricians, drillers, lead logistics specialists, and engineers which all require specific skills, education and training and work experience.

Communities expressed some fears about oil activity. People engaged in the fishing sector especially have doubts about the long-term effects of oil exploration on the fishing sector:

> Sometimes we fear for our lives and the future of our children. When this fishing industry dies what do we do? For the lot of us it is what we were born to do. Our husbands stay at home with no work and no money and we do not have fish to smoke. The children cannot go to school until I have given them money for food.
>
> (participant female, FGD, study district 1)

The most common fear of the communities is in relation to the economic activity they are engaged in. Households who depend on fishing having environmental fears stemming from an anticipated loss of their livelihood. Their fear is that the oil activity will contaminate the sea which will result in the destruction of aquatic life, the major means of livelihood for many of them. A caption from the *Daily Graphic* in 2012 reported that a dead whale had been washed ashore one of the coastal communities. No further explanation was given to the people of the communities and they believe this had to do with oil activity.

Another unfavorable event occurred in coastal communities which threatened their livelihood dependence is the bloom of algae. Algae are a green weed-like and slimy substance which appeared all along the coast. It has been an environmental threat for almost 20 years. Quite often it lasts between three weeks to a maximum of three months then diminishes in quantity until it finally disappears. However, in 2010 the algae lasted almost a whole year. Fisher folk especially began to suspect that the increased amount of algae was a result of the continuous disturbances in the ocean bed due to the construction of the oil pipelines linked to the FPSO which began production in November that same year. This assertion, though, has no scientific evidence. The EPA's investigation of the algae at the time found no toxic substances of potential health risk. A lot was also found in water bodies inland which flowed into the sea. In the caption on the appearance of the algae in 1997, the adverse effects of this was loss of income to fisher folk who now had to spend time mending their nets damaged by the weed.

The work of the Integrated Coastal and Fisheries Governance (ICFG) initiative otherwise referred to as "Hen Mpoano" has been involved in the investigation of the algae bloom and they dedicated a year of resources to finding the factors that influence the occurrence of the bloom. They again confirm there is a weak link between the bloom and oil activities until proven otherwise.

Other occupations also have fears and they are predominantly economical. Most people fear that the increased costs of living will lead to more economic hardship. "Everything has become expensive since the oil discovery was announced. It is because once foreigners enter your area they have more money to pay for goods and services" (participant female, FGD, study district 1). A few also feared increased immigration. Respondents, however, do not fear the loss of labor in their trade activities to oil activities, unemployment, and loss of income. If more income can be earned for them than loss in other activities which make use of the services they offer then the opportunity is beneficial to all.

The farming communities fear they are losing land. The resource has become even scarcer in the wake of oil discovery and now has an ever-increasing price. It implies a loss of livelihood and hence lower incomes for them. Issues of land are new to respondents. Subsistent farming is increasing in farming communities in recent times. The scarcity of land has resulted in smaller farm size. A preferred choice is to grow crops primarily for subsistence and then sell the excess if there is a good harvest. Households are concerned of the continuous conversion of existing farmlands into accommodation. In both farming communities where the survey was conducted warehousing facilities especially are seen to have been built recently. Respondents discuss that in the two communities most farmers have become artisans. Every year more people have joined the construction instead of farming sector as more farm lands are sold for non-farm purposes. When questioned on the reason for not wanting to keep farming, a male farmer retorts:

> I could try to rely on farming if I was not the breadwinner in my household. Aside land being so small, sometimes the rain does not come as expected. When this happens, crops fail and you get a low harvest. We don't know if it is the seeds or the soil.
>
> (male participant, FGD, district 1)

One notable situation existing in one of the farming communities that culminated in mistrust between the government and the people is the forceful acquisition of land by government. Pre-independence and post-independence government forcefully took land from the communities for agriculture. Ewusiejoe one of the farming communities in the study is home to the Norwegian Palm Ghana Limited (NORPALM) which has 4,000 hectares of oil palm. Some households have members who work as pruners on the plantation and as clerks (20%) of the total respondents sampled from this community. There was so little compensation for the land given to the state at the time that it does not make up for what the community lost at the time neither it can make up today. The IOCs are a part of the creation of social responsibility in communities. Aside the forums which always introduces communities and other stakeholders to a new IOC, the Jubilee partners engaged in actual CSR projects even prior to production in the communities of the six coastal districts. Panford (2017) notes that, Tullow Oil reportedly had been engaged in several activities in education, and health. GNPC is also known to be a sponsor of Ghana's participation in the 2012 World Cup. An observation was made in some community entertainment centers that televisions sets had also been donated by the jubilee partners.

The communities are appreciative of the efforts but there are questions raised about the purpose and the factors that influence the decisions that are made in the choice of projects. The PC community relations department wants to ensure that the development plans of districts are now used in selecting CSR projects. This step is in the right direction. The critics will however argue that CSR then becomes a supplementary development agenda and fully featured in most economic reform agenda in the past three decades. Slack (2011) supports that CSR has not provided the solutions to the environmental and social problems of the extractive sector because there is more rhetoric than actual incorporation of CSR plans in the activities of most IOCs. Besides this, the economic costs to be borne by the operator are often more of a priority that the social costs to be felt by the community. The early stages of oil production in Ghana involved gas flaring, and respondents discussed how this affected their lives. For some, there was a lot of apprehension and though they had been told it would not affect their health, they still had a lot of doubts.

There is no doubt that the costs of discovery, installation and final production of oil are all very high. A major part of the sea surrounding the Jubilee Field has been rightly cut off as a catchment to protect and safeguard the oil infrastructure which is worth millions of dollars. This area however is a part of the fishing grounds for a majority of the coastal communities who keep insisting on compensation. They support their argument with two pertinent facts: The cut-off zone means they have to go further into the sea at times to lay their nets, and this takes more fuel, which further increases the cost of going to sea. Second, the installation area is warmer and thus most of the fish tend to move to the cut-off area. This cut-off zone continues to be an issue of conflict and contention between the IOCs, PC, and the fishermen. Apparently, there is no open forum or dialogue where the fishermen would not raise this issue. Panford (2017) has noted that this issue offers potential grounds for conflicts in the sector.

Conclusion

Ghana's main aim is to ensure greater participation of Ghanaians in the oil sector. This is effectively being achieved through a proper implementation of the Local Content law in the oil sector. Previous natural resource development in Ghana perhaps did not emphasize the provision of support services in sector. Having identified the absence of specific skills needed for the industry, oil sector activity has gone the right direction in emphasizing that persons desiring jobs in the industry look more to development of skills which will be required in the provision of support services in the sector. The requirements for joint ventures in the absence of local expertise being enforced by the PC is also an effective measure. These initiatives are applauded, but the same effort needs to be put into encouraging CSR activities as a way of giving back to the communities in the resource-endowed regions.

The communities do not trust that both state and non-state institutions will guarantee that they benefit from the oil wealth. This is somewhat true. Oil revenue is quite thinly spread. There is the assumption that the long-term benefits will eventually trickle down. For the immediate communities in the resource producing areas, there is higher expectations which do not match the long term trickle-down effect. The EPA is also not accessible to communities, and study reports on environmental and social impact assessments are not made available to communities. It is no wonder locals rely on their own sources of information which often gins up popular discontent with no access to reliable information to provide them coping measures and help them remedy hardships that may result.

What the advocates of CSR need to do is to carry out a comprehensive record and documentation of projects. The PC should be tasked with such an endeavor. A specific and intentional budget should be dedicated to track social investment projects to avoid repetitions and increase the usefulness of such projects to communities. This will also encourage and provide more impetus for others to do the same. Three main factors often account for the decision to engage in a philanthropic act. The first is past history and activities in other countries. This is also dependent on feedback and information received over the years on previous social responsibility projects. The second is how the rest of the world reacts to these projects which is also based on feedback and data, and the international standards available. Third, how has the act benefited the core business of the corporation?

A lot of social responsibility decisions on the part of organizations is also based on the orientation, visons, and goals of the organization. As already discussed, the idea of social responsibility per se does not only refer to the occasional provision of social investments in the form of social infrastructure within resource bearing regions or communities close to the resource regions. Social responsibility includes a conscious effort to ensure that resource extraction does not become an enclave. The use of local support good and services is a necessary part of social responsibility. Local goods and services that need certification must be encouraged and assisted to receive the needed certification.

In a recent message broadcasted to the world, Shell publicly announced acceptance of not being socially responsible and as a result caused destruction to the livelihoods of the people of the Niger Delta. This should be a lesson for Ghana. The admission and apology does not atone for the harm and loss of lives and livelihoods in the Niger Delta. There is the need to initiate a paradigm shift and question the decisions being taken in Ghana's oil sector activities as part of general economic reforms and development agenda rather than an after-thought in the process of improving the economic well-being of the population. The worry with Ghana's oil development should be at two levels. At the national level, the object remains the avoidance of the resource curse, rent seeking, Dutch disease, and the concomitant issues. At the community level, the resource development need not destroy or endanger the lives and livelihoods. Consequently, oil exploration and production should be environmentally and socially responsible and it should aim at creating strong forward and backward linkages which can provide sustainable benefits to grow local economies.

References

Acemoglu, D., Johnson, S., & Robinson, J. A. (2002). *An African success story: Botswana.* Centre for Economic Policy Research. Retrieved March 6, 2019 from https://economics.mit.edu/files/284

Ackah-Baidoo, A. (2013). Fishing in troubled waters: Oil production, seaweed and community-level grievances in the western region of Ghana. *Community Development Journal 48*(3) 406–420.

Aguilera, R. V., Rupp, D. E., Williams, C. A., & Ganapathi, J. (2007). Putting the S back in corporate social responsibility: A multilevel theory of social change in organisations. *Academy of Management Review 32*(3) 836–863.

Akabzaa, T. (2001). *Impact of mining sector investment in Ghana: A study of the Tarkwa mining region.* Washington, DC: SAPRI.

Akpan, W. (2006). Between responsibility and rhetoric: Some consequences of CSR practice in Nigeria's oil province. *Development Southern Africa 23*(2) 223–240.

Arku, F. S., & Arku, C. (2011). The up and down sides of oil and gas development in the Wood Buffalo region of Alberta, Canada: Positioning Ghana for progressive gains. *International NOG Journal* 6(1) 001–009.

Asamoah, J. (2013). *Making the oil and gas find in Ghana a blessing* (pp. 6–15). Accra, Ghana: Joasa Publications.

Boohene, R., & Peprah, J. A. (2011). Women, livelihood and oil and gas discovery in Ghana: An exploratory study of Cape Three Points and surrounding communities. *Journal of Sustainable Development 4*(3) 185–195.

Campbell, B. (2011). Corporate social responsibility and development in Africa: Redefining the roles and responsibilities of public and private actors in the mining sector. *Resources Policy 37*(2012) 138–143.

Darkwah, A. K. (2013). Keeping hope alive: An analysis of training opportunities for Ghanaian youth in the emerging oil and gas industry. *International Development Planning Review 35*(2) 119–134.

Friedman, M. (1970, September 13). The social responsibility of business is to increase its profits. *New York Times Magazine*, pp. 173–178.

Garvin, T., McGee, T. K., Smoyer-Tomic, K., & Aubynn, E. A. (2009). Community–company relations in gold mining in Ghana. *Journal of Environmental Management 90*(1) 571–586. doi:10.1016/j.jenvman.2007.12.014

Ghana National Petroleum Corporation. (2013). History of exploration in Ghana. Retrieved October 10, 2011, from www.gnpcghana.com

Gilberthorpe, E., & Banks, G. (2011). Development on whose terms?: CSR discourse and social realities in Papua New Guinea's extractive industries sector. *Resources Policy 37*(2012), 185–193. doi:10.1016/j.resourpol.2011.09.005

Godfrey, P. C., & Hatch, N. W. (2007). Researching corporate social responsibility: An agenda for the 21st century. *Journal of Business Ethics* 70(1) 87–98.

Heuty, A., & Aristi, J. (2009). Fool's gold: Assessing the performance of alternative fiscal instruments during the commodities boom and the global crisis. Revenue Watch Institute. Retrieved March 6, 2019, from https://resourcegovernance.org/sites/default/files/RWI_Fools_Gold_Heuty_Aristi_FINAL.pdf

Hilson, G. (2012). Corporate social responsibility in the extractive industries: Experiences from developing countries. *Resources Policy 37*(2012) 131–137. doi:10.1016/j.resourpol.2012.01.002

Hilson, G., & Yakovleva, N. (2007). Strained relations: A critical analysis of the mining conflict in Prestea, Ghana. *Political Geography 26*(1) 98–119.

Idemudia, U. (2010). Corporate social responsibility and the Rentier Nigerian State: Rethinking the role of government and the possibility of corporate social development in the Niger Delta. *Canadian Journal of Development Studies 30*(1–2), 131–153.

Ikelegbe, A. (2005). The economy of conflict in the oil rich Niger Delta region of Nigeria. *Nordic Journal of African Studies 14*(2) 208–234.

International Monetary Fund. (2008). *Ghana: 2008 Article IV consultation: Staff country report* (IMF Country Report No. 08/344).

Jenkins, H., & Yakovleva, N. (2006). Corporate social responsibility in the mining industry: Exploring trends in social and environmental disclosure. *Journal of Cleaner Production 14*(3–4) 271–284.

Knight, J. (1992). *Institutions and social conflict* (pp. 16–19). Cambridge, UK: Cambridge University Press.

Larsen, E. R. (2005). Are rich countries immune to the resource curse? Evidence from Norway's management of its oil riches. *Resources Policy 30*(2) 75–86.

Le Billon, P. (2001). The political ecology of war: Natural resources and armed conflicts. *Political Geography* 20(5) 561–584.

Lee, K. (2008). Opportunities for green marketing: young consumers. *Marketing Intelligence & Planning* 26(6) 573–586.

Mackey, A., Mackey, T. B., & Barney, J. B. (2007). Corporate social responsibility and firm performance: Investor preferences and corporate strategies. *Academy of Management Review 32*(3) 817–835.

Mahler, V. A. (2010). Government inequality reduction in comparative perspective: A cross national study of the developed world. *Polity 42*(4) 511–541.

Min-Dong, P. L. (2008). A review of the theories of corporate social responsibility: Its evolutionary path and the road ahead. *International Journal of Management Reviews 10*(1) 53–73. doi:10.1111/j.1468-2370.2007.00226.x

Obeng-Odoom, F. (2012). Political–economic origins of Sekondi-Takoradi, West Africa's new oil city. *Urbani Izziv 23*(2) 121–130.

Obeng-Odoom, F. (2014a). Measuring what? "Success" and "failure" in Ghana's oil industry. *Society & Natural Resources 27*(6) 656–670.

Obeng-Odoom, F. (2014b). *Oiling the urban economy: Land, labour, capital, and the state in Sekondi-Takoradi, Ghana*. New York, NY: Routledge.

Panford, K. (2017). *Africa's natural resources and underdevelopment: How Ghana's petroleum can create sustainable economic prosperity*. New York, NY: Palgrave Macmillan.

PIAC. (2012). *Annual report on the management of petroleum revenues*. Ghana: Public Interest & Accountability Committee.

Ross, M. L. (2003). Nigeria's oil sector and the poor (Position Paper for DFID-Nigeria, UCLA, Los Angeles, CA).

Rupp, D. E., Ganapathi, J., Aguilera, R. V., & Williams, C. A. (2006). Employee reactions to corporate social responsibility: An organizational justice framework. *Journal of Organizational Behavior 27*(4) 537–543.

Slack, K. (2011). Mission impossible?: Adopting a CSR-based business model for extractive industries in developing countries. *Resources Policy 37*(2012) 179–184.

Tschakert, P. (2009). Digging deep for justice: A radical re-imagination of the artisanal gold mining sector in Ghana. *Antipode 41*(4) 706–740.

Tschakert, P. and Singh, K. (2007). Contaminated identities: Mercury and marginalisation in Ghana's artisanal mining sector. *Geoforum 38*(6) 1304–1321.

Yalley, P. P.-K., Atanga, C., Cobbinah, J., & Kwaw, P. (2012). The impact of the Ghana's oil discovery on land investment and its implications in the people, agriculture and the environment (case study: Cape Three Points, Ghana). *Journal of Environmental Science and Engineering B*(1) 922–930.

7 Ghanaian agency in economic engagement in the 21st century

The role of Chinese transnational oil corporations in Ghana

Isaac Odoom

Introduction

Ghana's post-independence economic performance and reform have long been influenced by complex domestic and external factors including foreign actors such as western countries and international financial institutions (IFIs) (Boafo-Arthur, 2007; Hutchful, 2002). While cooperation between Ghana and western actors, and the IFIs are intact, as with the rest of Africa, economic and political relations between Ghana and China have soared in the last decade with China becoming Ghana's single largest trading economy (see ACET, 2009; Aidoo, 2010; Amoah, 2014; Idun-Arkhurst, 2008; Mohan, 2015; Odoom, 2018). Ghana–China relations predate Ghana's political independence, however, since the turn of the millennium, China is increasingly becoming highly influential in Ghana's economic and political development given its critical assistance and investment in financing infrastructure projects in Ghana. What factors account for the growing economic linkage between Ghana and China? How do Ghanaian actors and institutions engage their Chinese counterparts?

Based mainly on information gathered from field research and other secondary sources, this chapter explores the role of Ghanaian agency in Ghana–China relations. I examine the question of how Ghanaian state officials respond to Chinese engagement in Ghana's energy sector particularly the oil and gas industry. How does China get access to Ghana's oil? Are Ghanaian actors able to influence China's engagement in Ghana's oil industry? Departing from the dominant approach in the literature (which focuses on how Chinese actors determine Ghanaian/African realities) this chapter examines the ways in which Ghanaian actors respond and react to Chinese involvement in Ghana's economy. By exploring the strategic ways in which Ghanaian actors engage Chinese involvement in the economy, the chapter sheds light on the extent of political and social agency of Ghanaian actors and institutions in their relations with external actors in contemporary times.

The chapter is structured into three parts as follows: the first section situates the rise of China, particularly Chinese transnational corporations (TNCs), in Ghana within the broader perspectives on the role and impact of TNCs in Africa.

The discussion on TNCs in Ghana is important as it offers the opportunity to interrogate their developmental impact in Ghana and in Africa and to understand their interaction with Ghanaian institutions and actors. The subsequent section offers an in-depth look into China's involvement in Ghana's oil and gas sector, specifically focusing on China National Offshore Oil Corporation's (CNOOC) interest in Ghana's Jubilee oilfield and China Development Bank's (infamous) $3bn loan facility to Ghana. Next is an overview of the role of domestic politics and the influence and agency of Ghanaian elites in shaping their engagement with the Chinese. The goal is to underscore the varied ways Ghanaian and Chinese actors attempt to influence each other's interest and strategies. The chapter concludes by highlighting the need for Ghanaian elites to balance their engagement with the Chinese and other western actors with an eye on prudent natural resource management.

The rise and impact of (Chinese) TNCs in Africa

As the literature on the spread of global capitalism shows, African countries are an integral part of the global capitalist economy. Their integration into the global system historically through colonization and through economic liberalization reforms after independence has meant that capitalist interest (including TNCs) from the metropolis but also from other regions have long had a foothold in African economies. The presence and role, particularly, of TNCs in Africa have increased with intensification of globalization, but especially since the economic reforms and trade liberalization in the 1980s. Being part of global capitalism, TNCs continue to play an increasingly dominant role in Africa and the developing world in general (Andebo, 2014; Dicken, 2007). The growing number and size of TNCs since the 1950s have raised controversy through both their economic and political power in especially weak states and the complexities in their operations.

There are varying perspectives on the role and impact of TNCs in the developing world including Africa. Some suggest that TNCs provide the capital, technological, and entrepreneurial capacity to spur economic growth and reduce poverty (Altenburg, 2000; Buckley & Casson, 1991; Wint 2006). Others are more skeptical of the role of TNCs and denounce their activities in developing countries. These scholars suggest that TNCs do not only exploit their host countries, but they actually hinder the development of structurally weak countries, creating *underdevelopment* (Frank, 1996; Onimode, 1982; Rodney, 1972). As market-driven entities, proponents of this school of thought argue that TNCs are solely interested in maximizing profit for themselves, with no interest in the development of the host countries and no loyalty to the countries in which they are incorporated.

There is a third perspective that holds that TNCs can have developmental effect in host countries under certain conditions (Buckley, 2006; Chan & Clark, 1995). These scholars argue that TNCs are capable of ensuring economic growth and alleviating poverty, but at the same time can cause destruction in host states and societies. Thus, the activities of TNCs are not necessarily negative or positive; a lot depends on the conditions in the host countries and the agency of the local actors (Chan & Clark, 1995). In a comparative study of East Asian and Latin American countries, Chan and Clark (1995, p. 187) argue that TNCs "can be either enabling or disabling in the pursuit of national development, depending on the coping capacity of the host state and society," a claim with direct significance for this chapter.

However, neither the traditional liberal nor the critical theoretical perspectives adequately explain China–Africa or Ghana–China political and economic relations, and this is certainly true with regard to Chinese TNCs. The Chinese TNCs in Africa present both opportunities and challenges. Therefore, their developmental impact has to be seen within the third perspective. Chinese TNCs have become major actors in ongoing relations between Africa countries and China. Before 1979, Chinese SOEs as well as other institutions were not permitted to operate outside China. Following the launch of the "Going Out Strategy" and consequently, the intensification of China's economic engagements in Africa, Chinese TNCs, mostly state-owned enterprises (SOEs) but also private firms, have increased their investment across Africa (Chen & Orr, 2009). These companies come in various sizes and capacity regarding ownership structure, methods of operation, overseas experience, and the level of capital and technology available to them (Burke, 2007, p. 327). At least five categories of transnational actors from China compete in African economic spaces: SOEs closely controlled by the Chinese government; private Chinese investment banks with government connections; PRC sovereign wealth funds (SWFs) such as the China–Africa Development Fund; medium-sized enterprises owned by Chinese local government structures; and small, private companies and individuals.

Some of these firms have decades of experience in the construction of large-scale infrastructural projects across urban and rural areas in China. It is therefore not surprising that some of these companies are at the forefront of China's efforts to engage Africa (Burke, 2007, p. 327). China's approach to development financing involves the participation of these entities (including petroleum and construction companies) and has become a mainstay for Chinese contractors to enter African countries (Chen & Orr, 2009, p. 1209).

In many ways, the Chinese government courts Chinese companies to promote Beijing's so-called win–win strategy in Africa. According to a Chinese official,

> China's approach is to try to encourage both Chinese SOEs and private SMEs to cooperate in the development of Africa. SOEs and SMEs are believed to better understand local African needs, and, when they report to the Chinese government, it will then try to address those issues.
>
> (cited in Gu, 2009, p. 581)

The Chinese government (whether national or provincial) is clearly very supportive of companies or will like to work with them in Africa, yet few Chinese private "firms share a sense of being part of an overall project, strategy or expectation" in Africa, leading to differences between the expectations of how Chinese firms' investments in Africa are supposed to bring developmental benefit to African societies (Gu, 2009, p. 581). Thus, regardless of the policy instruments put in place by the Chinese government, Beijing is incapable of controlling Chinese firms, especially small and private companies.

Contrary to some expectations of Chinese benevolence in Africa, the investment motives of these TNCs are purely market-driven. Their "investment motives reflect both the intensive competition being experienced in the Chinese marketplace today, as well as the attractiveness of African markets and the growth potential identified by the enterprises themselves" (Gu, 2009, p. 582). This is not to suggest that activities of Chinese firms cannot or should not contribute to economic growth and poverty reduction in their host societies. Far from that, Chinese investments can potentially deliver a number of benefits ranging from providing additional source of capital infrastructure investment to local employment to technology transfer to contribution to the alleviation of poverty. The point is that whether or not the development benefits of Chinese SOEs and private investments in Africa can be effectively realized rests with African actors, be it government, civil society, or individuals. The contractual setting in which Chinese companies operate and the governance setting of the host country are key factors that determine whether or not, for example, strict environmental protection measures or labor laws are implemented in projects with Chinese involvement (Hensengerth, 2013, p. 287).

It is within this framework that the rest of this chapter discusses Ghanaian interaction with Chinese state and transnational actors. What does the Ghana case tell us about the nature of interactions between African actors and Chinese state and transnational actors in China's search for overseas oil resources and opportunities for its construction companies? And what insight does it offer on the role and agency of local political and economic institutions in Ghana?

Chinese interest in Ghana's oil sector

The CNOOC and GNPC bid for Kosmos's stake in Ghana's Jubilee oilfield

In 2010 Ghana became an oil-producing country with a great potential for the industry to enhance the country's development prospects. The Jubilee oilfield was discovered through exploration by a UK oil company, Tullow, and a US oil company, Kosmos. EO group, a Ghanaian private company, and the state-owned Ghana National Petroleum Corporation (GNPC) were the other two parties involved in the exploration from the beginning. Production of crude oil started in December 2010 with an estimated deposit of 1.2 billion barrels of oil. Present production estimate is approximately 142,000 barrels per day (Tullow Oil, 2019). It is expected that gross oil production for 2019 will be 180,000 barrels per day (Tullow Oil, 2019). The Jubilee Field's potential revenue estimate is about $1bn per annum on an average crude oil price of $60 per barrel, and the

IMF has predicted that over the period 2012–2030, the Ghanaian government revenues from the field's oil and natural gas production could reach as high as $20bn (International Monetary Fund, 2008).

The discovery and production of offshore oil provided the opportunity for TNCs to invest in Ghana's energy sector. Since western companies have long dominated most oilfields in Africa, Chinese National Oil Companies have used a practical strategy of seeking access to newer discoveries in Africa where the competition is relatively more open, as in Ghana but also Sudan and Uganda (Mohan, 2015). China's first attempt to secure access to Ghana's oil came in the form of a partnership with the state-owned GNPC to make a bid for Kosmos's stake in Ghana's Jubilee field.

In 2010 Kosmos Oil wanted to sell a significant part of its stake in Ghana's operations. In September 2010 Kosmos signed an exclusive binding agreement with ExxonMobil to sell its stakes. But the GNPC, a partner in the Jubilee field, was unhappy about the deal and reacted negatively about the news of the Kosmos agreement with ExxonMobil, as GNPC was interested in buying the stake. Furthermore, GNPC accused Kosmos of breaching the Jubilee Agreement by sharing confidential geological data of the Ghana's Jubilee field with other parties without Ghana's approval (Cook, 2010). GNPC claimed that per the jubilee agreement all stakeholders who wish to sell their stake in the field to an external entity can do so only if none of the Jubilee partners was interested in buying (Cook, 2010).

GNPC's negative reaction to the ExxonMobil deal led to several months of high-level negotiations over the approval of the deal. On the one hand, the government of Ghana and the GNPC increased their pressure to have Kosmos consider GNPC as a potential buyer. On the other hand, intense pressure came on the Ghanaian government from lobbyists supported by the US embassy in Accra to accept or at least not block the deal between Kosmos and ExxonMobil (Cook, 2010). As negotiations were ongoing, China's Sinopec and CNOOC expressed interest in purchasing the Kosmos stake. Similarly, several other major IOCs such as Chevron, Total, BP, among others, were interested in buying stakes in Ghana's oil sector (Cook, 2010, p. 24).

In August of 2010, an advisory group set up to examine the deal by Ghana's President at that time, John Evans Atta Mills, advised the president to reject the deal between Kosmos and ExxonMobil. The committee also suggested that the government support GNPC to raise finance through either partnership with CNOOC or other western banks to enable it to buy the stake direct from Kosmos and select its own technical partner for the Jubilee project (African Confidential, 2010). The exclusive binding agreement between Kosmos and ExxonMobil expired in August 2010 following the GNPC's refusal to allow the sale agreement, thereby negating the sale. Consequently, Exxon announced on August 18, 2010 that it had decided to terminate its agreement with Kosmos (Hardus, 2014). Kosmos blamed the termination on the government of Ghana, which refused to approve the deal. Although it could be interpreted that ExxonMobil's decision to abandon its campaign to acquire stakes in Ghana's oilfield was a temporary victory for China against big western oil companies, it is instructive to say that ExxonMobil and Kosmos had to abandon the deal due more to Ghana politics than geopolitics, namely the stiff opposition of the GNPC, the Ministry of Energy and ultimately, President Atta Mills (Hardus, 2014).

Following the termination of Kosmos agreement with Exxon, in October 2010 CNOOC submitted a joint $5bn bid with GNPC for Kosmos's 23.5% stake in the Jubilee field. In November of 2010, Kosmos rejected the offer claiming that it was committed to staying on as an oil-producing firm in Ghana (Cook, 2010). Although it is not clear why Kosmos rejected the bid considering that the offer was $1bn more than the initial bid from ExxonMobil, two speculations have been adduced. On the one hand, it is suggested that the US government pushed Kosmos not to sell its stakes to the Chinese company for unstated geopolitical reasons (see Hardus, 2014, p. 599). These are unconfirmed rumors but reports suggest that there were intense discussions by US officials about the Kosmos–ExxonMobil deal with the government of Ghana (Hardus, 2014, p. 599). On the other hand, another potential reason suggested is that, considering ongoing new oil discoveries in Ghana at the time, the projected value of Kosmos shares would increase and so it would not make economic sense for Kosmos to sell its stake at the time (Hardus, 2014, p. 599).

After the CNOOC/GNPC bid was rejected, CNOOC entered into an agreement with BP and made another offer to Kosmos and was also rejected in March 2011. Kosmos's share of the field remains at 24.08%. Tullow Oil, the lead operator of the Jubilee Field, holds 35.48%; Anadarko Petroleum Corp has 24.08%, GNPC has 13.64% and Petro SA 2.73%.

The $3 billion CDB loan and China's access to Ghana's oil

Chinese interest in Ghana's oil remained after the failed bid as relations between CNOOC and GNPC continued. In September 2010, President Mills visited Beijing on the invitation of China's President Hu Jintao. During his visit, the government of Ghana and the China Development Bank signed the Master Facility Agreement (MFA) for a $3bn loan dedicated to the Western Corridor Gas Infrastructure Development Project in Ghana involving the construction or rehabilitation of roads, ports and oil and gas processing infrastructure. The loan facility was secured from the Chinese Development Bank (CDB) on a non-concessional basis through Ghana's Ministry of Finance and Economic Planning. The loan is to be paid at LIBOR plus 2.95% (for Tranche B) with an upfront fee of 0.25% and commitment fees of 1% per year. Additionally, the MFA required a minimum of 60% of all project contracts to be given to Chinese firms, as Ghana was only beginning to develop and build the skill and capacity in the petroleum sector (Ministry of Finance and Economic Planning, 2012). Details of the terms and conditions are summarized in Table 7.1.

The approval of the $3bn CDB loan took much longer than expected. At least two major issues account for the delay in the MFA becoming effective. The first was that as required by law Ghana's parliament needed to approve the terms of

Table 7.1 Terms and conditions of the original Master Facility Agreement (2011) Full loan

Availability period	6 years	
Upfront fee	0.25%	
Commitment fee	1% per year on the unwithdrawn and uncancelled amount[1]	
GoG contribution	15% of each subsidiary agreement amount	
	Tranche A	*Tranche B*
Amount	\$1.5bn	\$1.5bn
Interest rate	6 months LIBOR + 2.95% per annum	6 months LIBOR + 2.85% per annum
Repayment period	15 years	10 years
Grace period	5 years	3 years

Source: Ministry of Finance and Economic Planning, Ghana, 2012.

Note

1 Note that this part of the agreement has been expunged, following agreement between the government of Ghana and the CDB team in Beijing in March 2014.

the loan. As was revealed to me in an interview, the CDB loan was one of the most debated loan agreements in Ghana's parliament. The opposition NPP minority caucus in parliament were very critical of the terms of the loan as well as the entire process leading to the agreement with the Chinese. The main problems or criticisms of the opposition in parliament and outside parliament were the commitment fee, the lack of local content, and the use of Ghana's oil as collateral.[1] They also claimed it was not value for money. One senior party strategist had this to say:

> There was absolutely no way that the government would have found difficulty in getting sponsorship or funding for the gas infrastructure if it had done an open tender. Because the gas project will pay for itself, you do not have to have an off-taker agreement … gas plant is a profitable venture, we [Ghana] had previous proposals from countries that are known to have experience in building gas plants. Countries like Trinidad and Tobago, Italy, Japan, etc. All these countries have brought proposals costing around \$500 million and yet [government] rather go for a Chinese project of \$850 million, which has no ground element and is a purely commercial arrangement.[2]

Moreover, as the MFA was negotiated and signed months before the 2012 general elections, it became one of the talking points on campaign platforms, igniting heated political discussions on radio, at political rallies, and public forums. The leadership of the opposition NPP warned of the possibility of renegotiating the loan should it win power in the December 2012 elections.[3] In an election year, other party functionaries feared that the NDC government would redirect the loan into its political campaign.

Despite the opposition from the minority in parliament – they abstained from voting on the loan – the loan was approved in August 2012 by a majority vote.

The approval of the MFA by parliament was on condition that each of the separate components of the projects would be brought to parliament for approval.

Another major issue that delayed the signing or approval of the loan was the existing ceiling for non-concessional lending imposed on Ghana by the International Monetary Fund (IMF). In 2009 Ghana had signed with the IMF a three-year extended credit facility. One of the conditions of the credit facility was that Ghana's non-concessional debt had to be within a limit of $800m. Since the MFA was a non-concessional loan and was over the limit, Ghana had to request the IMF to waive the limit before the facility could be approved (see Hardus, 2014: 600). The request for waiver generated long discussions about Ghana's debt sustainability, but was eventually approved by IMF board and the limit was raised to $3.4bn.

While the MFA was finalized in December 2011 and parliament approved the loan in August 2012, the disbursement of the loan was not steady. Some have suggested that internal factors threatened the release of the bulk of the funds (Arhin, 2014). Among other things, as one interviewee claimed, Ghana was not meeting its part of agreement in time:

> We [Ghana] have to be serious and meet the requirements. If you don't, no cent will come from the Chinese. The fact of the matter is, we are talking about timelines, schedules ... the fact is that Ghana also needed to put up some money and so all the things you are seeing like the gas pipeline is Ghana money. They want to make it look as if it's the Chinese money; it is Ghana. That is part of the bargain, we start and they continue. Even on our own terms, we aren't even there yet. We've imported pipes and others will be coming, but that's just a little part. We [Ghana] had to do our part of the bargain. They wouldn't want to give you the money ahead.... Not even in a crucial election year.[4]

The Ghana government denied claims that it had defaulted in providing counterpart funding to allow disbursement of the loan (Myjoyonline, 2015). However, there were still concerns that some of the projects financed by the MFA lack the required feasibility studies. This feasibility study was to be conducted by the government and its inability or unwillingness to perform it caused delay in the disbursement of the funds (Arhin, 2014).

As part of the requirement of the MFA, the GNPC signed a commercial agreement with UNIPEC in March 2012 for the sale and purchase of oil from the Jubilee field. This agreement committed Ghana to supply 13,000 barrels of crude oil per day to the Chinese for the period of 15½ years to repay the $3bn loan. The payment by UNIPEC goes into a special escrow account at the Bank of Ghana meant for the repayment of Ghana's debt under the MFA. The oil agreement will end if Ghana is able to repay all outstanding amounts before the expiration of the MFA or if the GNPC discharges the agreement amount of oil to be delivered.

Ghana contracted Sinopec to undertake the first project under the MFA: the $850m Atuabo Gas Infrastructure project. The Atuabo Gas project located on the coast of western Ghana is part of the Western Corridor Gas Infrastructure Project of the government of Ghana. The project included the installation of offshore pipeline from the Jubilee Field; a gas processing plant with a capacity to process 150 million standard cubic feet of gas, a natural gas liquids export system for the export of LPG; a construction of a 120-kilometer pipeline to further transport processed gas to the Aboadze thermal power station; and an office complex. Construction work on the gas plant started in August 2012 with the Chinese state-owned enterprise Sinopec International Petroleum Corporation as the lead contractors. The plant will receive and treat raw gas from the offshore floating production, storage, and offloading (FPSO) facility named "Kwame Nkrumah" after Ghana's first president.[5]

The Atuabo Gas plant has since begun processing gas (SpyGhana, 2015) but not without controversy regarding the disbursement of money for its construction as part of the $3bn loan. In 2012, CDB made an advance payment of $225m to Sinopec to prefinance the project awaiting parliamentary approval. However, Sinopec temporarily halted work on the Atuabo project in April 2013 awaiting payment of $309m from the Ghana Gas Company (managers of the Gas Project). But Ghana Gas Company claimed that because CDB had only disbursed a little over $200m (out of $850m), they are unable to pay Sinopec. The CDB, on the other hand, was awaiting the approval of Ghana's parliament for proposed amendment to the original MFA. This amendment became necessary following the need to resolve conflict between the MFA and Ghana's newly passed Petroleum Revenue Management Act 2011 (Act 815). Originally the Bank of Ghana (party to the MFA) was required under the MFA to transfer 70% of the commercial invoice value of the crude oil lifted by UNIPEC into the Collection Account, but the amendment now requires the Bank of Ghana to transfer a defined amount into the Collection Account after each lifting, and will also be limited to Ghana's debt service obligation in each interest period (see Parliament of Ghana, 2013).

By January 2014 the full disbursement of Tranche B of the MFA was still not forthcoming. President Mahama made an appeal to the CDB to expedite the process for the release of the $3bn loan to Ghana to support infrastructure development. The President made the call during a courtesy call on him by the Chinese Foreign Minister, Mr. Wang Yi, at the Flagstaff House (office of the President). Mr. Mahama said that although Ghana had received only about $600m from the $3bn loan, the country continued to pay commitment fees on the whole loan. In response, the Chinese minister expressed the hope that the CDB team would help address the challenges confronting the loan during their visit to Ghana in February. According to minority spokesperson on finance, Dr. Akoto Osei, Ghana had accrued up to $54m in commitment fees after receiving only about $600m of the loan (Ghanaweb, 2014). As expected, the payment of the commitment fee had raised much criticism from the opposition party and civil society organizations that wanted Ghana to renegotiate for the commitment fees to be waived and the disbursement mechanisms streamlined. The CDB team's visit to Ghana in February did not lead to negotiated terms on the loan. Instead it came out after days of speculations that they wanted an increase in the daily quota of Ghana's oil from 13,000 barrels to 15,000 barrels. The team argued that ongoing downward pressure on international oil prices has meant a reduction in the value of the amount of oil originally agreed. Furthermore, it was said that the fall in both Ghana's gold revenues and its cocoa revenues, leading to $1.3b in foregone foreign exchange revenues in 2013, has made the loan riskier than the Chinese originally imagined (Ghanaweb, 2014a).

This call for revision to the MFA did not go well with opposition party. In February, the minority caucus in parliament increased their call and urged President Mahama to fly to China as a matter of urgency to renegotiate the terms of the loan. In mid-March 2014, Ghana's finance minister led a high-level government delegation to China to facilitate an agreement on the release of the remainder of the loan. The Ghana team were able to convince the CDB team to expunge the controversial commitment fee clause in the agreement. This mitigation meant that government of Ghana would no longer be required to pay for a loan it has not fully received. The government was to pay $12.5m commitment fee under the former terms, but only paid $2.5m under the new changes (Ghanaweb, 2014b).

In a rather surprising and unprecedented twist to the saga of the $3bn CDB loan, on July 16, 2014, the then Finance Minister, Mr. Terkper, announced during his mid-year budget review to parliament that based on the advice of the Attorney General's department and with the approval by Cabinet, he is requesting parliament to approve the proposal to take only $1.5bn instead of the $3bn as originally signed. The Finance Minister later explained that unrealistic demands by CDB forced government to abandon the $1.5bn of the $3bn loan facility. He said the Chinese were unwilling to renegotiate the terms of the loan but instead insisted on using $85 per barrel as the price to pay back the loan, although the oil price has gone beyond $100 (Myjoyonline, 2014). Moreover, the Minister announced,

> CDB has introduced a new condition precedent to the effectiveness of the subsidiary agreements of the two additional projects, namely a side agreement to amend some of the terms of the MFA as well as the five-party agreement and account agreement.
>
> (Ministry of Finance and Economic Planning, 2014)

He further explained that:

> The Side Agreement is to primarily ensure that starting from the 10th shipment of crude oil to Unipec Asia, in support of the facility, GoG [government of Ghana] will transfer an amount equal to 49 percent of the price of the shipment into the debt service account to ensure that GoG has sufficient funds to service the debts when principal repayments become effective in 2015; and the CDB facility is recognised as an oil-backed transaction contrary to the agreed position between CDB and GoG during the initiation of the transaction that the facility is not an oil-backed facility.
>
> (Minister of Finance and Economic Planning, 2014)

The minister therefore submitted the Side Agreement to parliament for approval and concluded that because the government did not agree with the new requirements, it had decided not to draw the second tranche of the loan.

The politics of saying "no": Legal framework, local politics, and parliamentary scrutiny

To return to the questions posed at the beginning of this chapter, what insight does the interaction between Chinese state actors, companies and local political and social actors, and institutions in Ghana offer us about how they influence each other? What role do Ghanaian actors play in this influence? And what are the implications of China's entry into Ghana's oil industry? With regard to the strategies Chinese actors use to achieve access to Ghana's oil, it is evident from the above that their first preference was direct access to the oil. But since GNPC was itself interested in buying the Kosmos stake in the Jubilee Field, CNOOC had no option than to partner with GNPC to make a competitive rival bid. The bid was rejected. Yet, the Chinese used another strategy for access. The Chinese offered credit lines to the Ghanaian government in return for a long-term supply of oil. Thus, although Chinese companies failed to secure upstream oil access through the MFA, they achieved access to Ghana's oil through the off-take agreement under the MFA (see Hardus, 2014). The success of Chinese actors' access to Ghanaian oil was thereby dependent on a number of factors. In the case of the direct acquisition, it was dependent on the role of other oil companies that are already in the market and the existing legal framework with the industry.

In the case of the resource-backed loan (MFA in Ghana), it is fair to say that local politics was the biggest threat to its success. Chinese access to oil through the MFA shows that in relatively stable democracies like Ghana, Chinese actors need more than a good relationship with government functionaries; the capacity and role of parliament, civil society and other institutions is crucial and could make or unmake any deal with a government for access (Hardus, 2014). These variables suggest that Chinese actors do not always make their way easily in getting access to resources in Africa as conventional assumption suggests.

The interaction between Chinese actors and Ghanaian political, social and economic actors and institutions is clear evidence that domestic politics in host African countries are capable not only of complicating the strategies of Chinese actors, but could actually determine some of the realities. Domestic politics in Ghana and the influence and agency of Ghanaian elites were evident in the MFA. The adjustment of the MFA to solve the conflict with the PRMA and more importantly the Cabinet decision not to take the second half of the MFA show that in democratic Ghana, parliamentary scrutiny and civil society pressure could to lead to adjustment in the host's country's engagement with China.

The decision to say no to the second part of the MFA further supports the emerging evidence of African agency in interaction with Chinese state actors. By arranging partnership with CNOOC, Ghana increased its bargaining power and position toward powerful multinationals like ExxonMobil. Furthermore,

Ghana's parliament was able to push for adjustment to already signed agreements under the MFA. The government's success on the commitment fee waiver is another indication that African government can bargain and amend their deals with Chinese actors. The Cabinet proposal to cancel half of the MFA and the parliament's subsequent approval are yet further evidence of Ghanaian agency.

Chinese and western oil companies in Ghana: What difference? What impact?

While Ghanaian actors wield influence in their engagement with the Chinese, the involvement of both Chinese and western oil companies in Ghana's nascent oil and gas industry holds implications for the management of the sector and developmental impact on Ghanaians. Since the discovery and subsequent production of oil, most analysis of Ghana's oil and gas sector have been framed within the "resource curse" or blessing framework (see Alagidede & Akpoza, 2012; Dagher et al., 2010; Gyampo, 2011; Gyimah-Boadi & Prempeh, 2012; Kopi'nski et al., 2013; Okpanachi & Andrews, 2012). Some scholars have challenged the resource curse analysis in at least two ways: (a) that the resource curse focuses on only the local state for causes and solutions to "oil-related problems" (Ayelazuno, 2014); (b) that curses and blessings are not necessarily independent, in most cases coexisting (Obeng-Odoom, 2012, 2014). Some observers also point out that there is actually a resource cure (Bazilian et al., 2013).

While domestic factors play a large role in conditioning the developmental impact of natural resources, sometimes the causes of resource-related problems in host countries are externally driven through exploitation by global capital, which perpetuate the existence of enclave extractive industries and a dependence on the export of low-value commodities (Ayelazuno, 2014). In this sense, whether a TNC is a Chinese or western company says less about the potential benefit of its activities in the host country. It can be argued, of course, that the presence of Chinese companies in Ghana and Africa in general challenge the dominance of western companies who have had undisputed command over natural resources exploration and production with their accompanying political ties over the years. Within that logic, Chinese companies may offer Ghanaian policymakers yet another choice and also open an avenue for competition in the oil and gas sector that may be of some benefit for Ghana.

Chinese companies' interest and involvement in Ghana or elsewhere in Africa, however, should not be seen as mere altruistic gesture or some sort of magic bullet for Ghana's development. In many ways, Chinese companies are no different from other large multinationals operating in Ghana and Africa who both engage with the state, on one hand, and abstract themselves from local responsibilities, on the other hand (Mohan, 2015, p. 51). Certainly, Chinese state-owned multinationals, like Sinopec and CNOOC, have a hybrid position of being both profit-seekers and state-influenced entities, thereby becoming involved in Chinese development assistance in Ghana. Yet, while Beijing's influence over Chinese SOEs is obvious, Hardus (2014) shows that Chinese oil companies in Ghana are fairly independent of the Chinese state and are driven by profit motives. They are as opportunistic as other western companies. This finding challenges the assumption that Chinese companies are merely part of some kind of large scale Chinese strategy to help with Ghana's development.

In the case of the $3bn CDB loan to Ghana, it may appear on the surface as a win–win agreement for Ghana and China: Ghana uses its new oil find as a guarantee to get loans that significantly help to develop its energy infrastructure, especially the construction of a gas plan for uninterrupted supply of electricity to businesses and homes in Ghana; China obtains the much-needed oil to fuel its economy and is also guaranteed that the loans will be repaid. However, as parliament, think tanks and opposition parties in Ghana have highlighted, aspects of the terms of the loan agreement (such as the upfront management fees, the requirement that 60% of the work must go to Chinese firms or vendors, and the fact that the loan had serious implications on Ghana's debt sustainability) were not favorable to Ghana, suggesting that the terms could have been better negotiated from the onset.

Concluding remarks

This chapter examined Ghanaian political agency in Ghana–China economic relations. It explored how Ghanaian actors negotiate their relations with their Chinese counterparts by studying the interaction between Chinese state actors and Ghanaian institutions in Ghana's oil and gas industry. Media reports and the growing "China in Africa" literature highlight increasing volume of Chinese investment in Africa, projecting China (and Chinese enterprises) as a formidable competitor for African energy resources and diplomatic influence across Africa. Yet, as this chapter shows, it is only through grounded analysis on how these investment projects operate, on how the diverse agents and local conditions enable their interplay with local elites and communities can we properly contextualize and understand the dynamic of encounters between Chinese investments and African actors. The cases examined more broadly highlight ways in which Ghanaian and Chinese actors influence each other's interest, policies, and strategies, countering the notion of Ghanaian or African passivity. While Chinese interests in Ghana are not different from that of western countries and institutions, what is curious and perhaps attractive about China's practice is the nature of the approach, terms of engagement and the tools China uses to develop and leverage its relations with Ghanaian institutions.

Ultimately, the chapter shows that in relatively democratic states like Ghana, parliamentary scrutiny and civil society pressure may not only lead to adjustment to harmful contractual agreements with Chinese institutions, but also state institutions can ensure that existing legal frameworks for public procurement are followed. There is, nonetheless, an urgent need for Ghanaian policymakers to be conscious of the long-term implications of when they mortgage huge volumes of oil against the acquisitions of commercial loans, even if such loan agreements have some developmental benefits such the CDB loan. They must be circumspect in scrutinizing offers from transnational corporations, whether from China or any other foreign investor. This need for due diligence is consistent with the wider calls to study the procurement strategies of Asian oil companies in Africa (Barclay & Smith, 2013).

Notes

1 Interview with party official in Accra, 2012.
2 Interview with Gabby Otchere Darko, NPP Party Strategist and Director of Danquah Institute, a policy think tank with affiliation to the NPP party, August 2012.
3 Interview with Gabby Otchere Darko, August 2012. The NPP did not win the presidential elections in 2012.
4 Interview with Mr. Franklin Cudjoe, CEO of IMANI Ghana (a policy think tank), August 2012.
5 Interview with Ghana Gas Official in Accra, September 2012.

References

African Confidential. (2010). The politics of no. Retrieved June 21, 2015 from www.africaconfidential.com/article/id/3638/The-politics-of-no

Africa Center for Economic Transformation (ACET). (2009). *Looking east: China–Africa engagements: Ghana country case study*. Accra, Ghana.

Aidoo, R. (2010). *China–Ghana engagement: An alternative economic liberalization in sub-Saharan Africa*. Ph.D. dissertation, Miami University, Oxford, OH.

Alagidede, P., & Akpoza, A. (2012). Sovereign wealth funds and oil discovery, lessons for Ghana: an emerging oil exporter. *African Growth Agenda 9*(4) 7–10.

Altenburg, T. (2000). Linkages and spill-overs between transnational corporations and small and medium-sized enterprises in developing countries – Opportunities and policies. Berlin, Germany: German Development Institute.

Amoah, L. G. A. (2014). China, architecture and Ghana's spaces: Concrete signs of a soft Chinese imperium. *Journal of Asian and African Studies* (Online First version) 1–18, doi:10.1177/0021909614545854

Andebo, P. P. (2014). Presence of transnational corporations in Africa: An assessment of tax justice and poverty implications in the light of Catholic social teaching (Topical Essay No. 2 of research project Tax Justice & Poverty).

Arhin, F. (2014). NDC pays US$54 for US$600m Chinese loan. *Stateman Online*, 16 January.

Ayelazuno J. (2014). Oil wealth and the well-being of the subaltern classes in sub-Saharan Africa: A critical analysis of the resource curse in Ghana. *Resource Policy* 40 (June) 66–73.

Barclay K., & G. Smith. (2013). Introduction: The international politics of resources. *Asian Studies Review* 37(2) 125–140.

Bazilian, M., Onyeji, I., Aqrawi, P.-K., Sovacool, B. K., Ofori, E., & Kammen, D. M., et al. (2013). Oil, energy poverty and resource dependence in West Africa. *Journal of Energy Natural Resource Law 31*(1) 33–53.

Boafo-Arthur, K. (2007). *Ghana: One decade of the liberal state*. New York, NY: Zed Books.

Buckley, P. J. (2006). Multinational enterprises in less developed countries: Cultural and economic interactions revisited. In J. C. Subhash (Ed.)., *Multinational corporations and global poverty reduction* (pp. 31–58). Cheltenham, UK: Edward Elgar.

Buckley, P. J., & Casson, M. (1991). *The future of the multinational enterprise*. London: Macmillan.

Burke, C. (2007). China's entry into construction industries in Africa: Tanzania and Zambia as case studies. *China Report 43*(3) 323–336.

Chan, S., & Clark, C. (1995). Do MNCs matter for national development outcomes? Contrasting East Asia and Latin America. In S. Chan (Ed.), *Foreign direct investment in a changing global political economy* (pp. 166–187). London, UK: St. Martin's.

Chen, C., & Orr, R. J. (2009). Chinese contractors in Africa: Home government support, coordination mechanisms, and market entry strategies. *Journal of Construction Engineering and Management 135*(11) 1201–1210.

Cook, N. (2010). Ghana, an emerging oil producer: Background and US relations. Washington, DC: Congressional Research Service.

Dagher, J., Gottschalk, J., & Portillo, R. (2010). Oil windfalls in Ghana: A DSGE approach (IMF Working Paper, WP/10/116, pp. 1–36).

Dicken, P. (2007). *Global shift: Mapping the changing contours of the world economy* (5th ed.). New York, NY: Guilford Press.

Frank, A. G. (1996). The underdevelopment of development. In Sing C. Chew & R. A. Denemark (Eds.), *The underdevelopment of development: Essays in honour of André Gunder Frank*. Thousand Oaks, CA: Sage.

Ghanaweb. (2014a). CDB loan: To be or not to be. Retrieved February 23, 2014, from www.ghanaweb.com/GhanaHomePage/NewsArchive/artikel.php?ID=301563

Ghanaweb. (2014b). $1.5bn CDB loan: Commitment fee successfully re-negotiated. Retrieved July 2, 2015, from www.ghanaweb.com/GhanaHomePage/business/artikel.php?ID=317679

Gu, J. (2009). China's private enterprises in Africa and the implications for African development. *European Journal of Development Research 21*(4), 570–587.

Gyampo, R. E. V. (2011). Saving Ghana from its oil: A critical assessment of preparations so far made. *Africa Today 57*(4) 49–69.

Gyimah-Boadi E., & Prempeh, H. K. (2012). Oil, politics, and Ghana's democracy. *Journal of Democracy 23*(3) 94–108.

Hardus, S. (2014). Chinese national oil companies in Ghana: The cases of CNOOC and Sinopec. *Perspectives on Global Development and Technology 13*: 588–612.

Hensengerth, O. (2013). Chinese hydropower companies and environmental norms in countries of the global South: The involvement of Sinohydro in Ghana's Bui Dam. *Environment, Development and Sustainability 15*(2) 285–300.

Hutchful, E. (2002). *Ghana's adjustment experience: The paradox of reform*. Geneva, Switzerland: United Nations Research Institute for Social Development.

Idun-Arkhurst, I. (2008). *Ghana's relations with China*. Braamfontein, South Africa: South African Institute of International Affairs.

International Monetary Fund (IMF). (2008). Ghana: 2008 Article IV consultation: Staff country report (IMF Country Report No. 08/344).

Kosmos Energy. (2014). Ghana: Jubilee field. Retrieved June, 21, 2015, from www.kosmosenergy.com/operations-ghana-jubilee-field.php

Ministry of Finance and Economic Planning. (2014). 2014 Mid-year review and supplementary estimates. Retrieved July 16, 2014, from www.mofep.gov.gh/sites/default/files/budget/2014%20Mid%20Year%20Review%20and%20Tables.pdf

Mohan, G. (2015). Queuing up for Africa: The geoeconomics of Africa's growth and the politics of African agency. *International Development Planning Review 37*(1) 45–52.

Myjoyonline. (2014, July 17). Chinese asking for too much oil – Finance minister explains abandoned $1.5bn CBN loan. Retrieved July 3, 2015, from www.myjoyonline.com/business/2014/July-17th/chinese-asking-for-too-much-oil-finance-minister-explains-abandoned-15bn-cbn-loan.php#sthash.qaQ6zTf4.dpuf

Myjoyonline. (2015). Gov't access US500 CDB facility. Retrieved June 25, 2015, from www.myjoyonline.com/business/2013/September-18th/govt-accesses-us500-million-cdb-facility.php#sthash.oSD2XjHg.dpuf

Obeng-Odoom, F. (2012). Problematising the resource curse thesis. *Journal of Developing Societies 41*(1) 1–29.

Obeng-Odoom, F. (2014). Measuring what? "Success" and "failure" in Ghana's oil industry. *Society & Natural Resources 27*(6) 656–670.

Odoom, Isaac (2018). South–South cooperation, SDGs, and Africa's development: A study of China's development intervention in Ghana. In K. T. Hanson, K. P. Puplampu, & T. M. Shaw (Eds.), *From Millennium Development Goals to Sustainable Development Goals: Rethinking African development* (pp. 90–109). New York, NY: Routledge.

Okpanachi E., & Andrews, N. (2012). Preventing the oil resource curse in Ghana: Lessons from Nigeria. *World Futures, Journal of Global Education 68*(6) 430–450.

Onimode, B. (1982). *Imperialism and underdevelopment in Nigeria. The dialectics of mass poverty*. New York, NY: Zed Press.

Parliament of Ghana. (2013). *Report of the Finance Committee on the term loan facility amounting to three billion United States dollars (US$3.0 billion) between the government of the Republic of Ghana and China Development Bank (CDB)*. Retrieved February 24, 2015, from www.parliament.gh/publications/44/549

Rodney, W. (1972). *How Europe underdeveloped Africa*. Washington, DC: Howard University Press.

SpyGhana. (2015). Ghana's Atuabo gas plant begins commercial production. Retrieved May 1, 2015, from www.spyghana.com/ghanas-atuabo-gas-plant-begins-commercial-production

Tullow Oil. (2019) Jubilee Field. Retrieved April 18, 2019, from www.tullowoil.com/operations/west-africa/ghana/jubilee-field

Wint, Alvin G. (2006). FDI and poverty alleviation in small developing countries. In J. C. Subhash (Ed.), *Multinational corporations and global poverty reduction* (pp. 83–104). Cheltenham, UK: Edward Elgar.

8 The politics of galamsey and anti-Chinese populism in Ghana[1]

Richard Aidoo

I don't blame the Chinese, I blame our politicians and local chiefs.
(resident of Awaso in the Western Region)[2]

Situating China in Ghana's political economy

Between 2013 and 2014, Ghana's relations with China gained much global attention through activities of Chinese illegal miners in parts of the country, and the brouhaha over the disbursement of the $3bn Chinese loan facility secured by the Ghanaian government in 2011. Though these situations have dogged recent Ghana–China engagements, China has always had constructive diplomatic and economic engagements with Ghana. The post-independent relationship between the two countries has evolved from a political ideological one to currently an economic pragmatic partnership. A framework for this relationship will be incomplete without looking back to the anti-imperialist struggle and the initiation of South–South cooperation at Bandung, in 1955. Ghana (then Gold Coast) was one of the African countries that encountered China at the Bandung Conference (Vang, 2008). Five years after Bandung, and three years after its political independence, Ghana officially recognized China, despite the very valued comradeship that Kwame Nkrumah had with the Soviet Union. To avoid any attempt at stirring up a Sino-Soviet contest, Nkrumah defined the ambits of this diplomatic relationship as mainly development and security oriented (Shinn & Eisenman, 2012).

As Nkrumah and the Convention People's Party (CPP) rode the populist wave into office as the first leader of the country, he began to scour for resources to build infrastructure and jump-start a development agenda for a new Ghana – both of which fostered his own political plan. Aside the Soviet Union, China became a keen supporter of Nkrumah's statist development agenda. In 1961, Nkrumah agreed to a $20m, interest-free loan repayable in Ghanaian exports – a better deal then was being offered by the Soviet Union at that time. In character with China's current relations with its African partners, Beijing also offered technical experts to Ghana. This was followed by another $22m pledge during the Zhou Enlai African tour in 1963–1964 (Shinn & Eisenman, 2012). Second, as these resources enabled the government to invest in infrastructure and pursue other development goals, Nkrumah cautiously welcomed Chinese military advisors to also help strengthen the military infrastructure of Ghana and other neighboring countries. The growing Ghana–China fraternity came to a halt in 1966 when the Nkrumah administration was overthrown in a military takeover. The relationship soured as accusations of Chinese interference by Ghana severed diplomatic ties until 1972. Arguably, scholars like Ogunsanwo (1974) contend that China took advantage of Ghana's hospitality to advance its ideological interest and agenda throughout the Africa continent.

Since the reestablishment of diplomatic relations in 1972, China's relationship has gradually evolved away from Nkrumah's socialist–statist ideological engagement to a more market-oriented economic relationship. This nature of economic relationship has evolved with political and diplomatic exchanges between the two countries, especially, as Ghana upheld the One-China policy. Apart from Zhou Enlai's visit, Ghana has later played host to high-profile Chinese politicians such as Hu Jintao and Wen Jiabao in 2003 and 2007 respectively. Ghanaian leaders have also returned these series of visits, from leaders like Jerry Rawlings, John Kufuor, to the leadership of John Mahama. These high-level visits came along with economic benefits ranging from a series of infrastructure loans, to business exploratory missions in both China and Ghana. Generally, most of the development support that Beijing has offered to Ghana in the postcolonial era has been in reciprocity for crucial diplomatic support that the latter had extended to the former, and also to maintain the fraternal links meant to exemplify and sustain the South–South cooperation initiated at the Bandung Conference in 1955. These include Nkrumah's campaign for the reinstatement of China at the United Nations, as well as Ghana's support during the border dispute with India in 1962 (Shinn & Eisenman, 2012). Later, in 1989, the Rawlings administration also displayed some sense of solidarity during the infamous Tiananmen Square protests. As many African countries alternated political systems, China's diplomatic overtures were extended to different political regimes – from one-party states, through military regimes to multiparty democratic states. Beijing had to adapt as the political landscape in Africa quickly moved toward democratization. In the 1970s and 1980s, about 85% of the governments across Africa had suppressed various forms of open political competition and in the 1990s the institutions and their political stories started to change as 50% allowed elections, in which opposition parties were allowed to openly compete (Bates, 2012, pp. 224–231).

So, the political change or reforms have often been tied in simultaneously with economic reforms, a feat that Bienen and Herbst (1996) argue is difficult to achieve in Africa compared to other regions of the world. In Ghana, Beijing's support and funding of the socialist–statist agenda under Nkrumah's administration gave way to different development plans most importantly the liberalization policies that took flight with the structural adjustment policies adopted by Ghana, especially in the 1990s. Ndulu et al. (2008) observed that government economic policy changed in the 1990s as the control regimes that characterized the immediate post-independent era, gave way to the "syndrome-free" policies – that were set to achieve economic growth and accommodate the forces of the market. Often described as the "model for adjustment," Ghana's set of IMF/World Bank-stimulated growth policies and arrangements in the 1980s followed Deng Xiaoping's reforms in the 1970s that led to the "Going Out" policy. This set the stage for a liberalized, natural resource exploitation, export-driven, Ghanaian economy, and a transitional China ready for a global economic outreach. Hence, Beijing's support of the Ghanaian economy largely consisted of various forms of loan packages as development assistance, trade, and technical cooperation, especially since Ghana was then a non-oil economy unlike Nigeria, Angola, and Sudan.

According to existing research, China's economic activities in Ghana have become varied and helped by the liberalization arrangements, these range from major mining operations to small-scale businesses – some of which are joint ventures with Ghanaian partners, and yet many more unregulated. Some of the recent big projects include the Bui hydroelectric dam construction, which was to add up to $622m, and an $850m agreement for a gas project between the Ghana National Gas Company and the China Petroleum & Chemical Corporation in Beijing (Bloomberg News, 2012). In spite of the selected attempts by a few big Chinese companies to direct equity into Ghanaian firms, and sign partnership agreements such as Alcaltel Shanghai's investment in Ghana Telecom and the international trade and investment partnership between Ecobank Ghana and Bank of China, most Chinese investments are small to medium-sized. Both the large Chinese businesses and small-scale private actors interacting with Ghanaian business counterparts and population, at various levels diversely serve as agents or actors of Beijing's foreign policy agenda – an effort that may threaten the coherence of China's foreign policy agenda in Africa, as have been documented in different studies that refer to the varying impacts of paradiplomatic efforts among subnational actors (Hess & Aidoo, 2016; Michelmann, 2009).

With the Ghana–China relationship characterized by the building up and rehabilitation of infrastructure to address Ghana's bequeathed collapsing colonial infrastructure, trade initiatives, aid and technical assistance, and the gradual growth in investments, the number of Chinese actors in Ghana has shown a sturdy increase. Apart from the Chinese diplomats serving in Ghana, teeming groups of Chinese continued to arrive in Ghana to implement infrastructure projects. For instance, Baah and Jauch (2009) note that the construction of the Esipong stadium at Sekondi-Takoradi employed 150 Chinese (representing 65% of the workforce) out of a total of 230 workers employed at the project. The Bui hydroelectric project was pegged to attract over 3,000 workers (of which the Chinese were the majority).

Presently, with the increasing economic engagements between Ghana and China, the benefits from complementary contributions by the Chinese are often eclipsed by the competition with local businesses for the domestic market. Apart from the struggle over market, the presence of the Chinese in the Ghanaian economy has also introduced what Lee (2014) describes as globalization from below – the human trafficking and its concomitant prostitution, and increasing illegal mining activities in parts of the country. First, Axelsson and Sylvanus (2010) recount the complexities and hardships that the Chinese competition brought upon the Ghanaian textile industry as some textile manufacturers had to fold, leaving thousands of workers redundant (see also Quartey, 2006). Second, Lee (2014) provides harrowing accounts of trafficked Chinese sex workers in Ghana who were lured into this business with the promise of working in honest, well-paid jobs in Africa. Third, and also the focus of this chapter is the menace and complexities that have swelled around Chinese involvement in "galamsey" – a local term for illegal and unregulated artisanal gold mining in Ghana – (henceforth referred to as galamsey). Apart from the diplomatic difficulties created by the involvement of Chinese natives and operatives in this underbelly of the Ghanaian mining industry, which for long has been the preserve of the poor and underprivileged local people, the environmentally destructive effects of the galamsey by both local and foreign agents have been well noted in various research (Armah et al., 2013).

Even though the Chinese and other foreigners have been involved in this unregulated mining activity in Ghana for a while, from 2013, its nuisance became a full-fledged crisis. The onslaught of Chinese natives, largely from China's Shanglin County in China's Guangxi Zhuang Autonomous Region invaded most gold-rich regions in Ghana, to either engage in illegal extraction of gold by themselves or partner with local natives (Chengcheng, 2013; Hancock, 2013). By law, Ghanaian natives can apply for licenses to operate small-scale gold mining. The Chinese as foreigners can provide resources for machinery and also the technical knowledge. This has led to a series of joint ventures between the Ghanaians and the Chinese in which the latter have no legal ownership since their documentation for living and working in Ghana are mostly invalid (Chengcheng, 2013). The fallouts from the Chinese galamsey crisis in Ghana, which peaked in 2013, were widespread, and transcended the locations that these activities took place in, becoming a diplomatic disaster that impacted the politics and economics of Ghana–China relations.

Methodological considerations

This chapter largely draws on interviews and information gathered in 2013 and 2014, from Ghana, particularly Awaso, in the Western Region of Ghana – an area known for Ghana's major bauxite mine, currently operated by the Chinese, as well as increasing galamsey activities in surrounding areas. As this qualitative study broadly emphasizes the interactions among different political actors and the resultant change in socioeconomic arrangements, it is framed around the evidence of the influences of the Chinese as external actors in shaping an unregulated economic activity and culture – galamsey – that is largely dominated by local actors.

To achieve the research objective, this work combines both primary and secondary sources. Published accounts and books on the subject matter were very resourceful secondary evidence. Primarily, information was gathered through unstructured interviews from respondents/participants that were selected through purposive and snowball sampling. It also includes general observation of the dynamics surrounding the activities of the galamsey operators, and the local populations that are impacted in both positive and negative ways. There were two main groups of participants. The first group consists of key respondents made up of community leaders, traditional leaders or their representatives, and leaders of businesses. These interviewees were essentially selected through purposive sampling as their positions and roles in the community were key to their selection, and contribution of responses. The second group of respondents included the local inhabitants who partake in galamsey or are generally impacted by this unregulated mining activity. This group also consists of Chinese migrants who have come to engage in galamsey. These respondents were reached through snowball sampling, as one interviewee would usually contact other respondents or would bring in other respondents into an ongoing unstructured interview. In some cases, the local inhabitants or Ghanaians that were jointly working with the Chinese served as useful contacts to reaching their Chinese partners. This was extremely helpful, given the tense nature and politicization of the galamsey crisis, especially in 2013 (which was the period when most of the interviews were conducted).

In a two-month period in 2013, and a series of follow-ups in 2014, the unstructured interviews were conducted with 12 key respondents and 33 interviewees within the communities (including Chinese migrants). Most of the respondents sought anonymity, which was also provided for those that did not. This is to protect the respondents from any impact that their statements might cause, especially given that most of these individuals held positions and businesses that could easily be jeopardized by statements made during the interviewing process. Anonymity was particularly crucial due to the upwelling popular fury that was generated during the crisis that gained national and global attention. The predominantly male respondents requested anonymity to protect their livelihoods, since they were heads of household and breadwinners who saw the interviews as opportunities to vent their grievances over an ongoing menace – Chinese galamsey, but to stay out of the political frustration and popular anger that characterized this issue in 2013. Respondents that owned or managed businesses that benefit from Chinese involvement in this unregulated activity – hotels, restaurants, and equipment rental – were circumspect in their responses, to avoid public retribution or loss of business. The palpable anxiety and uncertainty of the situation was also reflected in some respondents' reluctance to agree to audio recording of the interviews. In general, the information gathered through the unstructured interviews and the observations provided a good basis for the evaluations and arguments of the political undertones and impacts that the actors had on the socioeconomic environment in the communities and the country as a whole.

The politics of Chinese galamsey in Ghana

> I have known these Chinese people [referring to a Chinese couple] for the past two years, since I started working for my uncle in this hotel. When they come to Ghana, they stay for about a year and then return to their home country with some gold. When they come, they rent and pay for the rooms for about six months at a stretch, but they hardly sleep in the rooms. They spend all of their time in galamsey. The stay, eat, and sleep in the forest for almost a month. The only time you see them back here at the hotel is when the security forces come after them.... We have a weak government that cannot control the Chinese, and with local people like us, that help them, Chinese galamsey will never stop.
>
> (hotel receptionist, Awaso, Western Region, Ghana)[3]

The above is an account rendered by a hotel worker and a native of Awaso in the Western Region of Ghana, a region that represents the fulcrum of two major mining economies – the recently discovered and celebrated oilfields in Ghana dominated by western companies, and the main bauxite mines, which is currently run by the Chinese. At this location and surrounding towns and villages, like other gold-rich areas in the country, there have been a surge of different actors, both domestic and foreign, involved in the unregulated and illegal galamsey activities, which has drawn mass public anger, and recently impacted Ghana–China engagements. In Awaso and surrounding villages, the Chinese have come to engage in the extraction of gold through artisanal mining, on a very small and unregulated scale. However, unlike the natives who use rudimentary tools like pick axes, shovels, and head pans in their galamsey exploits, the Chinese have turned to the use of heavy machines such as excavators and the use of toxic chemicals in the refinery process.

Evidently, this practice is against Ghana's Minerals and Mining Act of 2006 (Act 703) which seeks to prevent foreign nationals from purchasing or mining on plots of land smaller than 25 acres. This law is meant to ensure that small-scale mining remains the preserve of the local population (Parliament of the Republic of Ghana, 2006). Additionally, the practice of galamsey has been connected to the extensive destruction of the environment through the pollution of sources of drinking water, which has been linked to myriad health concerns such as arthritis, respiratory failure, miscarriages, neurological problems, and death (Armah et al., 2013, p. 95). These excesses have been compounded by some of the violent acts that have characterized the clash and competition over land plots for galamsey purposes. Consequently, the deadly clashes have persistently stoked and increased public anger. However, culpability for the Chinese involvement and excesses of galamsey has been directed at both the Chinese actors as well as their Ghanaian counterparts. He Wenping, the Director of the Chinese Academy of Social Sciences argues that low-level Ghanaian officials and businessmen have contributed to the nebulous nature of the legal perceptions of galamsey. He asserts that "Many times [Chinese miners] are not clear about

Ghana laws since there are middlemen who bring them over and help them sign a contract" (Bloomberg News, 2014).

Most research and reports on Chinese involvement in the galamsey crisis in Ghana bifurcate the blame vaguely on both Ghanaian political actors and Chinese diplomats and nationals. Nevertheless, the nuance overlooked by these reports and studies is the preponderant role played by the local and traditional political forces and actors such as the constitutionally non-partisan local chiefs, district assembly members, and community leaders that serve as conduits between the "corridors of power" and local people. Consequently, the activities of the Chinese illegal miners (and their middlemen) through the help of the local and traditional leaders are sustained by the existing frailties in the relationship between government monitoring institutions and the local/traditional structures in Ghana. These existing weaknesses that played out at both the national and subnational levels, aided by other given factors, resulted in complicated outcomes for governments in Beijing and Accra, especially, during the 2013 Chinese galamsey crisis in Ghana.

First, the increasing Chinese involvement in galamsey, and the attendant excesses of violent clashes, raids, and death could not have happened at a worse time for both the Chinese and the Ghanaian governments, especially, the latter. Amid such promise and prospect, Ghana's then vice president John Mahama (and then president from 2012 to 2017) signed the first tranche of a $3bn loan with the China Development Bank (CDB) in April 2012, and also had another $6bn loan in the works with the China Exim Bank. During the signing ceremony at the Kempsinki Hotel in Beijing, then vice president John Mahama purported that, "With the current financial crisis, it's very difficult to go anywhere in this world and get $3 billion" and "this is the single largest loan Ghana has taken; actually, it's the single largest credit facility to an African country" (Sanderson & Forsyth, 2013). With such appreciation for this Chinese financial lifeline, which was meant for infrastructure development, Ghana proceeded to accessing the loan. However, after the disbursement of less than $1bn by 2013 (approximately $600m), the agreement hit a snag as demands for renegotiation of the terms, which were based on Ghana's newly discovered oil resources remained contentious (Ghanaweb, 2014a). To further complicate a relationship that was under strain through the tug-of-war that had ensued over the $3bn, the galamsey crisis came to a head in 2013. This put the Ghanaian government in a rather complex and delicate situation as it was under pressure from the general populace to react to the increasing Chinese involvement in galamsey. The link between the two separate incidents shaping Ghana–China relations was undeniable, as put by one Ghanaian government worker, "we are in a very tough spot … it is either galamsey crackdown or a big loan from China."[4] After a series of government efforts to deal with the Chinese galamsey operatives, including the deportation of 713 Chinese nationals – representing 67% of deportations and repatriations in 2013 (see Table 8.1), it simultaneously became clear that the $3bn loan disbursements had stalled, pushing now President John Mahama to admit that "China is changing its policy" and "looking more at projects that have the potential to repay over time" (Wayne & Hinshaw, 2014). By the last quarter of 2014, Ghana found its way back to IMF for almost $1bn in loans while it explored other sources of funding to help finance the list of infrastructure projects, which were initially meant to be funded under the truncated $3bn Chinese loan agreement (Bax & Dontoh, 2014). Clearly, the anti-galamsey efforts by the Ghanaian government, which complicated Ghana–China relations in general, also somewhat constrained a monumental step in Ghana–China economic engagement (Ghanaweb, 2014c).

The second factor was the obvious mistrust that had developed between the masses and the newly elected National Democratic Party (NDC) government in Ghana. The local people and their traditional leaders in some of the areas hard hit by Chinese galamsey activities exhibited little faith in the government's ability and willingness to stop the Chinese. For diplomatic reasons that also included the promise of accessing Chinese financial resources for development projects in Ghana, the then newly elected John Mahama and the NDC administration had a tough balancing act. The gradual and piecemeal approach of the government seemed to have developed distrust in the NDC government's resolve to deal with the Chinese galamsey, which was perceived as a menace (Ghanaweb, 2014c; *Modern Ghana*, 2012). As sporadic clashes between locals and the Chinese galamsey operatives gained global media attention, the Ghana government was pressured to act through several crackdowns by the security forces and subsequent deportations of the Chinese. These efforts on the part of the Ghanaian government were perceived as short-lived, and inadequate in dealing with some of the Ghanaian officers and institutions that were complicit in Chinese galamsey operations. During interviews in Awaso, a local lamented at how the government was not doing much to stop the Chinese from exploiting their lands, by working through the local and traditional political structures.

> It is like everybody is doing their own thing, the government doesn't mind our chiefs, and the chiefs and local leaders [including the member of parliament] are not working together … I know some of the leaders are getting money benefits, but guess who loses in the end?[5]

The middle-aged woman from Awaso was frustratingly puzzled. The seemingly uncoordinated efforts among the local government structures allowed some of the local and traditional leaders to extract financial incentives from the Chinese in return for security and cover during their galamsey operations within their community. An apparent loophole was the absence of any system to check or monitor the immigration permits and documents of the Chinese who arrive at these local areas to acquire concessions from landowners for galamsey or work with their Ghanaian partners. To some of the inhabitants in Awaso and surrounding communities, the government was not doing a good job; leaving them to find the antidote to stem the onslaught of Chinese wealth seekers who endanger their communities.

Table 8.1 Showing deportations/repatriations by the Ghana Immigration Services, 2010–2013

Country/region of origin	*2010*	*2011*	*2012*	*2013*
China	43	5	130	713
Rest of Asia	19	32	56	53
Africa	30	25	46	289
Europe	6	4	11	8
Middle East	–	–	–	1
North America	3	2	–	1
Total	101	68	243	1,065

Source: Author's construct based on Ghana Immigration Service, Annual Report 2014.

The issue of Chinese galamsey in 2013, which unfolded in tandem with the $3bn loan saga also brought Beijing's well-known and often-touted foreign policy agenda in Africa under scrutiny (Bloomberg News, 2014). In the past decade, as China's engagements in Africa have expanded, it has been watched and scrutinized especially by western critics who have been suspicious of Beijing's engagements in Africa (Reuters, 2011). China has consistently and persistently evoked its cornerstone policy of non-interference in diplomatic relations with the developing world. Though the ethos of this principle has been repeatedly used to justify Beijing's inaction or otherwise in the international community, in practice, Beijing has had to defend its actions and that of its principal actors in Africa, which have been perceived as incongruous with the tenets of non-interference. This has particularly been so, as political regimes and economies change in Africa, along with China's expanding partnerships on the continent (Aidoo & Hess, 2015). The illegal and unregulated involvement of Chinese nationals in galamsey in Ghana render an image far from the non-interventionist, non-meddling partner that Beijing has continued to project in its diplomatic and economic engagements in Africa. Hence, any attempts that China made to contain the galamsey crisis were also to ensure the upholding of its core policy of noninterference, which often comes under intense scrutiny with such unwelcome accounts of reports of Chinese galamsey from Awaso, and other communities in Ghana (*Xinhua*, 2013).

Furthermore, the politics that ensued between China and Ghana during the peak of the galamsey crisis occurred in the shadow of the negotiations for the disbursement of the $3bn loan from the CDB. This loan was somewhat an indication of the maturity of Ghana–China engagement as well as a gesture that cements a relationship that has had its highs and lows through the decades from the 1960s. Conversely, the difficulties encountered by both states in reaching a deal with regard to the disbursement of the loan, which additionally stalled efforts to access the financial resources for a list of infrastructure projects earmarked by the Ghanaian government, also challenges a general rhetoric of China's provision of non-conditional loans to African economies (Chen, 2016). The issue of Chinese non-conditional loans has been touted in juxtaposition with loans from western financial institutions that mostly come with stringent conditions of economic and political reforms. A major disagreement on the terms of the CDB $3bn loan, which was guaranteed with Ghana's oil, was China's insistence on $85 per barrel as payback price instead of the over $100 per barrel proposed by the Ghanaian government. This is in addition to the commitment fees and a stipulation that offers 60% of contracts under the loan agreement to Chinese companies (Ghanaweb, 2014b). In Ghana, this loan and its legality was a subject of parliamentary debates and protests with the opposition party – New Patriotic Party (NPP) – accusing the ruling NDC administration of not using the appropriate political processes to seek parliamentary approval for the Chinese loan. Particularly, the opposition claimed the NDC government was breaching the Petroleum Revenue Management Act, which stipulates that Ghana's oil cannot be collateralized for more than 10 years (Hardus, 2014). As the debate over the conditions of the loan agreement and its disbursement became intense and partisan, it became distinctly clear that negotiations over the loan terms will stall its use, and hence the Mahama administration would have to look elsewhere for the resources. As aptly put by an investment banker in one of Ghana's premier investment houses, "China's loan sounds too good to be true, and now we know the hidden costs."[6]

Galamsey and anti-Chinese populism

> My husband and me have all our paperwork, why these people hate us? … We love this country
>
> (Chinese woman in Awaso, Western Region, Ghana)[7]

The above sentiment infuriatingly expressed by a Chinese woman who accompanied her husband to Awaso to work in galamsey, captures the tensions that were at play among the various actors, especially during the 2013 galamsey crisis. Fearing any form of local retribution or anger, she initially claimed her husband was working with the bauxite mine in Awaso – currently run by a privately owned Chinese company. The palpable anger expressed in some of the communities hard hit by galamsey by foreign nationals like the Chinese was in stark contrast with the generally positive nature of varied perception surveys that represent the Chinese in Ghana. In a 2009 survey conducted by the *BBC World Service*, Ghana was one of the three most favorable countries among 20 countries, with positive perceptions ranging from 62% to 75% (Rebol, 2010). This is further corroborated by another 44% of Ghanaian respondents considering China's path to development as a very positive model – one of the top three countries with the most positive perception out of nine countries (Sautman & Hairong, 2009). A more recent survey of global attitudes and perceptions by Pew indicates that 63% of the Ghanaian respondents see China as a good influence on the country's economy (3% more than the perception towards the US) (Pew Research Center, 2013).

Despite the embrace of Beijing as an exemplary influence through complementary gains like the infrastructure, and loan concessions, the competitiveness that is currently associated with the presence of the Chinese in some sectors of the Ghanaian economy – the textile industries – has contributed to a gradual upwelling of anti-Chinese sentiments in Ghana. Lately, increase in anti-Chinese sentiment can be correlated with Chinese involvement in activities like galamsey, especially as the Ghana government is often impelled by popular dissent to crackdown on the Chinese, which has mostly led to a series of arrests and deportations. Though galamsey is an age-old unregulated economy activity that has largely been the preserve of the locals, it is currently a representation of complex economic and political interrelationships between local Ghanaian inhabitants and foreign nationals like the Chinese – a nuanced nexus of global and domestic actors. The role of multiple actors and politics of galamsey are intrinsically and broadly linked to the emerging resentment against the Chinese in Ghana.

Essentially, galamsey depicts competition between the teeming Chinese migrants and local populations in economically challenged areas, similar to Awaso and surrounding communities in the Western Region of Ghana. In some of the poverty-ridden, yet resource-rich rural environments in Ghana, inhabitants are driven into galamsey as a means of survival, and this then convert these small mining concessions into complex and dangerous environments as the Chinese fight to protect what they deem to be their legitimately acquired piece of mining concession. This nature of competition often ends up in a deadly contest (BBC, 2012). Additionally, this fuels local popular anger, as the Chinese are perceived as usurping critical resources that are meant for locals in these low-income village communities.

A second source of popular frustration that fuels anti-Chinese sentiment is the ineffectiveness, and in some cases connivance of government institutions in galamsey issues. Ghana's Minerals and Mining Act of 2006 (Act 703) was enacted to replace the Minerals and Mining Law of 1986 (PNDCL 153), as a statute that prevents intrusions by foreign nationals in small-scale economic activities, which include unregulated ones like galamsey. In different situations, Ghanaian immigration officials and security forces take advantage of the existing laws to either cover up or exploit situations that involve vulnerable and frustrated Chinese nationals (Hille, 2013). Hence, despite the illegal implications, this is one of the elements that have sustained the practice of galamsey, and essentially emboldened foreign actors like the Chinese. Undoubtedly, incensed by the blatant Chinese involvement in galamsey around the communities in Awaso, a hotel receptionist at one of the hotels which lodges some of the Chinese nationals engaged in galamsey lamented about the kick-backs and bribes that some of the local leaders are receiving from the Chinese galamsey operators. "It was rumored that some the Chinese recently paid a certain amount of money to some of our own local leaders … I know it is true" she opined.[8] More flagrantly, some of the local leaders have established small income-generating ventures that rely on the activities of the foreign galamsey operators. Some of the leaders and elites rent out excavators, tractors, and standby generators, which are certainly beyond the very limited budgets of local galamsey operators. Thus, increased popular anger toward the Chinese nationals engaged in galamsey is concurrent with the frustrations regarding an ineffectual government institutional setup, from top to bottom, which struggles to deal with a situation that has far-reaching implications on Ghana–China diplomacy.

Though the Chinese galamsey crisis was an immediate cause that easily stoked the challenges of a weakening Ghanaian economy, and visibly widening income gap between the rich and the poor, other proximate causes that contribute to anti-Chinese sentiment in Ghana include the incursion of Chinese traders and products into the textile industry leading to a near collapse of this once resourceful industry. The other two are the increased presence of the Chinese in unlawful business ventures like trafficking and prostitution, which directly flouts domestic regulations; and, third, the political and partisan brouhaha over the $3bn Chinese loan.

The challenges of Ghana's textile industry predate the recent Chinese galamsey problems as Ghana's embrace of the structural adjustment policies in the 1980s affected the textile manufacturing sector – an instance of the general ill effects of the manufacturing sector under the series of policy directives (Hutchful, 2002). This situation was further exacerbated by liberalization arrangements adopted by the Rawlings administration through the 1990s. This increased competition as the deregulation measures implemented by the state opened up the market for foreign products. Ghana's textile industry was greatly impacted by Chinese competition. Quartey (2006) alludes to the thousands of workers that were displaced and factories that were closed down as a result of the liberalization policies. Over the decade, the textile-manufacturing sector has experienced intense competition from cheap, low-quality knock-off textile prints from China, which ironically serve the low-income consumer base in Ghana (Axelsson & Sylvanus, 2010). The Chinese competition in the textile industry and the accompanying deindustrialization effects has garnered anger from different parts of the political and economic spectrum – from politicians to local textile traders who can collectively convert the anti-China fervor into political gain, but has yet to do that, given the clear roles played by other Ghanaian actors in this rather intricate tale shaping the fate of Ghana's textile industry.

An issue that is connected to galamsey, and also undergirds the growing anti-China fury in Ghana, is the increasing and visible presence of the Chinese in shady business ventures – ones synonymous with Lee's (2014) "globalization from below," which accounts for the involvement of the thousands of Chinese migrants at the non-hegemonic level in African countries such as Ghana. As Chinese economic activities increase in Ghana, with sectors like construction, energy, and communication experiencing a surge in Chinese labor, so is other associated economic activities such as the trafficking of Chinese women to serve in the sex industry. This is to meet the demand by the growing community of Chinese expatriate workers who are mostly away from their spouses and families for long periods at a time. As documented in other African countries, an undercover report by known Ghanaian investigative journalist, Anas (2009), carefully documents the modern-day slave economic exchange that takes place between the Chinese perpetrators and their victims in Ghana. According to Anas the

Chinese women "are lured here with promises of honest, well-paid jobs, only to have their passports and tickets confiscated.... They are beaten and threatened with a high debt to be repaid only through the sale of their bodies."

Though such activity may be common among other nationals in Ghana, the current preponderance of several other acts of unlawful behavior by the Chinese, including galamsey, overwhelmingly draws local anger directed at the wanton disregard by Chinese nationals for the domestic laws and regulations. In this regard, the response by the manager of a haulage company captures these sentiments:

> I have been to Beijing, and I can say with complete certainty that there is no way I can get away with some of the things the Chinese do here in Ghana.... They are taking us for granted by disregarding our laws and security services.[9]

Such opinions reflect the palpable disfavor and compounding effect of recent unlawful Chinese behavior in Ghana.

Finally, the signing and disbursement of the $3bn Chinese loan was characterized by an impassioned discourse of fairness, timeliness, and accountability of the loan agreement for Ghana's struggling economy. Concurrently, and as already stated, the heated and largely partisan debate in Ghana coincided with the growing dissent toward the Chinese galamsey activities across the country. With a goal of infrastructure development and investment in energy, the loan would have been a major complementary offer and attempt toward the deepening of Ghana–China ties. However, as the democratic processes of parliamentary debate, and questions from the media wrung out the details of the Chinese loan agreement, some argued that the loan was a bad deal from Beijing, as the terms favored Beijing and exploited Ghana, and its resources (*Modern Ghana*, 2014). Despite the contentious and partisan nature of the debate, with the opposition party, NPP taking a vehement stand by abstention from the vote in parliament, one factor that united a large section of the Ghanaian public in opposition to the loan agreement was mistrust toward a Chinese-structured financial deal. The rhetoric from the opposition political parties and groups gained much attention and traction, in the light of the Chinese galamsey crisis. Though the opposition could not immediately thwart the processing of the loan agreement, the loan payment stalled as renegotiation terms failed. As various political actors continued to debate about the stalled $3bn Chinese loan, President Mahama made an about-face toward a rather familiar course of action – turning to the IMF for an almost $1bn loan that will certainly come with some restrictions and conditions (Bloomberg News, 2015).

Concluding remarks

As Beijing continues to expand its resources and role in Africa, countries like Ghana will gain from complementary economic engagement, which includes the development of roads and other forms of infrastructure. Additionally, China's emerging economy also serves as ready market for Africa's natural resources. However, these complementary gains are often eclipsed by the local dissent and anger toward the competition between Chinese nationals and the locals in many African economies. Often, the nature of subnational China–African competition centers on the exploitation of critical resources like gold or oil, in addition to the side-by-side competition for local market through general trade. The story of the inhabitants in Awaso and surrounding communities in the western region of Ghana represents another emerging political economic discourse, which attempts to capture the nexus between local dissent and the foreign encroachment on crucial resources and market. However, the uniqueness in this case is underscored by the evolving complexity associated with China–Ghanaian relations, which has often been generalized and simplified by limited surveys and anecdotes in the China–Africa discourse. As this chapter adds to the needed nuance in China–Africa research, it carefully and methodically offers some emerging insights through a country case study.

First, as China's effort to expand and sustain its activities in Africa grows and diversifies, so would Beijing's inability to control the myriad economic and political actors working in various African economies. In effect, this would endanger the brand that China has been assiduously trying to main in its economic and diplomatic engagements with African economies.[10] Furthermore, as these subnational actors related to China incur local anger and mistrust, like the case of the Chinese galamsey in Ghana, the resulting anti-Chinese sentiment often present huge diplomatic costs, as the masses in emerging African democratic polities pressure their governments to act. Second, most accounts of the anti-Chinese sentiment in Africa reported in the media often enable and urge China–Africa pessimism with lack of a clear emphasis on the connivance of local actors, making the reportage or research a tale of foreign exploitation of powerless or voiceless local dwellers (Hess & Aidoo, 2010). In this particular Ghanaian case study, the role of local political and economic actors, specifically, the alleged involvement of local traditional rulers, and political representatives underscore a less explored dimension in the development of accounts on anti-Chinese sentiment in Africa. To most of the locals interviewed in Awaso, the alleged collusion between Ghanaian political actors and their Chinese counterparts has further emboldened the galamsey operations, which led to the uncontrollable crisis in 2013 that necessitated the deportation of Chinese nationals from Ghana.

Finally, the Chinese galamsey crisis in communities in Ghana, and its attendant anti-Chinese fervor, represent the impact of activities in the shadow of a competitively diverse international political economy – what Lee (2014) terms "globalization from below" in developing economies. In this particular case of China–Ghana relations, the involvement of Chinese nationals in galamsey is part of a broad account of the effect that subnational elements have on foreign political economic relations among countries – emphasizing the effects of paradiplomacy in the developing world. In Awaso and surrounding communities in

Ghana, different nationalities from various regions of the world – Europe, Latin America, and North America – are involved in galamsey activities, nevertheless, the pervasiveness of Chinese nationals in this unregulated activity, especially in 2013, has become one of the dominant issues that define recent China–Ghana relations. For the locals who are either negatively or positively impacted by Chinese galamsey, this underbelly of globalization has certainly contributed to an already dichotomously aligned debate between skeptics and optimists of China's growing role in Africa. As appositely put by a manager of a haulage company in Awaso,

> the Chinese galamsey issue in Ghana represents the pluses and minuses of China's role in our economy ... here in Awaso, people like us have jobs because of Chinese investment in the main bauxite mine, but the involvement of Chinese nationals in galamsey takes away from this point.[11]

Acknowledgment

This research was made possible through support from Coastal Carolina University's Professional Enhancement Grant (PEG).

Notes

1 The original version of this chapter was published as "The political economy of galamsey and anti-Chinese sentiment in Ghana," *African Studies Quarterly*, *16*(34), December 2016.
2 Interview with a driver, Awaso, Western Region (this area and surrounding villages witnessed increased Chinese galamsey activity), Ghana, May 2013.
3 Interview with a hotel receptionist at one of the few hotels, Awaso, Western Region, Ghana, May 2013.
4 During an interview at Accra, May 2013.
5 Interview with middle-aged woman, Awaso, Western Region, Ghana, May 2013.
6 An interview with investment banker, Accra, Ghana, May 2013.
7 Interview with Chinese woman, Awaso, Western Region, Ghana, May 2013.
8 Interview with a hotel receptionist, Awaso, Western Region, Ghana, May 2013.
9 Interview with the manager of a haulage company, Awaso, Ghana, May 2013.
10 Hess & Aidoo (2010).
11 Interview with the manager of a haulage company, Awaso, Ghana, May 2013.

References

Aidoo, R., & Hess, S. (2015). Non-interference 2.0: China's evolving foreign policy towards a changing Africa. *Journal of Current Chinese Affairs 44*(1) 107–139.

Anas, A. A. (2009). Undercover: Inside the Chinese sex mafia. *The Crusading Guide*, 17–23 February. Retrieved March 18, 2015, from https://ec.europa.eu/europeaid/sites/devco/files/article-anasaremeyaw_en.pdf

Armah, F. A. et al. (2013). Artisanal gold mining and surface water pollution in Ghana: Have the foreign invaders come to stay? *Environmental Justice 6*(3) 94–102.

Axelsson, L., & Sylvanus, N. (2010). Navigating Chinese textile networks: Women traders in Accra and Lome. In F. Cheru & Cyril Obi (Eds.), *The rise of China and India in Africa* (pp. 132–141). New York, NY: Zed Books.

Baah, A. Y., & Jauch, H. (2009). *Chinese investments in Africa: A Labour perspective.* Accra, Ghana: African Labour Research Network.

Bates, R. H. (2012). Political economy of Africa's economic performance in the post-independence period. In Ernest Aryeetey et al. (Eds.), *The Oxford companion to the economics of Africa* (pp. 224–231). Oxford, UK: Oxford University Press.

Bax, P., & Dontoh, E. (2014). Ghana turns to IMF for help as currency crisis deepens. *Bloomberg News*. August 4.

BBC. (2012, October 15). Ghana probes death of "illegal Chinese gold miner." Retrieved March 25, 2019, from www.bbc.com/news/world-africa-19946787

Bienen, H., & Herbst, J. (1996). The relationship between political and economic reform in Africa. *Comparative Politics 29*(1) 23–42.

Bloomberg News. (2004). China's Africa role under new scrutiny as miners expelled. June 7. Retrieved June 15, 2015, from www.bloomberg.com/news/2013-06-06/chinese-county-warns-locals-from-going-to-ghana-to-mine-for-gold.html

Bloomberg News. (2012). Ghana signs $1billion loan with China for natural gas project. *Bloomberg News*, April 16. Retrieved March 5, 2015, from www.bloomberg.com/news/articles/2012-04-16/ghana-signs-1-billion-loan-with-china-for-natural-gas-project

Bloomberg News. (2015). IMF agrees to lend Ghana almost $1 billion to boost Economy. February 26. Retrieved March 21, 2015, from www.bloomberg.com/news/articles/2015-02-26/imf-agrees-to-lend-ghana-almost-1-billion-to-bolster-economy

Chen, T. (2016). What happened to China Development Bank's $3 billion loan to Ghana? *China–Africa Research Initiative Policy Brief.* February. Retrieved May 20, 2016, from http://static1.squarespace.com/static/5652847de4b033f56d2bdc29/t/56d64a9e01dbaef868231233/1456884389759/CARI_PolicyBrief_10_Feb2016.pdf

Chengcheng, J. (2013). Africa or bust: Chinese gold miners take huge risks. *Time Magazine*, July 4. Retrieved May 3, 2015, from http://world.time.com/2013/07/04/africa-or-bust-chinese-gold-miners-take-huge-risks

Ghana Immigration Service. (2014). *Annual report*. Accra, Ghana: Government Printer.

Ghanaweb. (2013, June 8). Chinese miner shot dead in galamsey shooting. Retrieved 28 March, 2015, from www.ghanaweb.com/GhanaHomePage/NewsArchive/artikel.php?ID=276353

Ghanaweb. (2014a, May 5). Anti-galamsey war failing due to China's $3b loan to Ghana – Sec. chief. Retrieved March 26, 2015, from www.ghanaweb.com/GhanaHomePage/NewsArchive/artikel.php?ID=308282

Ghanaweb. (2014b, July 17). CBD loan: Chinese asking for too much oil, says Terkper. Retrieved March 25, 2015, from www.ghanaweb.com/GhanaHomePage/NewsArchive/artikel.php?ID=317382

Ghanaweb. (2014c, May 6). Don't mortgage Ghana's destiny for $3b loan. Retrieved March 26, 2015, from www.ghanaweb.com/GhanaHomePage/NewsArchive/artikel.php?ID=308314

Hancock, T. (2013). China miners' African gold rush tarnished by terror. *AFP*, June 13. Retrieved March 20, 2015, from https://sg.news.yahoo.com/china-miners-african-gold-rush-tarnished-terror-111148227.html

Hardus, S. (2014). Chinese national oil companies in Ghana: The cases of CNOOC and Sinopec. *Perspectives on Global Development and Technology 13*(5–6) 588–612.

Hess, S., & Aidoo, R. (2010). Beyond the rhetoric: Noninterference in China's African policy. *African and Asian Studies 9*(3) 356–383.

Hess, S., & Aidoo, R. (2014). Charting the roots of anti-Chinese populism in Africa: A comparison of Zambia and Ghana. *Journal of Asian and African Studies 49*(2) 129–147.

Hess, S., & Aidoo, R. (2016). Charting the impact of subnational actors in China's foreign relations: The 2013 galamsey crisis in Ghana. *Asian Survey 56*(2) 301–324.

Hille, K. (2013). Chinese gold miners' hope for riches shattered by Ghana crackdown. *Globe and Mail*, June 9. Retrieved March 30, 2015, from www.theglobeandmail.com/report-on-business/international/business/african-and-mideast-business/chinese-gold-miners-hope-for-riches-shattered-by-ghana-crackdown/article12444597

Hutchful, E. (2002). *Ghana's adjustment experience: The paradox of reform*. Geneva, Switzerland: United Nations Research Institute for Social Development.

Lee, M. C. (2014) *Africa's world trade: Informal economies and globalization from below*. London: Zed Books.

Michelmann, H. (Ed.). (2009). *Foreign relations in federal countries*. Montreal, Canada: McGill University.

Modern Ghana. (2012, August 18). Are NDC now desperately conniving with the Chinese government to fool Ghanaians because of elections? Retrieved March 26, 2015, from www.ghanaweb.com/GhanaHomePage/NewsArchive/artikel.php?ID=308282

Modern Ghana. (2014, January 11). $3 billion loan: Is China defrauding Ghana? Retrieved March 28, 2015, from www.modernghana.com/news/513093/1/3-billion-loan-is-china-defrauding-ghana.html

Ndulu, B. J. et al. (2008) *The political economy of economic growth in Africa, 1960–2000*. New York, NY: Cambridge University Press.

Ogunsanwo, A. (1974) *China's policy in Africa 1958–1971*. London: Cambridge University Press.

Parliament of the Republic of Ghana. (2006). *The Mineral and Mining Act*, 703, March 22. Retrieved June 15, 2015, from http://faolex.fao.org/docs/pdf/gha85046.pdf

Pew Research Center. (2013, July 18). Global image of the United States and China. Retrieved June 15, 2015, from www.pewglobal.org/2013/07/18/global-image-of-the-united-states-and-china

Quartey, P. (2006). The textile and the clothing industry in Ghana. In H. Jauch & R. Traub-Merz (Eds.), *The future of the textile and clothing industry* (pp. 133–146). Bonn, Germany: Friedreich Eberhart Stiftung.

Rebol, M. (2010). Public perceptions and reactions: Gauging African views of China in Africa. *African Journal of Agricultural Research 5*(25) 3524–3535.

Reuters. (2011, June 11). Clinton warns against new colonialism in Africa. Retrieved November 14, 2014, from www.reuters.com/article/2011/06/11/us-clinton-africa-idUSTRE75A0RI20110611

Sanderson, H., & Forsyth, M. (2013) *China's superbank: Debt, oil and influence – How China Development Bank is rewriting the rules of finance*. New Jersey, NJ: Wiley-Bloomberg.

Sautman, B., & Hairong, Y. (2009). African perspectives on China–Africa links. *China Quarterly* 199: 728–759.

Shinn, D. H., & Eisenman, J. (2012). *China and Africa: A century of engagement*. Philadelphia: University of Pennsylvania Press.

Vang, P. (2008) *Five Principles of Chinese Foreign Policy* Bloomington, IN: AuthorHouse.

Wayne, A., & Hinshaw, D. (2014). China takes wary steps into New Africa deals. *Wall Street Journal*. May 6. Retrieved March 20, 2015, from www.wsj.com/articles/SB1000 1424052702303647204579545813194873656

Xinhua. (2013, June 12). Delegation in Ghana to deal with illegal mining. Retrieved March 26, 2015, from www.china.org.cn/world/2013-06/12/content_29103708.htm

9 The search for economic self-determination

Senegal and Ghana's destiny

Saliou Dione

Introduction

The 1950s and 1960s marked the independence of many formerly European-held territories after their partition (Ratcliffe, 1981, p. 3) during the 1884–1885 Berlin Conference. Ghana secured its independence after Kwame Nkrumah's Gold Coast government issued a white paper with a proposal for the end of colonization on March 6, 1957 even though self-government with a local Ghanaian prime minister had already been started by the British colonial government in 1951 following a period of political turmoil after World War II (WWII). Senegal, for its part, formed with French Sudan, a territorial entity known as the Mali Federation, which became fully independent on June 20, 1960, but the transfer of power with France was signed on April 4, 1960. Internal political difficulties contributed in breaking up the federation and Leopold Sedar Senghor became the country's first president in August 1960, but the date April 4, 1960 was retained as the date marking its independence from French colonial domination.

In fact, Adam Smith (1776), widely considered the father of economics, labeled the machine the "invisible hand" and emphasized the economy's self-regulating nature that agents independently seeking their own gain may produce the best overall result for society as well. In the case of Senegal and Ghana, this "invisible hand" is articulated in their economic self-determination. The concept has its historical origin in the laws of nations of the western world. By 1945, historical imperialism and fascism had come to an end while colonialism was yet to be dismantled. So, the so-called Third World, Africa in particular, embarked on a political battle against colonial rule and in the process looked to whatever legal tools were available that might help back up its demand. One of the tools its political leaders resorted to was the right to self-determination (Grovogui, 1996, p. 112). The idea is then closely related to the European concept of nation-state and its classical corollary state sovereignty. The western democratic definition is associated with former US President Woodrow Wilson, for whom the right to self-determination is the right of peoples to govern themselves, implying that no one can legitimately govern a people without that people's consent. Self-determination, in its political origins, was deeply connected to statehood. But as the doctrine developed into a legal concept, it came to be referred to as a peoples' right.

But in a modern application of economic self-determination for Senegal and Ghana, there are numerous problems with this de facto, state-centered concept. The de facto state-centered application of self-determination over the last four decades witnessed the emergence of a persuasive legal doctrine that backed up the idea that peoples are the bearers of the right to economic self-determination. As a matter of fact, the economic self-determination-related discourse that was put forth after WWII denoted some ambiguity in its understanding and use, as to whether it was the state or the people who bore the right to economic self-determination. The resolutions that emerged from the United Nations General Assembly of that period used "people" and "state" interchangeably. Therefore, far from a mainstream categorization in relation to limiting self-determination to anticolonialism, the context of Senegal and Ghana's search for economic self-determination does not make any definitional distinction between the state and people. It rather reserves the right and undertaking to Senegalese and Ghanaian peoples and their states, as having the right to individually and collectively dispose of their wealth and natural resources. The traditional nations of economic self-determination are still relevant in the contemporary political and economic realities of the two West African countries that are marked by new world challenges such as neocolonization and globalization under the conceptual banner of western imperialism. These represent the forces by which foreign countries' control and domination are still felt on the continent (Davidson, 2014, p. 19).

The problem of destiny touches other angles that raise other historical questions related to the search for economic self-determination. These are the history of development policies, the history of industrial enterprises, and the assessment of the standard of living of the populations, the management of natural resources, the political economy, political decisions, and so on. Indeed, the relevance of analyzing the destiny of Senegal and Ghana in their search for economic self-determination and their related development policies and strategies allow seeing where their commonalities and differences lie as they struggle to secure economic sovereignty.

The analytic approaches and socioeconomic and political practices of the postcolonial, as opposed to pillars of western politics of *in-dependency* and subordination theory-based hegemonic economic imperialism, making it both a political and epistemic project (Mignolo, 2011, p. 8), documents how the postcolonial approaches to understanding Senegal and Ghana's economic self-determination processes are related to the nature of neoliberalism, neocolonization, globalization, transnational flows of capital and workers, and the making and remaking of territorial borders assume center stage in debate about contemporary economies and policies. As an ideological framework which looks at how postcolonial Senegal and Ghana, as preys in the global village of the West, it serves as a measurement and analytical tool, as well as a response to the relation of direct political, social, and economic domination established by Europeans (Quijano, 2007, p. 168). In any event, postcolonial thought cannot be easily jettisoned because of the present biased globalized world marked by new (re)configurations and new challenges for the two countries as they seek to encompass three senses (a) temporal, (b) spatial, and (c) ethico-cultural, and economic, and political regardless of the questionable past (colonial) legacies that are regimented in present international relations and exchanges within western globalism.

However, this chapter does not reflect any willingness to propose a product of "combat" or a thorough political and economic assessment of their political economies. It seeks to report on and analyze development in contemporary Senegal and Ghana by developing a framework that allows reading the evolution of reforms and policies, as well as their nature and leaders' ways of exercising power and authority in their search for economic self-determination. To this end, the study leans on a postcolonial and on an *in-dependency* theory so as to analyze their political and economic destiny using a cross-analysis as an analytical methodological tool to unearth the differences and commonalities in their economic policies, with the different regimes that have governed these cases. Aware of the fact that a greater proportion of the scholarly literature on the two West African countries was produced by foreign scholars who inevitably handled the subject matter within an external frame of reference, this study is concerned with reconstituting the changing trajectory of the (re)configuration processes which marked the economic and political life in Senegal and Ghana, from the period of independence with the founding fathers, Nkrumah and Senghor, the first regime changes and the post-2000 period. It shows the changes and ruptures in the political, sociocultural, and economic fields, and reveals the responses of the two states and societies to the most important shifts observed since their independence. It looks to identify the main cycles of the construction of the economies and modes of political and economic regulation they used from 1957 to the present day, and highlight the consolidation of an effective political bureaucracy, which sometimes bore significant economic performances and weaknesses as well.

The (post)colonial search for economic self-determination and the construction of the economies of Senegal and Ghana

Between the 1870s and 1900s, Africa faced European imperialist aggression, diplomatic pressures, military invasion, and eventually conquest and colonization. At the same time, African countries initiated various forms of resistance against the attempt to colonize and exploit their natural resources and impose foreign domination. In fact, the most important cause of colonization was economic. The idea came after the industrial revolution when Europe's needs of natural resources could mainly be met by Africa as it was hit by economic depression. To make money in Africa, France and Britain depended on the many raw goods of Senegal and Ghana, respectively. Because of cheap labor force, hoarded oil, ivory, rubber, palm oil, wood, cotton, and gum were easily acquired for the colonizer's financial boon. They set up new African markets to produce more commerce and boost the capitalist industrial revolution. The imperatives of capitalist industrialization, including the demand for markets and profitable investment outlets, spurred their scramble and eventual conquest of Africa. Therefore, the primary motivation of France in Senegal and Britain in Ghana was economic.

However, the decade after WWII was characterized by the revival of development economics which, like most field of economics, had its ups and downs. Economic development then remained the main preoccupation of many countries across the world, with leading western economists such as Thomas Robert Malthus (1982), John Stuart Mill (2000) among others who devoted their attention to explaining the long-run course of the economy. After WWII, a study of economic development, particularly the economic problems of the less developed countries or the "Third World," as they came to be described, attracted the attention of economists once again. Partly as an offshoot of the Marshall Plan aimed at reconstructing war-devastated Europe but mainly due to the experience with planned development in the Soviet Union elaborate theories and models were molded as solutions to the poverty and instability of the large number of countries, some of which were beginning to emerge from western colonial rule: Senegal and Ghana.

State building and nationalist economic spirit formation

Senegal and Ghana's search for economic self-determination began during the colonial period. In Ghana, it was the British that eventually gained control of the territory, buying all the trading posts the other countries had installed over the years. Apart from the westerners, they also had to face the Ashanti and Fanti tribes that were nowhere near ready to cede their land to British invaders. In fact, two reasons account for the emergence of the rise of nationalism in Gold Coast. Among them, are internal and external factors that involved the presence of a conscious intellectual elite, urbanization, the emergence of political parties and trade unions as well as the development of communication channels (roads and railways), the impact of WWII and the British postwar politics and consensus failure. Likewise, the decolonization process in Senegal had to follow the prevailing politics of French-held territories. It was a phase of major political advancement consecutive to the Brazzaville Conference, whose goal was to reform the administration of the colonies as a "reward" for their participation in World War II. Though no African attended the meeting, it heralded a new African consciousness for the need to govern themselves as the only way to freedom and economic self-determination. This resulted in the adoption of a new constitution that changed the status of the colonies, making them French territories overseas, and leading to the settlement of a territorial assembly with an involvement in political and economic decisions, the suppression of French denizenship, and forced labor. Consequently, Leopold Sedar Senghor and Lamine Gueye, on the Senegalese side, and Kwame Nkrumah and Joseph Boakye (J. B.) Danquah, on the Ghanaian one, started working with other African elites to reach the goal of independence.

A political and economic changing trend occurred in the Gold Coast with the rejection by the country's elites of the 1948 constitution that Governor Sir Alan

Burn was tasked with implementation. The economic situation was bad as a result of the swollen shoot, a plague that ravaged the cacao trees, thus depriving thousands of families of their anticipated incomes. The colonial government's response to the plaguing tree diseases, that all the trees of the concerned district be removed, raised the suspicions of the elites, and motivated them to face the ruling colonial power. The opposition grew stronger with the former servicemen back from India who requested equal treatment as Asian countries that had just secured their independence. All the country's protesters gathered around one man, J. B. Danquah, a lawyer and aristocrat who believed that the only way for his people to reach economic self-determination was to implement the authority of an enlightened minority politics. To this end, he created his party, the United Gold Coast Convention (UGCC), and solicited a young college student in London to be the secretary, Kwame Nkrumah. The first thing he did was to turn the political party into a party of the masses, as dictated by his Marxist ideology, allowing citizens to be engaged in the road to political and economic independence. In 1948, he initiated a boycott of European products as a way of protesting against their high prices. He further developed a radicalism politics within the UGCC which was used against the British colonial administration. That marked the beginning of a huge riot across the country, most known in Accra in 1949 that killed 29 Ghanaians and resulted in the arrest of hundreds of people, including Nkrumah and Danquah. The Watson Commission concluded after the riot that there was a strong popular resentment spreading in the country and that the political autonomy of the Gold Coast was the only alternative that could curb it. In reaction to the Empire's proposition of reforms two voices emerged, the UGCC with "discussing the autonomy as soon as possible," and the Convention People's Party (CPP) with its "self-government" now. After years of political struggle, Great Britain eventually ceded to Nkrumah's demands and started working with him toward the goal of independence, which was declared on March 6, 1957. The country was named Ghana, a name that symbolized the political renaissance of Black Africa.

In fact, the newly independent African countries of Senegal and Ghana embarked on a new economic enterprise which they had no mastery and control over. Despite all, their leaders engaged their countrymen in a state- and economy-building processes with the articulation of similar and different paths, as reflected in their destiny, in their proper historical, political, and economic contexts. The postcolonial economies of the two countries, characterized by dire economic conditions with mass starvation and widespread pauperization of the peasant masses, massive unemployment, and rising inflation in the urban areas of Dakar and Accra. The dire situation resulted in total dissatisfaction among the populace as a whole. Thus drought and famine in some rural areas, the global oil shock resulted in deterioration in the general economic situations. This precipitated the need for alternatives to economic self-determination aimed at putting their countries on the right track to decolonial development.

Early economic decolonization processes

The period from 1951 to February 1966 was under the leadership of Kwame Nkrumah and the CPP. Under him, Ghana experienced important economic transformation and development. His economic strategy was modest industrialization based on import substitution. Indeed, fighting for the self-management of the natural resources accounted for the awakening of the masses in both Senegal and Ghana. Being part of the Commonwealth of Nations, Ghana continued cooperating with Great Britain economically. The collaboration between the two countries resulted in the former colonial power's initiated natural resources management programs, thus allowing Ghana to benefit from other experiences while having full power of decision regarding its natural resources. In the early years of independence, the economic strategy of both Ghana and Senegal mainly focused on industry and trade development with the intent to achieve the same level of development as their former colonizers. Therefore, Presidents Nkrumah and Senghor oriented their economic strategy toward growth-oriented development approaches and strategies and rapid industrialization. It was the same key-to-growth process that was adopted in the 1970s with more policies toward poverty reduction as proven by a lax government. As for Senegal, since in the 1960s, it did not have enormous potential to establish enviable economic growth, it experienced ups and downs because of its poor colonial heritage that could not facilitate its takeoff. Despite possessing some economic infrastructures (Autonomous Port of Dakar, the international airport, and road and railway infrastructure) and being a trade transit for West Africa, however, the heavy-handedness of France was an obstacle to the realization of some of Senegal's potentials. The country needed more energy to build a sovereign state. At that time, Senegal and Ghana had the same GDP as South Korea. But the poor performance of the reform policies undertaken by Presidents Nkrumah and Senghor to boost their countries' economies had led to deficient growth caused by the oil crises (bankruptcies of many companies, the closure of factories, and the fall in the price of oil, peanut and poor agricultural yields). The primary sector, which was one of the sectors that employed the labor force surplus, suffered a regrettable decline, because many of them were affected by poor economic growth. Faced with this, the government of Senegal decided to implement development policies in order to revitalize all sectors through cooperation with international financial institutions (IFIs) such as the French Development Agency (FDA), the World Bank (WB), and the International Monetary Fund (IMF).

In the same period of time, between the 1960s and the 1970s, Ghana's Nkrumah sought to exploit the country's natural resources and lay the foundation for the development of other economic sectors. The goal was to provide Ghanaians with basic infrastructure, create jobs, and offer possibilities for technological progress. The policy was characterized by import substitution, administration controls, and public sector investment. The restrictive initiative of foreign exchange regime and an overvaluation of Ghana's domestic currency, the cedi, also played an important role in the implementation process of the president's economic system. Nkrumah's self-reliance approach involved reducing Ghana's economic dependence on Britain. Yet, the initiative was not successful because it produced a negative balance of payment due to stagnant export and rising imports. Both Presidents Senghor's and Nkrumah's export industrialization failed to meet the expectations of the masses since their industrialization strategy did not fully materialize. Yet, the regime changes that occurred in Ghana in the 1970s did not continue the industrialization process of Nkrumah. Focus was mostly placed on poverty reduction and assuring the population's basic needs under rural development programs with slogans such as "Operation Feed Yourself" and "Operation Feed Your Nation." There were poor economic performances as the main macroeconomic policies generally led to economic deterioration.

Senegal and Ghana, on their road to economic self-determination, faced the disillusionment and breakdown that dulled the early achievements of the postcolonial period. However, much has been achieved since independence.

Post-Senghorism, post-Nkrumahism and the construction of an economic utopia

Senegal's Senghor and Ghana's Nkrumah had great economic and political ambitions for their countries. They were both concerned with improving their populations' living conditions. Such convictions became stronger as for instance there was a powerful anti-state wave stirred up by the main donors of Senegal, Indeed, conceived in the 1960s as an effective apparatus that could serve to promote economic and social development, the state was later on seen by donors as an inefficient device. The post-Senghorism and post-Nkrumahism eras were characterized by regime changes in Senegal and Ghana. This was illustrated by the succession process between Presidents Senghor and Diouf (Diop & Diouf, 1990, p. 10) as a way of shedding light on how the Senegalese bureaucracy operated in the postcolonial succession of its first generation of leaders. Unlike Senegal that experienced a smooth power change, Ghana's second republic following a coup was established under the presidency of Kofi Abrefa Busia in 1969 before he was overthrown by a military coup three years later. In 1979, Hilla Limann came to power and established Ghana's third republic. But he did not last in power since he was, in turn, toppled by a coup led by Jerry Rawlings who presided over the destiny of Ghana from 1981 to 1993. From 1966 to 1981, the country was in a continuous period of political instability marked by successive military coups that toppled three elected civilian governments and one military government. It was the era when Ghana's politics recorded a cyclical nature comprising both civilian regimes and military interventions. The period of political unrest did, however, not usher in ideological unrest. The policies rather resembled each other more than the protagonists wanted to admit (Nugent, 1995). The tenures of the two democratically elected civilian governments, respectively, ranged from October 1969 to January 1972 and from September 1979 to December 1991. It was the military coup that took place in December

1981 that ended the third experiment with multi-party elected civilian government, and marked the establishment of the Provisional National Defence Council (PNDC) under President Jerry Rawlings.

Both Senegal and Ghana were more concerned with modernization of their governments. That enabled them in the early 1980s to put their countries' economy back on the right track to development. But their economies worsened later on due to huge fiscal deficit, compelling their governments to seek loans from the domestic and international banking systems and leading to inflation and a currency overvalued. Like in Senegal, in Ghana it resulted in a decrease in trade, export earnings and a shortage of imported goods, lack of private investment, and a massive public sector. The agricultural production of both Senegal (1982) and Ghana (1983) was at its lowest level because of the drought that hit the two countries. Ghana's President Rawlings embarked on a decentralization of the governance with a view to contributing to Economic Recovery Programs (ERPs) which was imposed by external donors. The objective was to initiate an economic liberalization and reduce state involvement in the economy. Senegal experienced the same situation under President Diouf since the economic "takeoff" promises in the early years of independence were yet to be kept.

The political and economic management patterns observed between December 1962 and the late 1970s plunged the two countries into serious difficulties. That opened up the way for some reforms, spurred by the IMF and the WB, to improve the management of public finances and reenvision of relations between the state, economy, and society. The IMF and WB-backed SAPs were part of the initiatives undertaken to overcome the structural deficiencies facing these two postcolonial African economies. This was evidenced by the reforms Senegal's President Diouf and his administration undertook from the 1980s up to the 1990s. Both Senegal and Ghana had then to undertake a process that would gradually free them from the post-independence ideological, political, and economic materials. That was the beginning of the IMF and WB-backed SAPs in which they had to put in place political and economic strategies that would enable them to limit the damages and turn their economies around.

The Structural Adjustment Programs

To get Senegal and Ghana out of their economic malaise, the WB and the IMF decided to allocate financial aid to their respective governments in order to facilitate the implementation of their development plans for real economic expansion. Both decided to implement SAPs intended to liberalize their economy and boost investments. Prior to that, between 1981 and 1990, resistance from the government administration of both countries to structural adjustment failed to revive the economy on the basis of the recommendations of the Bretton Woods institutions. That resulted in a weak internalization of President Diouf's power as well as some constraints related to the adjustment and structural programs, despite relatively large external financial outlines. It also led to a deterioration of the economic and social situation, together with serious budgetary difficulties, and the donors' hardening of the conditions of access to economic resources. The early 1990s were thus characterized by a severe deterioration of the relationships between Senegal's central government and its main donors. The structuring politics of the French cooperation and the aridity of the government of Edouard Balladur's policies, indicating the limits of France's financial support, constituted new objective constraints which the ruling class had also to include in its development agenda (Diop, 2013, p. 23). Meanwhile, in the early 1980s, a new development policy was adopted in Ghana since the country had little choice to make due to poor economic conditions in a post-Nkrumah era. Like Senegal, Ghana was then compelled to accept the help of the capitalist West. The only alternative was to accept the IMF and WB-imposed reforms aimed at maximizing the freedom of the market and minimizing government's involvement in the economy. The initiative was opposed to Marxist perception of the economy and gave way to neoliberal thinking that believes in market efficacy as a precondition to reach economic development. As in Senegal, the state in Ghana was seen as one of the major obstacles to economic growth instead of constituting the solution (Diop & Diouf, 2000). To better implement the reforms, Ghana instituted the Economic Recovery Program (ERP) with the main objective of stabilizing the economy and laying the foundation for sustainable growth rates. From then on, a better management of public resources, of the exchange, and trade system had become prerequisites toward stabilization and flexibility in both countries, forcing them to embark on deregulation, trade liberalization, privatization, and stable macroeconomic management (Dordunoo et al., 2000, p. 125).

In fact, Ghana's ERP was implemented in three phases. The program's first phase rested on stabilization, the second on rehabilitation of the economy, and the third on economic liberalization and development. The targeted objective was to renew the public sector and bring changes in the private one. With the liberalization and privatization-generated profits, the whole country was expected to reach prosperity (Aryeetey et al., 2002). The SAPs sought to remove structural barriers, which would lead to a 5% annual growth rate in GDP, a decrease of inflation to 8%, and a healthy balance of payment (Aryeetey et al., 2002). The production of cereals such as maize and rice was promoted and Ghanaian farmers were provided with guaranteed minimum prices through subsidies for fertilizers, machinery, and other agricultural chemicals. It was in the third phase of the programs that the agricultural sector was liberalized and the guaranteed minimum prices for maize and rice dropped along with subsidies, thus paving the way for more competition and weakening the Ghana Cocoa Board. Still, there was no real structural change insofar as the ERP failed to reach its goal of attracting flows of private investment (Gyimah-Boadi & Jeffries, 2000, p. 37).

While the Structural Adjustment Programs totally failed in Senegal, they were modestly successful in Ghana as they enabled a slight hike in economic growth rate with increased poverty among the lower and middle classes. While increasing the regime's dependency on the outside world, the SAPs exacerbated social tensions; in particular, they had depressed incomes, especially among the middle class. Unfortunately, behind the seeming acts of goodwill of the Bretton Woods institutions, there were some debilitating economic effects which the two countries continue to manage.

The post-Structural Adjustment Programs era

The early 1990s were marked in Senegal by difficult relations between the central government and its traditional economic partners and donors. Indeed, mixed results were gained from the IMF and WB-backed SAPs due to the partial implementation of the envisaged political and economic reforms. In some cases, both Ghana and Senegal were paralyzed by resistances from the government administration. But in Ghana, economic stabilization, rehabilitation, and liberalization contributed in boosting the economy, even if it generated development problems. Access to a good education system and health services still posed a problem for the Ghanaian population. Meanwhile, in Senegal in the second half of 1993, after a period of procrastination and tense relations with its donors, the government was forced to confront the social claims of the country's trade unions and political parties by adopting an "Emergency Plan" called the Sakho–Loum Plan, named after the respective finance and budget ministers. The plan aimed at reducing, in the short term, the budget deficit. In 1993, the government faced a financial situation due to a significant drop in its budgetary revenues, while the wage bill, a major item of its public expenditure, was at a high level. Following the same trend as Senegal to fill the remaining gap in access to education and health services, which the SAPs had failed to provide, the Ghanaian government had to look for alternatives that would allow it to reach social and economic development. To this end, it decided to implement a long-term plan called the National Co-ordinated Programme of Economic and Social Development Policies (popularly referred to as Vision 2020). The initiative became the development guide for all the major sectors with a view to reducing poverty. It was expected to put the country on the right track to reaching the status of middle-income country by 2020. Because of its holistic nature, it focused on the Ghanaian people's standard of living in relationship to human development, rural development, and urban policies. Yet, like Senegal's Poverty Strategy Reduction Program, Ghana's Vision 2020 is yet to be fully realized (though it has reached middle-income status) due to poor coordination between the National Development Planning Commission (NDPC) and the Ministry of Finance (MOF). It was also not well connected to the population's needs, the country's economic management reality, and budget allocations. Therefore, the government expenditure on poverty reduction and growth programs were low during the 1990s, thus forcing the country to supplement the gap with foreign aid from multilateral and bilateral partnerships (IMF, 2010).

Considering the outcomes of the SAPs, the WB and the IMF seemed to have had other objectives more important than their cooperation. Indeed, the reform policies, encompassing the policy of restricting wages to ensure balance of payments, imposed by these two institutions did not necessarily consider the standard of living of the Senegalese and Ghanaian people. The two states had no choice but to accept these standards, because they needed to implement their economic projects to help reach their so-awaited economic self-determination. In a context where the economic growth and poverty rates were still increasingly high, protests and movements that opposed the adjustment policies resulted from the execution of these policies. Indeed, the economies of Senegal and Ghana were punctuated by development plans, which were gradually supplanted by stabilization and adjustment programs. Thus, one can argue that the two international financial institutions were the main sources of the depletion of funds in the two states. That happened despite the bilateral and multilateral cooperation, to fund their programs such as the Central Bank of West African States (BCEAO), the African Development Bank (ADB), the West African Economic and Monetary Union (WAEMU).

Monetary in-dependence

The Sakho–Loum Plan did not prevent the devaluation of Senegal's domestic currency, the CFA franc in 1994, despite President Diouf's resistance. But the plan managed to take daring and fruitful steps after the country's assets were divided by two while those of France, which keeps the reserves and guarantees of the currency, were multiplied by two. From that episode, Senegal undertook important structural reforms aimed at consolidating the bases of a sustainable growth, improving its economy competitiveness, reviving exports, and cutting the state's scope of intervention in order to ensure financial viability thereof. Ghana had its own currency devalued, which marked the country's currency redenomination exercise, from cedi to the new currency, the Ghana cedi in July 2007. That gave a transfer rate of one Ghana cedi for every 10,000 cedis. Despite its monetary *in-dependence*, Ghana is still dependent on the fluctuation of the dollar for its exports and imports. Like Senegal, its degree of monetary *in-dependence* is still limited. Compared to Ghana, Senegal, for its part, has to pay currency guarantee fees to France annually. The Ghanaian government undertook a huge awareness campaign to explain to its citizens what re-denomination entails.

In the Senegalese case, attempts at *technocratizing* and rationalizing the government's size after the devaluation of the CFA franc currency, however, did not rid the state of its patronage and predominant logic of social pacification and economic efficiency. The devaluation and the associated subsequent reforms had improved the government's performance in fiscal consolidation (Diop & Diouf, 2000). In the late 1990s, outstanding results were achieved by Prime Minister Mamadou Lamine Loum and his administration with regard to restoring the country's financial viability. The efforts made since the devaluation period paid off from 1998, after a better internal revenue mobilization. Indeed, an improvement of the fiscal yield and the broadening of the tax base were noted with Senegal having recorded significant performances in budgetary revenues mobilization over the period 1995–2005. Domestic revenue grew at a 10.25% average annual rate, reflecting both a base-growth effect and an expansion effect, and representing the country's most sustained economic growth (World Bank, 2012, p. 31). This was the period when it recorded its most steady economic growth since independence.

Post-2000 and the latest episode of a long political and economic chronicle

In the second half of the 1990s, despite a worsened social situation noted since the devaluation of Senegal's domestic currency, there was still a sharp rise in the government's lifestyle, impunity for embezzlement of public funds, the resistance of the wealthy to pay taxes, the proliferation of expensive institutions to reward political partners such as the creation of a senate, boroughs, growth of government posts. This situation and other factors (Diop, 2000) favored change in the political leadership and led to the election of President Abdoulaye Wade in March 2000. In power, he initiated projects that were original, but disproportionate in their denomination, architecture, and financial arrangement. These numerous projects indicated, to a certain extent, his personal concern with extending his time in office. He developed projects called the "President's Major Projects" which were executed by the Agency for Promotion of Investment and Major Projects (APIX). What was striking in President Wade's leadership approach was that he did not allow donors to decide and do everything in all sectors within the society. He rather sought to build a singular identity which would distinguish him from his predecessors and African peers by coining the *Wade formula* (Wade, 2008). Meanwhile, Ghana also witnessed a power change in 2000 with the election of John Kufuor as president, marking the beginning of the country's safe and peaceful transition of power.

Two years after his election, President Kufuor, like his Senegalese counterpart, joined the debt relief initiative of the IMF and the WB intended for Heavily Indebted Poor Countries (HIPC) Initiative. Prior to that, the country was expected to prepare the Ghana Poverty Reduction Strategy (GPRS) over the period 2003–2005 (see IMF, 2003–2005). As Africa's second-biggest gold producer and rich in diamonds, manganese ore, bauxite, and oil (like Senegal in the late years of President Diouf's tenure), most of its debt was cancelled in 2005, marking the two West African countries' new perspectives on economic self-determination, and giving them more room for political and economic maneuver.

New perspectives on economic self-determination

As both Presidents Wade and Kufuor were fond of infrastructure development, they embarked on modernization programs. They initiated projects to modernize their agriculture for rural development, boost social services, and promote good governance and the private sector. To this end, they adopted policies looking to efficiency, capacity building, accountability, and transparency, which would, in the long run, make the private sector the engine of growth and poverty reduction (IMF, 2005). Ghana released GPRS which comprised two phases, GPRS I and II, and Senegal published the Poverty Reduction Strategy Paper (PRSP) which also comprised two phases, PRSP I and II. The two strategies made giant strides in reaching their targeted objectives. But, relatively, the two countries' Poverty Reduction Strategy (PRS) had limited outcomes as they focused too much on macroeconomic stability. Consequently, the participatory process was still ineffective and gender focus specification was insufficient (IMF, 2005). A second GPRS was designed over the period 2006–2009. GPRS I was an anti-poverty and Millennium Development Goals (MDGs) attainment program whereas GPRS II was tasked with reaching the goal to become a middle-income country through economic growth. The four priorities of GPRS included continued macroeconomic stability, accelerated private sector-led growth, vigorous human resource development and good governance and civic responsibility (IMF, 2005). In fact, GPRS I and II played a significant role in providing the country with resources and mainstreaming the United Nations-backed MDGs. Ghana's strategies succeeded in connecting development plans with realities on the ground compared to previous plans. Whereas Senegal's strategy discussed economic, social, an environmental performance of policies, the political and institutional environment, and the constraints weighing on its growth as well as the challenges (IMF, 2013). It succeeded, to some extent, in filling in the gap in infrastructure shortage, especially upcountry, compounded by lack of infrastructure for individual sanitation, and in reducing the poverty of households, and limited resources of local communities. Therefore, in Ghana, if the objectives of macroeconomic stability and the achievement of poverty reduction goals were within reach, there were still large fiscal and balance-of-payment deficits, with decrease in remittances and private external financing becoming more difficult as a result of the global financial crisis. GPRS II was followed by a medium-term development policy framework, named the Ghana Shared Growth and Development Agenda (GSGDA) which ran from 2010 to 2013. The initiative targeted structural problems which the SAPs failed to address – large fiscal and balance-of-payment deficits.

In 2007, Ghana started drawing a new chapter with its oil discovery. During the same period, Senegal discovered gold in the southern part of the country and later some oil. These discoveries led to changes and great challenges for the two governments since they were expected to positively impact economic growth and reduce poverty. But, the fall in oil prices, which resulted in some economic difficulties, forced Ghana to negotiate an extended credit from the IMF. Unlike his predecessors, President Wade (and his counterpart Kufuor) did not lead the country under France's and Britain's interests respectively. In Senegal, that was evidenced by the arbitrations carried out against major French companies about some public markets (Diop, 2013, p. 45). Both also diversified their countries' economic partnerships by forging strong ties with China, India, Brazil, Iran, Pakistan, North Korea, Qatar, Saudi Arabia, among others, to fund some of their major infrastructure projects. It was in that economic self-determination approach that in 2010, President Wade railed against the monetary management politics of the BCEAO as the Bank's reserves placed in France (estimated at billions CFA), could have been used to boost the Union's member countries' weak economies. With his OMEGA plan for Africa, he also played an important role in shaping the New Partnership for Africa's Development (NEPAD) along with Presidents Bouteflika of Algeria, Obasanjo of Nigeria, and Mbeki of South Africa. With the substantial financial and political resources available to him when he came to power, President Wade's government had powerful means to give an impetus to the country's economic activities, and ethically manage public resources. But these were thwarted by an economy of predation and unprecedented waste. Practices related to his art of governing deprived people of important resources that could allow them to meet their basic needs. Charges of corruption and misappropriation of public resources multiplied, so the management of public resources failed to improve even if good results were recorded in many sectors of the economy amid shattered dreams, hopes, and failures.

Therefore, the management practices noted in Senegal and Ghana between 2000 and 2012 were in contradiction with social equity and redistribution requirements that were likely to reduce social inequalities and poverty. The situation was aggravated by the lack of transparency in the handling of public contracts, and management of projects and, the unprecedented amount of presidential power. Their heavy-handedness and human-centered models of economic management, despite the existence of regulatory bodies, and the circumvention of rules for political purposes, led to escalating waste of public resources. In Senegal, the management of the public sector was dominated by the mushrooming of project executing agencies, which, according to some, was a way of decentralizing some ministry responsibilities to structures that were deemed to be more flexible and self-sustaining, to strengthen policy interferences in public sector (World Bank, 2012, p. 56). These agencies executed most of the country's public investments (World Bank, 2006, p. 27).

Despite numerous references to liberalism, Presidents Wade's and Kufuor's governments' economic self-determination strategies were based on interventionism in different economic sectors. Indeed, President Wade's government once took a step of quasi-nationalization of the state-owned power company – SENELEC – by canceling the cessation contract granted to Hydro-Quebec and Elyo. After SONAGRAINES was dissolved, SONACOS was privatized in 2005 in favor of Avens (Diop, 2013, p. 50). In 2008, he withdrew the management of the Port of Dakar from the French company Bollore and handed it to Dubai Port. As for the capital of the country's telephone company SONATEL, the government only possessed a small share in 2009. In the agricultural sector, he initiated some projects, notably the Grand Agricultural Offensive for Food and Abundance (GOANA) aimed at reaching food self-sufficiency and reducing imports. In addition, the Senegalese government adopted the Accelerated Growth Strategy (AGS) document in order to promote strong growth, reduce poverty and make Senegal an emerging economy in 2015, coinciding with the year dedicated to achieving the MDGs. But the deterioration of the state accounts was highlighted by various sources, despite a fairly high tax return and the debt cancellations obtained under the HIPC initiative and the Multilateral Debt Relief Initiative (MDRI) (IMF, 2017). Senegal and Ghana had several achievements in their diverse economic sectors between 2000 and 2012.

Senegal and Ghana in today's global apartheid economy

In the 1970s, critical scholars such as Andre Gunder Frank (1976), Samir Amin (1974), and Walter Rodney (1972) were concerned with explaining the problems of underdevelopment that were manifest within the formerly colonized parts of the world. Their intellectual interventions grappled with the impact of today's (re)colonial matrix of power on development within African countries dubbed peripheral societies. They interrogated the dialectics of the center–periphery relations that were created by (re)colonial modernity, and located the roots of underdevelopment in this exploitative and *in-dependency* relationship within which the ex-colonial powers, the emerging, and the so-called developed countries continue to reap economic benefits from Africa to develop their nations, and assure their survival at the expense of African peoples. The predicaments of Africans are visible if one carefully analyzes and weighs the state of the economies of Senegal and Ghana on the global scale where they are being apartheidized. Their populations are today connected to western economic powers in the global apartheid economy and politics as an international system of minority rule which include: differential access to basic human rights, wealth and power structured by race and place, structural racism, embedded in global economic processes, political institutions and cultural assumptions, and the international practice of double standards that assume inferior rights to be appropriate for certain "others," defined by location, origin, race or gender (Booker & Minter, 2001, p. 11). Beyond a metaphor to describe the purported marginalization of Senegalese and Ghanaian peoples, politics and economy, this global apartheid is characterized by the current world order sustained by ideologies, theories, and philosophy such as "neoliberalism," "capitalism," "globalism" or "globalization," or even "corporate globalization." Most important, it clearly defines what is fundamentally unacceptable, abnormal, and unhuman about the current economic, political, social, and cultural systems, together with pretexts such as human rights, global justice, and democracy on the agenda as requirements for the "others."

Indeed, since the concept of the global village was coined (McLuhan, 1968), the economies of the world have become increasingly interlayered, mixed, and juxtaposed. Largely, a product of technology, of instantaneous media access by means of which anything that takes place at the global scale can instantly be seen everywhere. Unfortunately, what Senegalese and Ghanaian peoples can see or are allowed to see is, in practice, controlled. The inexorable forces of globalization have increasingly brought the world economies into a single system in which Senegal and Ghana have no control over their economies. They are the victims of multinational and transnational companies that look to global markets for growth, which has now become impossible to achieve in the markets of the West alone, and lower their cost base by outsourcing manufacturing, call centers to any country that is poor and reasonably politically stable. An analysis of the "qualities" of the global village shows nothing but global apartheid determined by categorizations such as race and geography, as well as market (Booker et al., 2001, p. 11). Western imperialism and globalization are then expressions of egoism in a mode of interaction codified as "racial," "ethnic," "anthropological," or "national" in relation to specific historical, social, and geographic contexts (Quijano, 2007, p. 168). It perpetuates a politics of inequalities and destruction of the postcolonial economies of Africa. The benefits of the West always outweigh those of Africa though the continent offers the natural resources needed in most of world production. With neocolonialism and neo-exploitation in the postcolonial period, Senegal and Ghana's destiny is being designed and controlled by foreign multinational, transnational corporations, and foreign countries as well. Trade partnership patterns like debt arrangements, investments policies, and the overall political economies are being controlled by former colonial powers backed by the United States of America. The WB, IMF, and WTO that are expected to be supportive and regulatory organizations, unfortunately, negatively impact Senegal and Ghana as they become more dependent on foreign powers' investments, financial flows, technology, information highways, byways, and thoroughfares that are directly and undoubtedly beneficial to predatory western corporations, and countries that also apply predatory pricing on their imported and exported products.

To cope with this new economic deal and protect its population, Senegal has adopted under President Macky Sall a new development model aimed at accelerating progress towards economic emergence. This strategy, called Plan for an Emerging Senegal (PES), establishes the framework for the country's economic and social policy over the mid and long term through a new development path likely to lead to a sustainable growth potential, as well as drive creativity and private initiative to cater to people's aspiration for a better life. The PES seeks to get Senegal onto the road to development in 2035. Meanwhile, President Nana Addo Dankwa Akufo-Addo's Coordinated Programme of Economic and Social Development Policies (2017–2024) of the government falls within the same framework which targets job creation, prosperity, and equal opportunity for all. Both Presidents Sall and Akufo-Addo's plans usher in a new era of hope and prosperity. They want to see their countries beyond the realm of aid from donor countries and western-led financial institutions. They seek to build up self-reliant and prosperous economies away from the exploitation of their countries' natural resources. Both have stressed the need for an effective fiscal management as a prerequisite toward making their visions and economic self-determination strategy successful.

Conclusion

Ghana and Senegal have known rich histories of development policy. Since they secured their independence in the late 1950s until the present, their respective leaders have initiated political and economic approaches and strategies that have had checkered outcomes. Because they have not followed a linear trajectory, every new approach and strategy had its own strengths and weaknesses. Senegal and Ghana aimed at political and economic independence. So, they first adopted the development route of their former colonizers – France and Britain. That was the reason why Presidents Senghor of Senegal and Nkrumah of Ghana opted for industrialization as key to development and economic growth. That approach failed to take into account the basic needs of their people – food, shelter, clothes, and education that are also keys to development. Thus, they realized the need to focus on agriculture to satisfy their citizens' food needs. The idea was embraced by the second generation of leaders who came to power from the 1970s and 1980s and attempted at combining economic development with the basic needs of the people.

The neoliberal approach to economic development was established with the WB and IMF-backed SAPs, leaving Senegal and Ghana with no alternative but to accept the initiative in the 1980s and 1990s. As a result, the two countries' export and import markets were liberalized followed by a deregulation of their economic sectors. This led to the devaluation of Senegal's domestic currency, the CFA franc, which is guaranteed by France. Following the same trajectory as Senegal, Ghana also embarked on a redenomination exercise. This monetary instability denotes the two countries' monetary *in-dependence* as their currencies are dependent on exchange rates fixed by western countries and institutions. Strikingly, Senegal and Ghana have continuously found postcolonial economic alternatives to overcome their economic challenges and turn them into success stories.

This chapter touches on the problem of growth in a search for economic self-determination by Senegal and Ghana. Addressing the issue has helped to better understand the history of development policies in the two countries from the early days of independence to now, and their impact on "endogenous" economic growth. Senegal and Ghana do share few destinies in their postcolonial efforts towards economic self-determination as they have initiated many similar development strategies aimed at reaching the same objectives, the needs of their populations. Documenting their economic and political trajectory shows how perspicacious they were in implementation of poverty reduction initiatives and overcoming the WB and IMF-designed SAP traps and some of the "successful results" they produced despite the oil price shocks which had far-reaching consequences (capital recycling, inflation, and the savings-investment balance) on their economy. The political and economic strategies of Senegal and Ghana en route to economic self-determination continue to mold the ways their populations live and work. The major challenge they both face in this critical process is that they are caught up in a world economy of production, technology, and competition that can impact them negatively.

References

Amin, S. (1974). Vers une nouvelle crise structurelle du système capitaliste. *Sociologie et société 6*(2) 7–33.

Aryeetey, E., Harrigan, J., & Nissanke, M. (Eds.). (2002). *Economic reforms in Ghana: The miracle and the mirage*. Trenton, NJ: African World Press.

Booker, S. & Minter, W. (2001). Global apartheid. *The Nation*, *273*(2).

Davidson, B. (2014). *Modern Africa: A social and political history*. Abingdon, UK: Taylor & Francis.

Diop, M. C. (2010). *Le Sénégal sous Abdoulaye Wade*. Paris, France: L'Harmattan.

Diop, M. C. (2013). Le dernier épisode d'une longue chronique du Sénégal contemporain. In M. C. Diop (Ed.), *Sénégal (2000–2012): Les institutions politiques à l'épreuve d'une gouvernance libérale*. Paris, France: Karthala.

Diop, M. C., & Diouf, M. (1990). *Le Sénégal sous Abdou Diouf: État et société*. Paris, France: Karthala.

Diop, M. C., & Diouf, M. (2000). *Le Sénégal sous Abdou Diouf: État et société*. Paris, France: Karthala.

Dordunoo, C. K., & Dogbey, G. Y. (2000). Globalization and economic reforms in Ghana. In D. Bigman (Ed.), *Globalization and the developing countries: Emerging strategies for rural development and poverty alleviation* (p. 125). Wallingford, UK: CABI Publishing.

Frank, A. G. (1976). Economic genocide in Chile. Open Letter to Milton Friedman and Arnold Harberger. *Economic and Political Weekly 11*(24) 880–888.

Grovogui, S. N. (1996). Sovereigns, quasi-sovereigns, and Africans. In A. Anghie (Ed.), *Imperialism, sovereignty and the making of international law* (pp. 111–142). Minneapolis: University of Minnesota Press.

Gyimah-Boadi, E., & Jeffries R. (2000). The Political Economy of Reform. In E. Aryeetey et al. (Eds.), *Economic reforms in Ghana: The miracle and the mirage* (pp. 32–50). Trenton, NJ: Africa World Press.

IMF. (2003–2005). Ghana Poverty Reduction Strategy (pp. 143–145).

IMF. (2005). Ghana Poverty Reduction Strategy (GII) (pp. 2–3).

IMF. (2010). Ghana Shared Growth and Development Agenda (GSGDA), 2010–2013 (pp. 2–3).

IMF. (2017). Heavily Indebted Poor Countries (HIPC) initiative and the Multilateral Debt Relief initiative: Statistical update.

McLuhan, M. (1968). *War and peace in the global village* design/layout by Quentin Fiore, produced by Jerome Agel; 1st ed. New York. NY: Bantam.

Malthus, T. R. (1982). *Principles of political economy*. Cambridge, UK: Cambridge University Press.

Mill, J. S. (2000). *Essays on some unsettled questions of political economy* (2nd ed.). Kitchener, Canada: Batoche Books

Nugent, P. (1995). *Big men, small boys and politics in Ghana: Power, ideology, and the burden of history* (pp. 6–8). London, UK: Printer Publishers.

Quijano, A. (2007). Coloniality and modernity/rationality. *Cultural Studies 21*(2–3) 168–178.

Ratcliff, B. M. (1981). The economics of the partition of Africa: Methods and recent research trends. *Canadian Journal of African Studies 15* 3–31.

Rodney, W. (1972). *How Europe underdeveloped Africa.* Washington, DC: Howard University Press.

Smith, A. (1776). *An inquiry into the nature and causes of the wealth of the nation* (2nd ed.). London, UK: W. Strahan.

Wade, A. (2008). *The Mathematics of Modern Economic Analysis.* Economica.

World Bank. (2006). *Public Finance Review.* Washington, DC: World Bank.

World Bank. (2012). *Public Expenditure Review.* Washington, DC: World Bank.

10 The "new Gambia" and Ghana collaboration

Potential lessons from Accra

Abdoulaye Saine

Introduction

In the heady days of pre-independence Africa, the Gold Coast was the beacon of hope and inspiration for African-liberation leaders in the continent. Seeking to end colonial rule in their subjugated territories, they flocked to Accra from where Kwame Nkrumah provided them intellectual and strategic directives for continent-wide unity. At independence in 1957, Ghana was hailed as a model, as well as the shining black star for liberation struggle(s) not only in Africa itself but throughout the black world. Nkrumah had argued in his numerous publications and speeches that Ghana's independence was meaningless unless it was tied to the liberation of all African peoples and states.

Nkrumah's tenure (1957–1966) witnesses the fastest economic growth rates in Ghana particularly due to his aggressive approach toward industrialization. Notwithstanding, a confluence of falling cocoa prices, personalist rule, discontent within Ghana's military, and strained relations with the West combined to put great strain on the economy. As Ghana's economic crisis deepened, Nkrumah was forced to continuously reach out even to international political opponents of his rule in Ghana and growing allegiances in the wider developing world. Politically, critics argued that Nkrumah had become overly ambitious, perhaps obsessed with building his power base at home, and continental unity at the expense of domestic economic priorities. These factors precipitated a legitimacy crisis, which the military brass seized, with tacit support from the West, to oust Nkrumah from power in 1966.

In the years following Nkrumah's ouster from power, Ghana went through a dark period of political instability punctuated by successive military regimes, and interrupted only by short interludes of weak civilian government. The Rawlings-led December 1981 coup promised a "national democratic revolution, which would wrest control of Ghana's economy from imperialism and end corruption which had ruled the country's political life for so long" (Hutchful, 1979, p. 56). Rawlings's revolutionary rhetoric would later change into an IMF-inspired and directed liberal foreign economic policy. Agyeman-Duah (1987, p. 632) argued that the PNDC's internal development strategy while having the pretentions of a Socialist revolution, was, in effect, a liberal economic policy couched in defensive political rhetoric. In 1994, Yahya Jammeh, a junior officer in Gambia's new army ended Dawda Kairaba Jawara's 32-year tenure, as Africa's longest and continuously serving head of state. Appropriating Rawlings's own political rhetoric, Jammeh engineered a political transition program that replicated Ghana's in its repressive and managed political outcomes. Apart from the politically dictatorial and destabilizing ways of the Jammeh administration, the Gambian economy suffered as the government housed in Banjul oversaw a hopeless and most severe economic crisis since the country's independence from Britain (Saine, 2009). In fact, a 2004 IMF report noted several examples of government mismanagement, poor execution of monetary and fiscal policies, and characterized the existing economic policies as "far off track" with incomplete, missing and/or fabricated data (IMF, 2004). Under the protracted and squelching political regime of Jammeh, politics often got in the way of good policy attempts to rescue the economy from politically inflicted challenges. On assumption to power under the Armed Forces Provisional Ruling Council (AFPRC), forward-looking development objectives were established that could have propelled Gambia ahead under good political management. For instance, mirroring Ghana's reform attempts under Rawlings's Economic Recovery Programme (ERP), Gambia's Vision 2020 blueprint adopted in 1994 was directed at transforming the Gambian economy to make it more competitive, diverse, and highly integrated into the global economy. Nevertheless, Saine (2009, p. 99) submits that regrettably, while the Vision 2020 sounded good in concept, and had received a programmatic nod from IFIs, it had no basis in reality, considering the then Gambian political economy scenario. After more than two decades in office, akin to the term of rule of Ghana's Jerry Rawlings, Gambia had very little to show in terms of political economic reform outcomes.

In December, 2016, President Jammeh lost power to an eight-party coalition headed by Adama Barrow. Almost two years into his tenure, the Coalition Government has crumbled-leaving in its wake the United Democratic Party (UDP), of which Barrow is a member, as de facto government of the day. Highly anticipated political and economic reforms under President Barrow have been piecemeal and slow in coming – occasioning a popular backlash against the president's and the first lady's jet-set lifestyle, as close to half of Gambia's population wallows in abject poverty. Accusations of corruption against President Barrow are rife while cabinet ministers also travel excessively to earn lucrative per diems to the combined total of $6m in six months. Critics have derogatorily characterized the government, as "clueless, heedless, and careless." Though harsh, the characterization, to some degree captures growing frustration over the new government, and failure to meet popular expectations.

This chapter, explores ways in which Gambia (emerging from 22 years of military, and quasi-military dictatorship) could potentially glean from Ghana's own democratic and economic successes to institute key reforms in all vital sectors of its economy and polity. Now a consolidated democracy, Ghana possesses exemplary political and economic governance credentials for countries emerging from years of dictatorship, war, or both, to emulate. The chapter also argues that a renewed and strengthened Gambia–Ghana relationship, is a win–win proposition, and a replicable example of improved intra-Africa trade connections, and deepened South–South cooperation.

After winning the 2016 election to succeed, the NDC's John Mahama, President Nana Akufo-Addo (following meetings with several world leaders, and his historic address to the US Houses of Congress), has amply demonstrated that he has the intellectual pedigree and requisite skill sets to propel Ghana into filling the leadership vacuum in West Africa. In doing so, Ghana, and its current leadership would serve as models worthy of emulation by countries and leaders like Gambia's. Thus, in spite of the enormous benefits of Ghana's past experiences – both progress and mistakes – developing a contemporary collaboration with the current Ghanaian regime will enable Gambia to carefully position these learning opportunities in its contemporary and future politics.

Though the political histories of Gambia and Ghana differ, some may argue, they, nonetheless, have more in common. A shared colonial legacy that include shared democratic norms, civil service and legal systems are but a few. What differentiates them, in particular, is at the time of Ghana's 1966 coup, Gambia was only one year into independence. Under Dawda K. Jawara's leadership the country enjoyed a little over 30 years of a functioning democracy with regular and relatively free and fair elections. Thus, when Ghana suffered from deep political troubles from the mid 1960s to the early 1990s, Gambia enjoyed over three decades of political stability. Paradoxically, as Ghana began its own transition toward political liberalization while navigating major economic reforms in the early 1990s, Gambia's democratic experiment was abruptly ended by the 1994 coup – resulting in severe democratic reversal contrary to the continent-wide liberalization trend at the time (see Saine, 2009).

Yet, ease of communication in English between Gambians and Ghanaians, use of a regional creole dialect, add to the synergy to support collaborative relations between Gambia and Ghana. The sister states also continue to face challenges in their efforts to improving the well-being of their respective populations. In addition, similarities in fundamental cultural values between the two peoples (tolerance, openness, kindness, faith in God, and family), bode well for improved collaboration between the two sister states and their peoples. Thus, Ghana's over a quarter century of sustained economic and political reforms augurs well for countries like Gambia, as they stand to potentially benefit by adopting important reform lessons from Ghana's successes.

By January 1993, Ghana had begun a new democratic/liberalization strategy that would culminate in the election of successive democratic governments with important alternations of political power. In fact, Ghana, is today considered one of the most stable democracies in Africa with impressive economic growth rates to show for it (Daddieh, 2008, p. 644). As in the heady days of pre-liberation Africa, Ghana today represents a beacon of hope and an example of what is possible when a people are committed to new political and economic reforms despite the costs. Yet, in looking at what lessons the Gambia could likely glean from the successes and challenges of its fellow West African neighbor, Ghana, it is important that we briefly explore historically Gambia–Ghana relations.

Gambia–Ghana relations: A brief retrospect

Gambia–Ghana relations predate their respective independence from British colonial rule in 1965, and 1957. In the years following World War II, a few Ghanaian servicemen were settled in Gambia, as part of the West Africa Constabulary Force. Resulting intermarriages between the ex-servicemen and Gambian women, in time, led to the emergence of a small community of Gambians of Ghanaian heritage. As the first generation of ex-servicemen passed on, their off springs, through their maternal relatives, became increasingly acculturated into Gambian culture. Most blended seamlessly into Gambian society, with some remaining Christian, while others converted to Islam.

In the early 1950s, before Ghana's independence, one of Gambia's major nationalist leaders, Ibrahima Garba Jahumpa, and several others, frequented Ghana to consult with Nkrumah. Dawda K. Jawara, who would later become Gambia's first president, received a British Council Science Scholarship to study at Achimota, located in Accra, in the mid 1950s, before proceeding to the UK for further studies. Notably, and in unison with the predominant message of African unity espoused by Nkrumah, Jawara changed his middle name from Kairaba to Kwesi (name for a Ghanaian Sunday born boy in Akan) while in Ghana.

In the early 1960s, Jahumpa would arrange scholarships for many young Gambians to attend high school in Ghana. Called the "Ghana Boys," and now in their seventies they included: Koro Sallah, Lamin Janha, Musa Bittaye, Tamsir Jallow, Sidia Jatta, and several others. They returned to Gambia, schooled in the teachings and revolutionary principles of Nkrumah. Several were to later become important youth leaders in the quest for Gambia's independence. Sidia Jatta is a longtime politician of a progressive pan-Africanist-oriented party. Tamsir Jallow, was once active in the National Teachers Union before becoming ambassador to Washington. Musa Bittaye, is today a renowned attorney. It is Korro Sallah who perhaps exemplified the Nkrumahist revolutionary ethos the most. Following his studies in Ghana, he studied in Moscow, and became a major dissident-turned-exile during the First Republic. Some also stayed in Ghana. One such Gambian was the late Saul Ndow, who became a successful businessman in Accra, and was said to have been raised by Nkrumah's own mother. A strong opponent to Yahya Jammeh's authoritarian rule (1994–2016); Ndow was allegedly abducted and killed in 2012, by Jammeh's henchmen, while on a visit to Gambia.

At independence in 1965, Gambia attracted a few Ghanaian professionals to boost what were embryonic institutions. Also, young Gambian high school graduates with impressive A levels, flocked to various Ghanaian universities, and by the mid-1970s to Winneba Teacher Training College to complete higher teacher's certificate training. Gambian bankers, insurance agents, air traffic controllers and other young professionals also studied in Ghana. In fact, in the mid-1970s, the popular and much anticipated Nti Salary Review Commission tasked to evaluate Gambia's civil service salaries, was headed by a Ghanaian. And, during Ghana's dark days of military rule, and resulting economic downturn in the mid-1980s, many Ghanaians arrived in Gambia, as teachers to fill positions in an expanding education sector.

Since the founding of Ghana Town on the coastal waters of Gambia in the early 1970s, there has been a flourishing export trade in marine and other meat products for its Ghanaian–Gambian residents. Subsequent generations have since acculturated to Gambian culture, and speak local languages, adopted Gambian surnames, and converted to Islam. These sociocultural bonds between the two countries gives some support to the exchange of political and institutional strategies and personnel at different political eras in the Gambia.

Soldiers-turned-president(s)

Following the bloodless coup in 1994, Lt. Jammeh looked to Rawlings for counsel. Both men quickly became friends to the extent that Rawlings was in 1995, the first guest of (dis)honor to the first anniversary celebrations of the 1994 coup. Thereafter, Jammeh adopted several of Rawlings's own draconian policies and strategies, effected during Ghana's own "transition" program. The presidential elections in Ghana and Gambia in 1992 and 1996, respectively, showed remarkable similarities in both process and outcome. What was striking in the 1992 and 1996 presidential elections in Ghana and Gambia was the degree and extent to which Rawlings and Jammeh both micromanaged their own transition programs from the very start to ensure their electoral victories (Saine, 2000, p. 204). The advantages of incumbency, coupled with handpicked electoral commissions, routine violations of electoral laws, violence against and banning of political opponents and parties, culminated in favorable electoral victories for the incumbents. In fact, Jammeh's "radical" political rhetoric was also strikingly similar to Rawlings's own.

Characteristically, both leaders had to succumb to IMF/World Bank Structural Adjustment Programs to help rebuild their economies. Similarly, Rawlings introduced the Economic Recovery Program (ERP) in the 1980s around the same period of initiation of Jawara's ERP which led to a nominal depreciation of exchange rate that allowed for the increase in prices of groundnuts and stable prices for nontraded goods (Beddies, 1999). After the 1994 military takeover, Jammeh continued with the neoliberal approach to economic reform with the adoption of plans such as the Vision 2020 which had clearly laid out an agenda for development of food sufficiency, increasing and diversifying exports to help transform Gambia into a middle-income country (a development status Ghana was able to achieve in 2011) with higher incomes and improved living standards for its population.

The "new Gambia"–Ghana collaboration: Prospective lessons

Today, Ghana has enjoyed over two decades of stable democratic governance, while Gambia just ended, through its remarkable 2016 presidential election

32 years of Yahya Jammeh's autocratic rule. Reversing Jammeh's mishandling of the economy, the civil service, etc., will take time and support from sister countries like Ghana and the international community – this is crucial. Already, Ghana has built a wealth of experience in these and other institutional reforms efforts, and could be a repository of expertise to Gambia, with a much stronger collaboration between both countries.

In the area of security sector reform, Ghana could play an important supporting role to secure Gambia's territorial integrity, and support Gambia's efforts to evolve a new national security policy. Ghana already has a sizeable presence in Economic Community of West African States Monitoring Group (ECOMOG) forces currently securing Gambia. And, former President Mahama's shuttle diplomacy alongside other African leaders to end Gambia's political impasse after Jammeh refused to step down when he had a week earlier conceded defeat, averted a major military showdown. Therefore, Gambia, as well as President Barrow could look to Ghana and President Nana Akufo-Addo for continued support, as President Barrow seeks to put in place important institutional reforms in the military and judiciary. The newly established CRC could also benefit from Ghanaian expertise, and personnel, as the laborious task of drafting a new constitution is begun. The financial cost for these and other outlays are likely to be lower compared to European and other western expatriates.

Equally, establishing an Anti-Corruption Court, as Ghana, to litigate alleged instances of theft could potentially help ease the load on an already beleaguered justice system in Gambia. In this regard, Ghana, having gone and still undergoing several decades of state-wide reforms, could serve as a useful model for Gambia, and other states in the subregion emerging from decades-long dictatorship and war. Ghana's media laws and institutions also remain vibrant. These are examples to emulate in Gambia where a growing media landscape and training for media personnel could be vastly improved.

Similarly, Gambia's newfound oil wells, due to begin production in November 2018, bode well for the country's economic transformation. Prudent management of this new resource is imperative. Here, Ghana, as well as Norway could provide important strategies and lessons on management strategies, and long-term investments to benefit future generations. Failure to glean important lessons from these countries will likely result in deepening social inequality, waste, environmental pollution, corruption, and conflict leading to the proverbial resource curse – well known in many resource-endowed African countries. Thus, of vital importance for the new Barrow administration, is to exercise great caution in distributing funds from oil. It is important that Gambians be informed of the terms governing oil contracts, revenue, and training of local managerial personnel and workforce. Transparency, accountability, and probity must once more become the mantra for Barrow's government. Hiring a management team from Norway and Ghana, alongside Gambian counterparts could allay rising popular fears of mismanagement and graft in the oil sector.

Relatedly, Gambia's new Barrow government will also be well advised to explore, modify, and possibly adopt Ghana's policies toward China's growing investments in the country. With tensions already rising in Gambia over a Chinese fish-hatchery and pollution of vital water resources in Gunjur and Kartong, Ghana's experience in these and other areas could prove useful (Aidoo, 2017, p. 14). An integrated subregion-wide China policy spearheaded by Ghana could potentially reduce Gambia's state vulnerabilities, and curb China's growing abuse of sacred environmental grounds and waters (Hess, Aidoo, & Saine, 2011). The Gambia government does not need to reinvent the wheel, as a great reservoir of knowledge, best practices and goodwill exist to ensure proper management, environmental protection, and distribution of vital national resources.

Faced with similar development challenges, Gambia–Ghana collaboration could also extend to tackling energy distribution challenges to reduce, and possibly curb in the long term, rolling blackouts and water rationing. The Gambia government has undertaken a bold initiative on this front. Yet, rather than Turkish ships docked at Banjul's port to supply power to the Greater Banjul Area, collaboration with Ghana to explore alternative sources of power would have been more cost-effective. How both states potentially address these vexing challenges could yield creative and sustainable solutions/strategies for a "new Gambia" emerging from years of dictatorship. It would be prudent, therefore, for the new Adama Barrow administration to cultivate closer ties with Ghana, and President Nana Akufo-Addo, in particular, to help address priorities in Gambia's National Development Plan 2018–2021. Several alternations of political leadership, bodes well for Ghana and Africa (Daddieh, 2008, p. 646) This speaks to the important repository of skills and knowledge that could prove useful for Gambia's own efforts at reform. It is clear that Ghana, despite its challenges, or perhaps because of them, holds out hope for countries still struggling to institutionalize functioning democratic governance frameworks (Daddieh, 2008, p. 646).

Enjoying the singular status as the first independent black African country, peoples and countries of the Caribbean, especially Jamaica, see Ghana as the ancestral home of its majority black population. With these come high expectations and responsibilities for Ghana, its peoples, and especially it political leadership. Together, they must continue to build upon democratic and economic structures in place since independence, to realize the vision of its founding fathers of a truly economic and politically independent Ghana. And, in doing so, continue to be seen as the model for countries in the subregion and elsewhere to emulate.

Gambia–Ghana relations must take on added importance for Gambia's new administration, as it seeks to rebuild the entire country's civil service, education, medical, and agriculture infrastructure. Ghanaian expertise, as in the past, must be leveraged to help fill the personnel capacity gaps in vital sectors in Gambia. Rather than send Gambian students and professionals to Europe and the Americas, or deploy expensive expatriates, Ghanaian institutions, and personnel, as in years past, could fill these gaps at a much-reduced cost.

Attracting qualified Ghanaians with favorable incentive structures could complement Gambia's limited professional pool, and go a long way to addressing challenges in other sectors. Finally, with oil and gas production soon to begin in Gambia in November 2018, it is of paramount importance for Gambian authorities to consult with their Ghanaian and Norwegian counterparts so as to place this industry on sound footing. Gambia, like Norway, must consider establishing a sovereign wealth fund to safeguard the futures of Gambians unborn.

In the area of international human rights protection, Ghana has a special interest, as Gambia, to bring ex-president Yahya Jammeh to justice at the ICC, or other legally determined court, for the alleged murders of some 44 Ghanaians in 2005. This would be a great triumph for the two sister states, and a boon for Africa's commitment to human rights, generally. It will send a clear message to dictators in Africa, and elsewhere that the days of impunity are over. Therefore, Ghana, and its foreign policy, as in pre-independence Africa, must once more become more assertive, assume the mantle of leadership in Africa, or at least the subregion, and use its soft power to help shape, in its image, current and future events in the subregion.

Conclusion

Current Gambia–Ghana relations need careful assessment and strengthening in order to identify areas where Ghana government personnel, and civil society interventions would be most immediately needed in both the long and short terms. Given the geographic proximity, historic ties of both states in the colonial and post-independence eras, similar development challenges, experience with military rule and botched political transitions, it is only logical that the two sister states strengthen bilateral relations. This is a recipe for a win–win proposition for both sister states. Though reliance on the EU, and Bretton Woods institutions will likely continue into the future, it is imperative that Gambia–Ghana technical cooperation be given renewed special status and attention, to address daunting challenges, and leverage existing opportunities. In the long term, such technical relations could begin to slowly reverse external dependency on the EU, and international financial institutions. While enriching the economic prospects of both states, technical cooperation between the two sister states could also serve as a shining model in intra-Africa trade, and of South–South cooperation.

President Nana Akufo-Addo, has demonstrated in his speeches to the US Congress, as well as meetings with the French president, and German chancellor, that he possesses the requisite policy mix, and intellectual pedigree to lead and be taken seriously worldwide. Thus, a refocused Ghana–Africa policy that reprioritizes Ghana's national and African interests, take the lead to redefine Africa–China relations, specifically (even where it exists), must be boldly rearticulated and become known to all – leaving no doubt that Ghana by its demonstrable democratic and economic stability and credentials has the credibility and global standing to lead. In doing so, the Nkrumahist vision of Ghana's role in African, and global politics would be reestablished. There exists a perilous leadership vacuum in Africa, and West Africa, specifically, and Ghana must boldly step up to fill it.

Note

I would like to extend my gratitude to Abdoulai Jobe and Hatib Janneh for their insights on the "Nkrumah Boys" of Gambia during a conversation on Wednesday, September 12, 2018 in Fajara, Gambia.

References

Agyeman-Duah, B. (1987). Ghana: 1982–6, politics of the PNDC. *Journal of Modern African Studies 25*(4) 613–642.

Aidoo, R. (2017). Go global, meet the locals: Pragmatism, plunder, and anti-Chinese populism in Africa. *Journal of Diplomacy* (Winter) 11.

Beddies, C. (1999). Investment, capital accumulation and growth: Some evidence from the Gambia: 1964–1998 (Washington, DC: IMF Working Paper).

Daddieh, C. K. (2008). The presidential and parliamentary elections in Ghana. *Electoral Studies* (December) 642–647.

Hess, S., Aidoo, R., & Saine, A. (2011). Taming the dragon: Outlining an African response to growing Chinese engagement. *Africa Insight 40*(4) 59.

Hutchful, E. (1979). A tale of two regimes: Imperialism, the military, and class in Ghana. *Review of African Political Economy 14* 26–52.

International Monetary Fund (IMF). (2004). Country report, No. 04/42.

Saine, A. (2009). *The paradox of third-wave democratization in Africa: The Gambia under AFPRC-APRC rule, 1994–2008*, Lanham, MD: Lexington Books.

Saine, A. (2000). The soldier-turned presidential candidate: A comparison of flawed "democratic" transitions in Ghana and Gambia. *Journal of Political and Military Sociology 28*(2) 190–209.

11 Making democracy and development work in Kenya

Lessons from Ghana

Fatuma Boru Guyo

Introduction

The failure of the August 8, 2017 general elections was a major setback to the development of democracy in Kenya. The Supreme Court nullified the presidential election results over alleged irregularities. Although the court's decision was widely hailed as one of the rare manifestations of judicial independence in Africa, the celebration was short-lived. Far fewer people came out to vote in the repeat election held on October 26, 2017 relative to the earlier one that was fraught with challenges and violent protests that questioned the credibility of elections. This was particularly disquieting after the Independence Electoral and Boundaries Commission (IEBC) failed to effect the needed reforms for free and creditable elections.

The contentious general elections and the subsequent incivility by the participating political parties and their supporters offer a context to analyze issues challenging Kenya's democratic development. International partners have long considered Kenya a strategic and "indispensable partner" in East Africa (*Daily Nation*, 2009). However, underlying such accolades are questions of historical marginalization of minority ethnic groups. Until recently, Kenya has made slow progress, especially in addressing socioeconomic and political rights of minority groups, such as pastoralists who often remain in the margins of Kenyan society, both in policy rhetoric and sociopolitical realities.

Kenya's socioeconomic and political achievements including promulgation of new constitution in 2010 that paved way for a devolved county government was long overdue, and often eclipsed by issues of equality. These attendant issues and the existing bane of terrorism, particularly in the Northeastern part of Kenya present a significant threat to democracy, economic development, and long-term stability of the country. Nothing demonstrates more the limit of democracy than loss of rights over land because of the increased commodification and privatization of land under state control. This particularly impacts pastoral communities whose activities are often tied to the land. The would-be Vision 2030 plan to alienate pastoralists' land for the exploitation of mineral and construction of mega transnational infrastructure such as the Lamu Port-Southern Sudan–Ethiopia Corridor Project (LAPSSET) through arid and semi-arid areas will adversely affect pastoral communities (Bwanaadi, 2013).

This chapter analyzes Kenya's democratic trajectory in historical, political, and economic contexts, and assesses the features of the country's sociopolitical challenges in its democratization path. The main purpose of this work is to contribute to the contextualization of democratization and development in Africa, and Kenya in particular, and to examine and apply lessons from a known case of an African reformer – Ghana. More broadly, it analyzes issues of marginality and social exclusion within the context of socioeconomic and political developments in Kenya, as it makes references to the less studied regions and experiences of marginalized communities in Kenya. While Kenya has made some important strides in its development, questions of inequality and marginalization still remain. What features of Kenya's political culture threatens democracy and inclusion? Can Ghana's democratic experiences offer any insights or serve as guideposts to Kenya's political course? More precisely, this contribution is not meant to discredit the milestones Kenya has achieved, but to explore the political misnomer that challenges democracy and development in Kenya.

Conceptual considerations of democracy and development in Africa

Many parts of the world experienced the surge from the third-wave democratic movements from the late 1970s to early 1980s. The African continent experienced this increase in democratic movement beginning in the early 1990s. This was considered the second liberation, the first took place in the 1960s for majority states in Africa with the dethroning of colonialism (see Osaghae, 2005). Many particularly in the West approached the wave of democratic movements in the continent with doubt since Africa was perceived as poor and generally lacking conditions necessary for democracy. Additionally, many states in Africa were cited as operating under what is termed a patrimonial state, an antithesis of democratic governance, and hence critics had little hope for democratic triumph (Brown & Kaiser, 2007). African leaders too opposed democratic reforms and argued that democratic model was not ideal for the continent citing fear of ethno-religious divisions, and instead stressed the need to hold on to the one-party system and a strong centralized power that could hold the multiethnic and religious groups together (Schraeder, 1994).

However, amid popular protests in many parts of the continent, the move to democratize proceeded. The movements toward democracy also coincided with the introduction of 1980s economic reforms, notably, the Structural Adjustment Programs (SAPs) by the IMF and World Bank to ease the debt burden and economic crises that hit the continent hard after the late 1970s. By 1993, multiparty elections began and the idea of basic political rights started to make its way among various African populations, including Kenya (Bratton & van de Walle, 1997).

Internal and external factors explain the surge for democratic changes. Many scholars like Austin (2010) argued that democratization was one of the preconditions stressed by donor agencies for African countries to get financial assistance.

The authoritarian character of the post-independent states, and economic crises of the 1980s which contributed to the introduction of the SAPs requirements further bolstered the prodemocratic movements' call for continent-wide political change. Other external factors included call for universal human rights by international community, and their promise for unilateral trade relations with prodemocratic states in Africa. Political reforms required leaders to enforce legitimate governance, improve political institutions and develop their economies (Harbeson et al., 1994). While countries such as Ghana made immense progress toward democratic development, the call for democracy has not yet produced the much-anticipated changes in many other African countries, as cases of wars, other forms of internal conflicts, and corruption still afflict some states – part of what Diamond (2015) refers to as the "democratic recession."

It is most significant to note the meaning of democracy and its application in Africa. While the concept of democracy as a form of governance is ancient, differences in historic and geographic realities, shift in perception and processes of the concept make it more difficult to provide a universal definition of democracy. Variously, scholars have defined democracy in many ways, for example, Diamond (2008) adopts the classical "rule of the people." While Sorensen (2008, pp. 26–27) concurs with the basic concept of democracy as "rule by people," he notes that it is hard to precisely arrive at the meaning of the concept since "democracy is a dynamic entity that has acquired different meanings over the course of time." Others simply perceive democracy as an act that reflects the will of majority (Joyce, 2006), and at its minimum, affording the people their rights to cast their votes (Przeworski, 2011).

Another angle to the definition debate views democracy as an essential prerequisite for success of development (Alence, 2004; Knutsen, 2010; Olson, 1993) as the counterview holds that development ought to precede democracy (De Meur & Berg-Schlosser, 1996). Even though there is no agreement on what development means, the general assumption linking democracy and development is that people in a country with higher levels of economic development – measured in terms of education, income, and health indicators – are more likely to demand accountability from the government and hence with a better chance of democratic survival. An educated and well-informed population with growing income is said to have a better chance at participating in the processes of national development, and understanding the policies that impact their lives. These practices are said to contribute to the development of democracy, which in turn is equated as a mark of achievement in the process of development (Menocal, 2007).

While the question on how to measure development is still an ongoing debate, and beyond the scope of this chapter, however, according to Janvry and Sadoulet (2016), the general agreement dubbed Millennium Development Goals (MDGs) was established by the United Nations (UN) in 2000 to measure countries' development objectives. The UN developed sets of indicators, for example, education, health, and income as yardsticks to gauge a country's progress over a given period. Considerable evidence exists in the world today that almost all developed countries in the West are democratic and have kept their economies stable (Przeworski, 2000). However, the conception that democracy and development go hand in hand lacks universality. In Africa, although linkage between democracy and development is often made, the majority of countries point to an unproven attempt to consistently established some causality or correlation between both concepts. This study is cognizant of the fact that democracy promises equal socioeconomic and political rights, which has not been fully achieved in many African countries.

Bearing in mind the challenges of measuring a country's democracy, the case of Ghana remains a clearly positive example of democratic development in Africa. Apart from the designation of "free" by Freedom House (2012), and going by the minimalist definition of democracy as evidenced by citizen participation in free and fair elections, Ghana fits the model of a successful transition to democracy. Simultaneously, Kenya may have a developed liberal economy from the beginning, yet, it has not sustained its democratic growth to meet some global expectations.

In terms of development, Ghana and Kenya both former British colonies were with low human development in terms of indicators in education, health, and income in 1990 (United Nations Development Program, 1990), necessitating political and economic reforms. Intriguingly, under the regime of president Arap Moi, centralization of power became the hallmark of the presidency with only a few political elites at the top level, marginalizing the common people. In other words, the power resides with the elite and national decisions are passed from the top with little input from the masses, a process which hampered democratic transition. However, external pressure from the international community was decisive in return to multiparty democracy (Muigai, 1993).

In terms of economic ideology in the postcolonial era, Kenya adopted the capitalist agenda while Ghana initially embraced socialism, and later inched toward liberal economy in line with the conditions set by the international donor agencies. This is not to suggest that the two countries were exceptional in Africa, but the difference in democratic routes they took illuminates the lessons Kenya can learn from Ghana's experiences. For instance, Ghana's political parties have attempted traditions of organizing around party unity, rather than overemphasis on ethnicity unlike the case of Kenya, which has encouraged the element of negative ethnic consciousness and competition for state resources (Rutten & Owuor, 2009). Additionally, Kenya's democratic hurdles have also been exacerbated by concurrent development quandaries such as regional and ethnic marginalization, underscoring the importance of both concepts – democracy and development – in African examples.

Inequalities and marginalization in Kenya: A historical context

The foundation of Kenya's political economy is traced to the era of colonization (1895–1963). As a settler colony, privileged Europeans owned large portions of land in the so-called white highlands to grow cash crops for export to Europe, but with no returns to develop neither the colony nor African masses. Rather, natives occupied unproductive reserves and became landless providing cheap source of labor for European farms (Ogot & Ochieng, 1995). The colonial state sanctioned discriminatory policies, for example, Africans in major towns received poor and racially segregated services in education and health services and lived in separate quarters from Europeans (Mamdani, 1996). Generally speaking, European colonization integrated Africans into the colonial economic agenda, albeit on an unequal footing. The impact in Kenya as is true with other colonized countries was an uneven penetration of capitalism. The colonial government concentrated development projects in the regions presumed to have higher potential, mainly Central, Rift Valley, and Nyanza at the expense of communities in regions such as northern Kenya which remained at the periphery, lacking basic social services in education, healthcare, and infrastructure (Mutua, 2008). Independence brought not much structural difference and the colonial socioeconomic trend persisted.

Kenya established a representative legislative body with a national and regional administrative divisions after independence in December 1963. The seven autonomous regions had boundaries determined by indefinable ethnic settlement patterns; most notably large ethnic groups have a region to themselves. Particularly, farms in the highlands left by settlers became sites of contestation between the Kikuyu and Kalenjin ethnic groups. Additionally, according to Kagwanja (2010), the Kikuyu and Kalenjin political divide further pushed Kenya into politics of ethnicity, a feature that would later become synonymous with Kenya's political development. The political party Kenya African National Union (KANU), became dominated by majority ethnic groups by time Kenya became a republic in 1964. Jomo Kenyatta became the first president (1963–1978) and Oginga Odinga his vice. The minority party Kenya African Democratic Union (KADU), a coalition of small ethnic groups dissolved itself in 1964 and joined KANU. The KANU party remained the only political party up until 1966, when a faction led by Jaramogi Oginga Odinga broke away to form Kenya People's Union (KPU). Kenya reverted into a single party state after the government banned KPU and enacted economic and political sanctions on opposition leaders, and detained Odinga and top officials in 1969 (Kagwanja, 2010).

The Jomo Kenyatta administration placed emphasis on national unity and expansion of social services such as equal educational opportunities for Africans, an essential element of post-independent development plans. However, Kenya's postcolonial economic development was elite driven, and particularly, land redistribution employed discriminatory policies that facilitated privileged majority ethnic groups to acquire land at the former "white highlands" in Rift valley at the expense of pastoral communities like the Maasai (Nyawalo et al., 2011). This was evidenced in Kenya's Sessional Paper No. 10 (1963), the Government Development Plan of 1965 states that the government would invest in regions that offered "great potential." Such policies had negative impacts on minority pastoral societies who lost their lands not only to the creation of wildlife parks and to the establishment of industries with little or no benefits in return to the communities (Livingstone, 2005). Clearly, redistribution included the bid to reappropriate land and other resources for certain groups hence social marginalization for others, a product of ethnic politics in which elites favor their own to consolidate their political interests. By the end of Kenyatta's era, social marginalization had cut across ethnic, gender, class and geographic barriers with majority Kenyan citizens deprived of their socioeconomic rights and remained marginalized (Ogot & Ochieng, 1995).

Daniel Arap Moi succeeded Kenyatta (1978–2002) as Kenya's second president. Moi's regime, however, was equally marred by neo-patriomonialism and politics of exclusion. By June 1982, the constitution was amended making Kenya officially a one-party state. Like Kenyatta, Moi consolidated his power by fostering Kalenjin ethnic nationalism with a promise of political power, and there after marginalizing others in the process of national resource distribution (Mutua, 2008). Moi's ethnic nepotism elicited ethnic animosity in which dissatisfied communities attempted a coup d'état, but loyalist forces crushed the rebellion in 1982.

However, Moi adopted distributive policies and made an attempt at reaching historically marginalized areas by generally developing infrastructure, expanding basic school system and university education, among other projects. The role of education has been touted as one of the viable means to social mobility, by preparing graduates for white-color jobs and other economic opportunities. While national enrollment increased throughout post-independence era, however, among communities in northern Kenya enrollment remained disproportionately low (Republic of Kenya, 1979). While acknowledging cultural factors for low school enrolment, socioeconomic reasons, and lack of opportunity to access education, especially for females explain disparity in education access, retention and, graduation rates (Somerset, 2007).

President Moi generally decentralized development by introducing District Focus for Rural Development (DFRD), a program that made resource allocation at district level possible and encourage local participation. However, according to Barkan and Chege (1989), Moi's redistribution efforts focused mainly on Rift Valley province, and heavily funding healthcare and road projects. By the time of the economic downturn of the mid 1980s and 1990s, Kenya began to experience persistent national budgetary deficits. The external powers and Kenya's partners-in-development including international financial institutions (IFIs) such as the IMF and the World Bank began to meddle in the power structure, imposing policies supposed to emanate from the Kenyan government (Bates, 2011). Moi's government faced pressure to introduce cost cutting measures in provision of public services; education and healthcare included (Republic of Kenya, 1984). The preconditions that came with these financial and technical arrangements variedly impacted the development landscape of Kenya. Minorities including pastoral societies particularly bore the brunt of the stringent conditions for structural economic reforms, which often resulted in the overstretch of available and limited national resources to the neglect of the vulnerable and elements residing in the fringes of the state – farther from the seat of political power.

It was not until the advent of multiparty politics and movements for democratization in the 1990s that new political space for minorities began to emerge. In 1991, incumbent President Moi and KANU amended constitution, repealing one-party system to introduce a multiparty political system. This development was, however, not without challenges. Political interference by the incumbent KANU government continued with harassment of opposition parties, which made it possible for the Moi government to win the 1992 and 1997 general elections (Kavuti, 2014). The National Alliance Rainbow Coalition (NARC), a consortium of opposition political parties competed against KANU in the December 2002 elections. Mwai Kibaki won, ending the 24-year rule by Moi, but the voters not only rejected the proposed new constitution, but also demanded for the replacement of Kibaki's choice of cabinet ministers. Kavuti (2014) argues that these demands laid the foundation for the post-2007 election crisis. Although Kibaki came to power amid growing challenges including rapid population growth, poverty, growing income disparity, corruption, and unemployment (especially youth), nothing exacerbated these problems like the post-2007 presidential election violence in which more than 1,500 people died (Human Right Watch, 2008). This was a testament to the flawed politics of ethnicity and exclusion.

Kibaki's presidency was marked both by accomplishments and failures. Massive corruption and legal institutional failures – judiciary, electoral commission, and police administration – weakened the administration (Murunga, 2011). Alternatively, in the first term of the administration (2003–2007), the Kenyan economy grew to 7% in 2007 from 3.4% in 2003 apart from attaining reduction in deficit expenditure (World Bank, 2014). Also, realized were growth in state privatization of government owned enterprises and more foreign investment. By the second half of Kibaki's term, while economy remained strong, one of his key legacies was the introduction of primary education for all (Kagwanja & Southall, 2010).

With regard to marginalized communities, it was not until 2008 that Kabaki's administration created the Ministry of State for Development of Northern Kenya and other Arid and Semi-Arid Lands (ASALs). According to the Sessional Paper No. 8 of 2012, on the National Policy for the Sustainable Development of Northern Kenya and other Arid Lands, the government aimed at bridging inequality and taping into the potential of the ASALs. Changes envisioned for pastoralists have also been featured in the constitutional change and Kenya's Vision 2030. Constitutional change generally recognizes the inclusion of minorities and their rights to social, economic, political, and civil justice. Vision 2030, among other things, aims at revamping the livestock sector through disease control, improving market facilities and provision of water, and better educational services. While these undertakings of marginalization and demarginalization of Kenya's minorities remain a pertinent feature of the democratization and development processes in the country, political and economic developments elsewhere in countries like Ghana offer some identical or dissimilar insights to exploring various dimensions of these issues while lessons are educed within the same continental context.

Ghana: A brief historio-political context

Kenya and Ghana were both former British colonies, though Ghana became the first sub-Saharan African country to gain its independence in 1957 with the victory of the Convention People's Party (CPP) in the 1956 general election (Gocking, 2005). The political freedom made the young state a beacon of hope for other African countries still under colonial rule (Kwakye, 2011). The first president of Ghana, Kwame Nkrumah, emphasized his pan-African aspirations and support for the total liberation of African countries, and this was indicative of Nkrumah's postcolonial aspirations of projecting Ghana's political and economic ambitions onto other African countries on the continent throughout the decolonization struggle. An ambition that connected Ghana to other African countries, including Kenya.

The first few years of Nkrumah government witnessed development as well as political decay, as the CPP government was marked by the development of primary, middle, and secondary schools in the country as part of the first Five-Year Plan (Rooney, 2007). Otherwise, the implementation of the Preventive Detention Act (PDA) in 1959 gave the government leeway to arrest political opponents, and was perceived as a move in the wrong direction of political progress. On February 24, 1966, the military toppled Nkrumah while on diplomatic visits to Vietnam and China. The military accused him of violating democratic rights, instituting failed economic policies, and detaining political opponents without fair judgment (see Fobih, 2011; Skinner, 2011). The coup led to the establishment of the National Liberation Council (NLC) under General J. A. Ankrah's leadership. One of the accomplishments of NLC was the drafting of a new constitution for Ghana's Second Republic in addition to freeing political prisoners. After three years of military rule, the 1969 elections returned the country to democratic rule. Kofi Abrefa Busia became the prime minister after his Progress Party (PP) won the elections with majority parliamentary seats (Asare & Prempeh, 2010; Yidana, 2012).

In 1972, the military led by General Ignatius Kutu Acheampong overthrew Busia and formed the National Redemption Council (NRC). Unwilling to give power back to civilians, in 1976, Acheampong renamed the NRC as the Supreme Military Council (SMC) and introduced the Union Government (UNIGOV) which composed the police force, the military, and citizens in a bid to legitimize military rule (Gocking, 2005). According to Debrah (2015), the military rule was not only prolonged, but also characterized by corruption, inefficiencies, and human rights abuse issues. In 1978, General Acheampong was ousted out of SMC leadership and replaced by Fred Akuffo. Although Akuffo lifted the ban on political parties in an attempt to return Ghana to a civilian rule (Austin & Luckham, 2014), he was overthrown in June 1979 by Armed Forces

Revolutionary Council (AFRC) led by Jerry John Rawlings. Rawlings oversaw the execution of some former heads of state and military officers, but returned the country to a democracy with elections held in June 1979. The People's National Party's (PNP) presidential candidate, Hilla Limann won the elections. The promulgation of the 1979 constitution that established the Third Republic of Ghana placed legislative power in the hands of parliament for the first in Ghanaian history (Abdul-Gafaru, 2009).

The Third Republic, however, did not last since Rawlings returned in 1981 through another military takeover toppling Limann whom he accused of corruption, and rendered inept (Adedeji, 2001). Rawlings became the leader for the Provisional National Defense Council (PNDC), which, after the 1992 constitution, turned into a political party – National Democratic Congress (NDC). In the 1996 multiparty elections, Rawlings was reelected to complete two presidential terms (Brenya et al., 2015). Though not without shortcomings, one of the achievements of Rawlings's regime was implementation of radical economic reforms adopting redistributive policies, banned hoarding of goods, and effected market-wide price control of commodities (Brenya et al., 2015; Shillington, 1992).

Most significantly, it was the Fourth Republic that saw Ghana's transition from authoritative rule to democratic government through the concerted efforts of political parties and civil society, among other groups (Frimpong, 2017). At the end of Rawlings's two four-year terms, he stepped down to pave way for opposition New Patriotic Party (NPP) led by John Kufuor. In the 2008 election, the NDC's John Atta-Mills edged NPP's Nana Akufo-Addo in a runoff election after both candidates did not secure the 50% margin. After the sudden demise of President Atta-Mills, the country displayed rare democratic restraint as power was constitutionally transferred to the Vice President John Mahama in July 2012. In December 2012, Mahama and the NDC again beat Nana Akufo-Addo and the NPP in an election that was fraught with accusations and counter-accusations of electoral fraud. The defeated candidate, Nana Akufo-Addo challenged the election results in the Supreme Court (akin to the happenings of Kenya's 2017 elections) which tested the resilience of Ghana's constitution and its political institutions (Boafo-Arthur, 2018). In yet another milestone in Ghana's democracy and democratic turnovers, in 2016, opposition leader Nana Akufo-Addo finally won the presidency after three tries (Gyampo, 2017).

The intriguing, but rather circuitous path that Ghana has taken to become a worthy democratic example in Africa is one definitely instructive for other burgeoning democracies across the continent. In spite of Ghana's political imperfections and the uncertainties that characterize the democratic process in a developing region, there are still pertinent lessons for Kenya.

Kenya's developing democracy and Ghana's democratic development: Exploring lessons

Ghana and Kenya both experienced a similar political trajectory in the first few post-independent years. Ghana under Kwame Nkrumah and Kenya under Jomo

Kenyatta reverted to one-party state and experienced a period of dictatorship, but both countries returned to multiparty system in the 1990s. While both countries confront common challenges like corruption, Ghana's economic reform and democratic development trajectory have shown relative promise in recent years, compared to Kenya. Lessons from Ghana focus on the pivotal role of the Electoral Commission (EC), the function of informal institutions such as the Inter-Party Advisory Committee (IPAC), the vitality of ethnic balance in electoral process and other gains made over the years.

The mid-1980s introduction of SAPs forced the Rawlings regime to adopt neoliberal economic policies dubbed Economic Recovery Programme (ERP) to curb high inflation rates and national deficits. To secure loans from the IMF and World Bank, Ghana, like other African countries, had to accept economic austerity programs required by the donor agencies. Specifically, subsidies on basic commodities were to be removed, and budget cuts on education, healthcare, and basic infrastructure services implemented. Other measures adopted include privatization of state-owned enterprises, commodity prices control, and layoffs in urban and public sectors resulted in income decline affecting particularly low-income populations (Alexander, 2001; Konadu-Agyemang, 2000).

Although privatization and other unfavorable economic strategies were backlashed, the economic conditions leading up to the Rawlings's revolution suggest that a key challenge for democratization was finding ways to shift popular expectation from a government legitimacy based on subsidies determined by economic conditions to a democratic legitimacy and state commitment to the rule of law and its representative institutions. Arguably, this holds an important lesson for Kenya as Ghanaians have long learned that an alternative to military brutalities and dictatorial regimes is a bad civil government that can at least pledge people's liberty (Olukoshi et al., 1994). Political instability and civil wars are products of autocratic rule as witnessed in instances like Somalia, Liberia, and Congo. Ghana has so far avoided civil wars or widespread intrastate conflict despite the bane of political instability through many segments of its political history, along with economic hardships, even before and after the implementation of SAPs. Kenya may have been developing its economy with the embrace of free market principles; however, it has often experienced political strives that often slow the process of democratic development.

Presumptively, Ghanaians have created awareness on dangers of civil unrest in addition to the experience of military dictatorship, which has directed development of democracy and economic stabilization, however imperfect, which has depended on legitimate governance based on constitutional rule. Political legitimacy is thought to afford the country flexibility and leverage to negotiate with IFIs on more favorable terms. Limann's government had political legitimacy, but was considered ineffective and toppled amid negotiations with the World Bank and the IMF in a military intervention by Rawlings who also turned to donor agencies to resuscitate the economy (Boafo-Arthur, 1999a). Rawlings's leftist polices, however, brought general fear, however, was that as a reformed leftist, his negotiations strategies would plunge the country into more debts compared to Limann (Boafo-Arthur, 1999a). It is important to note that the initial negotiations phase was difficult because members who included leftist supporters, scholars, and bureaucrats had divergent views and could not come to a general agreement (Boafo-Arthur, 1999a). Despite the challenge, the central agenda remained building sustainable economy for Ghana. In effect, PNDC established a Committee of Secretaries composed of various state ministries to steer the ERP/SAP and drive the economic agenda. One of the significant lessons arising from Ghana's economic reforms is not only maintenance of political stability and constitutional rule based on elected governments, but also the political willingness, negotiation ability, and compromises of all the stakeholders involved in delivering the economic promises (Boafo-Arthur, 1999b).

Adoption of SAP policies had vast implications on the marginalized sections of the population. Ghana's experience in alleviating anticipated costs has lessons for Kenya, and Africa in general. In 1988, the country put in place the Program of Actions to Mitigate the Social Costs of Adjustment (PAMSCAD) with funds from donors to address the social cost of adjustment. The adjustment targeted a number of social projects including healthcare services, informal education, and road construction to meet the basic needs of common Ghanaians (Boafo-Arthur 1999b; Donkor, 1997). Such social endeavors are very necessary on the heels of major restructuring efforts which often produce wide-ranging uncertainties for populations in developing regions like Africa characterized by vast inequities.

Another lesson Ghana holds for Kenya is that the Rawlings's government made deliberate choices that contributed to successful transition to democratic development in Ghana. Whether by plan or political providence, Rawlings's engagement with the wide Ghanaian public helped to tie the people's views and commitments into Ghana's political (and economic) future through the National Commission for Democracy (NCD). This process enabled President Rawlings's government to build democracy from bottom-up including the creation of conditions necessary for district-level political engagement. In July 1987, the PNDC inaugurated the new District Assemblies. Although the general population doubted the democratic goals of the new local level organizations, it was not long before Rawlings and his PNDC supporters announced the first District Assembly elections of 1988 (Asante & Gyimah-Boadi, 2004). The elections were held in line with the decentralization program guidelines, in which District Assemblies took charge of local-level politics and administration. The aim was to make localities the loci of power with possibility of increasing public participation in the political process (Tsikata, 2006).

Ghanaian electoral institutions and politics also hold lessons of building institutional independence, credibility, and professionalization for Kenyan institutions. In Ghana, the Rawlings administration established independent institutions that worked autonomously from other state organizations. For example, the EC according to Levitsky and Way (2010, p. 303) was "professionalized, upgraded technically, and infused with resources." Operating alongside independent judicial system, the EC, not only remained neutral and fair in ruling against the government on many issues, but also openly condemned suppression of peaceful protests in 1993 by students and labor unions, and upholding the legality of such protests (Jeong, 1998). On the contrary, Kenya's electoral body has been for a long time marred by claims of incompetence, biasness, mismanagement, and corruption involving registration of noncitizens and underage voters, among other issues. Although one of the achievements that came with the reintroduction of multiparty system in 1992 was the formation of the Electoral Commission of Kenya (ECK), the ECK, however, was disbanded in line with the Constitutional Amendment Act of 2008 which repealed section 41 of the constitution and created the Independent Electoral and Boundaries Commission (IEBC). These changes were as a result of December 2007 general election violence that contributed to continued human rights abuses (Human Rights Watch, 2008). Bad governance and absences of strong institutions were cited as some of the factors that contributed to the outbreak of ethnic violence during elections. This development led Kenya to join the list of countries labeled with autocratic features where citizens are deprived of their rights of representation and participation in political processes (Odhiambo-Mbai, 2003; Opondo, 2014).

To ensure equal representation, the IEBC was mandated with the power to administer elections and boundaries. The IEBC administered six consecutive elections, safeguard election registers, manage election disputes, and determine constituencies and polling stations, among other duties (IEBC, 2017). However, in the 2013 general election, IEBC encountered its first sets of challenges from inconsistent decision-making that led to delays in voter registration, distribution of voting materials to recruitment of polling staff. These challenges brought other changes including late counting of votes. While many citizens regarded IEBC as an independent and credible institution following the proposed 2010 constitutional reforms, the outcome of the election led many to questions practices and the integrity of IEBC. The opposition leaders rejected the results citing electoral malpractice (Mutiga, 2017). Although they took their dissatisfaction to the Supreme Court of Kenya, on March 10, 2013, the court unanimously declared Uhuru Kenyatta as the president. The court's ruling received mixed reactions from observers. Some argued that the court rejected all evidences of malpractices and fraud by IEBC, and thus failed to exercise its independence (Maina, 2013).

This is not to overlook or discount tensions during election periods in Ghana. Lindberg and Morrison (2008) argue that the key to democracy in Ghana lies in the neutrality of its EC. What has made Ghana an insightful case is the potential of political contestants to accept election results based on the presumed confidence in the leadership and work of the EC. This is a key factor behind return to peace and normalcy in post-election periods in Ghana. The EC has consistently managed political transition and peaceful transfer of power, from the Rawlings era to date. Transitioning from military rule to govern two elected terms in office, Rawlings stepped down to peacefully transfer power to opposition NPP after his NDC party lost the December 2000 election. Many world leaders including Nelson Mandela and Bill Clinton saw Rawlings's act as the essence of democratic maturity, and a "mark of Rawlings' positive historical legacy" (Gyimah-Boadi, 2009, pp. 111–112).

Another Ghanaian experience constructive to Kenya's developing democracy is the work of civil society organizations (CSOs). While CSOs have played a role in the push for democracy since the 1990s, Kenya lacks CSOs that have the resolve to influence government polices like the case of Ghana. In 1992, constitutional change in Ghana's Fourth Republic provided enabling environment for civil society to participate in government policymaking to promote transparency and accountability on the part of the government. The Ghana Anti-Corruption Commission, for instance, has been awarded recognition by the World Bank in 2009 for working with government on anticorruption initiatives (Owono, 2012). While Kenya's CSOs often display a strong agenda, and have often displayed wide awareness on issues affecting citizens and helped in the implementation, e.g., policies on health, agriculture, and recently gas and oil natural resources, however, the CSOs are overwhelmed by government's regulations, and the lack of structure and operational focus which impacts participation in policymaking (Ndegwa, 1996). This limitation further hampers their role to explain government policies and its effects to citizens – a feature that has witnessed some progress in Ghana.

Conclusion

Kenya and Ghana have gone through democratic experiences marked by both success and failures since gaining their independence. While Kenya has achieved important milestones in many areas, still many others in its democratization process remain. In the context of Africa in general, and not only in Kenya, issues of democracy and development, particularly political engagement and economic development for minority groups remain unfinished and far-fetched from the efforts of current and past administration. Therefore, the discourse on democracy, marginalization and development in Kenya, and Africa will continue to resurface in contemporary political and economic debates.

The surge in acknowledging the plight of marginalized groups and the call for integration into the national agenda of the countries in question is a major step in the right direction. However, the case of Kenya raises questions of whether elites and government administrations have the right motive and political willingness to address issues of marginalization or to continuously perpetuate the recognition of the plight of the minorities without specific arrangements for redistribution. This still remains the case, as the Kenyan democratization has offered domestic political actors and elites opportunities to use the rhetoric of redistribution and development for their selfish political agenda of canvassing for votes. These is significantly clear as research shows that the elites and governments pay lip service to most of the issues confronting minorities, but are reluctant to address them consistently once in office. Hence, perpetuating policy objectives set by colonial administrators during the colonial era.

Central to the above concerns are issues of building a sustainable democracy and helps to offer significant well-being to the population. This chapter explored literature on the meaning of democracy and development in the context of Africa. While there are no general consensuses on the meaning of democracy, the key elements that make democracy a good system of governance, Ghana remains a credible example in Africa. Ghana's political journey through many of the transitional pitfalls associated with democratic governance includes institution of a functioning electoral system, judicial independence, and the management of peaceful transfers of power. However, this does not mean the Ghanaian political system is devoid of challenges. Characteristically, this West African state has dealt with the challenges of military interventions, and like any other African country have glaring issues of political corruption and economic inconsistencies in spite of countless reforms. On the other hand, electoral politics in Kenya need more astute reforms to strengthen the capacity of IEBC to professionally manage elections to help abate issues of ethnic politics and the attendant violence. To ensure that democracy and the concomitant economic development thrives in Kenya, introspective internal challenges could also use political and economic reform experiences generated on the African continent.

References

Abdul-Gafaru, A. (2009). Political context study – Ghana. Retrieved January 20, 2018, from www.polis.leeds.ac.uk

Adedeji, J. (2001). The legacy of J. J. Rawlings in Ghanaian politics, 1979–2000. *African Studies Quarterly 5*(2) 1–27.

Alence, R. (2004). Political institutions and developmental governance in sub-Saharan Africa. *Journal of Modern African Studies 42*(2) 163–187.

Alexander, N. C. (2001). Paying for education: How the World Bank and the International Monetary Fund influence education in developing countries. *Peabody Journal of Education 76* 285–338.

Asante, R., & Gyimah-Boadi, E. (2004). Ethnic structure, inequality and governance of the public sector in Ghana. United Nations Research Institute for Social Development. Retrieved September 5, 2018, from www.unrisd.org/80256B3C005BCCF9/(httpAuxPages)/8509496C0F316AB1C1256ED9004 66964/$file/Asante%20(small).pdf

Asare, S. K., & Prempeh, H. K. (2010). Amending the constitution of Ghana: Is the imperial president trespassing? *African Journal of International and Comparative Law*. Retrieved December 8, 2018, from http://danquahinstitute.org

Austin, D., & Luckham, R. (2014). *Politicians and soldiers in Ghana, 1966–1972*. New York, NY: Routledge.

Austin, G. (2010). African economic development and colonial legacies. *International Development Policy* 11–32. Retrieved March 10, 2018, from http://poldev.revues.org

Azikiwe, A. (2009). Nkrumah and Ghana's independence struggle. *Worker's World*. Retrieved March 7, 2018, from www.workers.org

Barkan, D., & Michael Chege. (1989). Decentralising the state focus and the politics of reallocation in Kenya. *Journal of Modern African Studies 27*(3) 431–453.

Boafo-Arthur, K. (1999a). Ghana's politics of international economic relations under the PNDC, 1982–1992? *African Study Monographs 20*(2) 73–98.

Boafo-Arthur, Kwame (1999b). Ghana: structural adjustment, democratization, and politics of continuity? *African Studies Review 42*(2) 41–47.

Boafo-Arthur, K. (2008). Democracy and stability in West Africa: The Ghanaian experience. *Claude Ake Memorial Papers No. 4*. Retrieved January 15, 2018, from www.pcr.uu.se

Boafo-Arthur, K. (2018). Democracy and stability in West Africa: The Ghanaian experience. *Claude Ake Memorial Papers No. 4*. Department of Peace and Conflict Research Uppsala University & Nordic Africa Institute Uppsala.

Bonafede, G., & Lo Piccolo, F. (2010, June). Participative planning processes in the absence of the (public) space of democracy. *Planning Practice & Research 25* 353–375. http://dx.doi.org/10.1080/02697459.2010.503430

Bratton, M., & van de Walle, N. (1997). *Democratic experiment in Africa*. Cambridge, UK: Cambridge University Press.

Brenya, E., Adu-Gyamfi, S., Afful, I., Darkwa, B., Richmond, M. B., et al. (2015). The Rawlings' factor in Ghana's politics: An appraisal of some secondary and primary data. *Journal of Political Sciences & Public Affairs* S1:004. doi:10.4172/2332-0761.S1-004

Brown, S., & Kaiser, P. (2007). Democratisations in Africa: Attempts, hindrances and prospects. *Third World Quarterly 28*(6) 1131–1149.

Bwanaadi, H. (2013). LAPSSET will bring a tsunami, government says: People of Lamu react with shock and dismay. *The East African* (Nairobi, July 27). Retrieved April 13, 2018, from www. theeastafrican.co.ke/OpEd/comment/Lappset-will-bring-a-tsunami-govt-says/-/434750/1928204/-/item/0/-/13b7j5tz/-/index.html

Daily Nation. (2009). Retrieved August 11, 2018, from www.nation.co.ke/news/politics/1064-670760-76t076z/index.html

De Meur, G., & Berg-Schlosser, D. (1996). Conditions of authoritarianism, fascism, and democracy in interwar Europe. *Comparative Political Studies 29* 423–468.

Debrah, E. (2015). Reforming Ghana's electoral process: Lessons and the way forward. *Journal of Politics and Law 8*(1).

Diamond, L. (2008). *The spirit of democracy: The struggle to build free societies throughout the world*. New York, NY: Henry Holt.

Diamond, L. (2015). Facing up to the democratic recession. *Journal of Democracy* 26(1) 141–155.

Donkor, K. (1997). *Structural adjustment and mass poverty in Ghana*. Farnham, UK: Ashgate.

Fobih, N. (2011). Challenges to party development and democratic consolidation: Perspectives on reforming Ghana's institutional framework. *Journal of Asian and African Studies 46* 578–592. Retrieved March 7, 2018, from http://dx.doi.org/10.1177/0021909611403268

Freedom House. (2012). Retrieved July 28, 2018, from www.freedomhouse.org/report

Frimpong, Kwarteng. (2017). Civil society organisations and good governance in Ghana. *International Journal of Development and Sustainability 6*(9) 956–971.

Gyampo, R. E. V. (2017). The state of electoral reforms in Ghana. *Africa Spectrum 52*(3) 95–109.

Gyimah-Boadi, E. (2009). Another step forward for Ghana. *Journal of Democracy* 20(2) 138–152.

Harbeson, J., Rothchild, D., & Chazan, N. (Eds.). (1994). *Civil society and the state in Africa*. Boulder, CO: Lynne Rienner.

Human Rights Watch. (2008). Ballots to bullets: organized political violence and Kenya's crisis of governance. Retrieved August 2, 2018, from www.hrw.org/report/2008/03/16/ballots-bullets/organized-political-violence-and-kenyas-crisis-governance

Independent Electoral and Boundaries Commission (IEBC). (2017). The mandate. IEBC Retrieved 7 July, 2017, from www.iebc.or.ke/iebc/?mandate
Gocking, R. S. (2005). *The history of Ghana*. Westport, CT: Greenwood Publishing. Retrieved April 2018, from https://knustesa.files.wordpress.com/2015/01/the-history-of-ghana-the-greenwood-histories-of-the-modern-nations.pdf
Hutchful, E. (2002). *Ghana's adjustment experience: The paradox of reform*. Geneva, Switzerland: United Nations Research Institute for Social Development.
Jeong, H. (1998). Economic reform and democratic transition in Ghana. *World Affairs 160*(4).
Joyce, P. (2006). *Teach yourself – Politics*. London, UK: Hodder Education.
Kagwanja, M. P., & Southall, R. (2010). *Kenya's uncertain democracy: The electoral crisis of 2008*. London, UK: Routledge.
Knutsen, C. H. (2010). Africa's growth tragedy revisited: weak states, strong rulers. Department of Political Science, University of Oslo Centre for the Study of Civil War, PRIO. Retrieved July 12, 2018, from https://warwick.ac.uk/fac/soc/pais/research/researchcentres/csgr/garnet/workingpapers/7109.pdf
Konadu-Agyemang, K. (2000). The best of times and the worst of times: Structural adjustment programs and uneven development in Africa: The case of Ghana. *Professional Geographer 52* 469–483.
Kwakye, J. K. (2011). *Africa's long road to development*. Accra, Ghana: Frontiers Printing & Publishing Limited.
Levitsky, S., & Way, L. A. (2010). *Competitive authoritarianism: Hybrid regimes after the Cold War*. Cambridge, UK: Cambridge University Press.
Lindberg, S. I., & Morrison, M. K. (2008). Are African voters really ethnic or clientelistic? Survey evidence from Ghana. *Political Science Quarterly 123*. Retrieved March 19, 2018, from www.class.ufl.edu
Livingstone, J. (2005). A comparative study of pastoralists parliamentary groups: Kenya case study. Pastoral and Environmental Network in the Horn of Africa.
Maina, W. (2013). Verdict on Kenya's presidential election petition: five reasons the judgment fails the legal test. *The East African* (Nairobi, 8 February). Retrieved June 6, 2017, from www.theeastafrican.co.ke/OpEd/comment/Five-reasons-Kenya-Supreme Court-failed-poll-petition-test/-/434750/1753646/-/297c6q/-/index.html
Mamdani, M. (1996). *Citizen and subject: Contemporary Africa and the legacy of late colonialism*. Oxford, UK: James Currey.
Menocal, R. A. (2007). Analysing the relationship between democracy and development: Defining basic concepts and assessing key linkages. Retrieved November 11, 2018, from www.odi.org/publications/1342-analysing-relationship-between-democracy-and-development-defining-basic-concepts-and-assessing-key
Muigai, G. (1993). Kenya's opposition and the crisis of governance. *Issue: A Journal of Opinion 21*(1–2).
Murunga, G. (2011). Spontaneous or premeditated: Post-election violence in Kenya. Uppsala, Sweden: Nordiska Afrikainstitutet.
Mutiga, M. (2017). Kenya: Avoiding another electoral crisis. International Crisis Group March 3. Retrieved June 6, 2017, from www.crisisgroup.org/africa/horn-africa/kenya/kenya-avoiding-another-electoral-crisis
Mutua, M. (2008). *Kenya's quest for democracy: Taming Leviathan*. Boulder, CO: Lynne Rienner.
Ndegwa, S. (1996). The two faces of civil society: NGOs and politics in Africa. Connecticut, CT: Kumari Press.

Nyawalo, P. A. et al. (2011). The invisible violence in Kenya: A case study of Rift Valley and Western Regions. Retrieved March 13, 2018, from www.researchgate.net/profile/Manasseh_Wepundi/publication/289252329

Odhiambo-Mbai, C. (2003). The rise and fall of the autocratic state in Kenya. In W. O. Oyugi, P. Wanyande, & C. Odhiambo-Mbai (Eds.), *The politics of transition in Kenya: From KANU to NARC* (pp. 51–95). Nairobi: Heinrich Böll Foundation.

Odoom, I. (2018). South–South cooperation, SDGs, and Africa's development: A study of China's development intervention in Ghana. In K. T. Hanson, K. P. Puplampu, & T. M. Shaw (Eds.), *From Millennium Development Goals to Sustainable Development Goals: Rethinking African Development*. New York, NY: Routledge.

Ogot, Bethwell A., & William Robert Ochieng. (1995). *Decolonization & Independence in Kenya*. Oxford, UK: James Currey.

Olson, M. (1993). Dictatorship, democracy, and development. *American Political Science Review 87*(3) 567–576.

Olukoshi, A. et al. (1994). *Structural adjustment in West Africa*. Lagos, Nigeria: Nigerian Institute of International Affairs.

Osaghae, E. E. (2005). The state of Africa's second liberation. *Interventions: International Journal of Postcolonial Studies 7*(1) 1–20.

Owono, J. (2012). Ghana: A democratic anomaly. Retrieved March 9, 2018, from www.aljazeera.com/indepth/opinion/2012/07/201273182115464514.html

Rutten, M., Owuor, S. (2009). Weapons of mass destruction: Land, ethnicity and the 2007 elections in Kenya. *Journal of Contemporary African Studies 27*(3) 305–327.

Przeworski, A. (2000). *Democracy and development: Political institutions and well-being in the world 1950–1990*. Cambridge, UK: Cambridge University Press.

Przeworski, A. (2011). Divided we stand? Democracy as a method of processing conflicts. *Scandinavian Political Studies 34*(2) 168–182. Retrieved March 9, 2018, from http://dx.doi.org/10.1111/j.1467-9477.2011.00265.x

Republic of Kenya. (1979). *Ministry of Education annual report*. Nairobi, Kenya: Government Printer

Republic of Kenya. (1984). District Focus for Rural Development. Nairobi, Kenya: Government Printer.

Rooney, D. (2007). *Kwame Nkrumah: Vision and tragedy*. Accra, Ghana: Sub-Saharan Publishers.

Schraeder, P. J. (1994). Elites as facilitators or impediments to political development? Some lessons from the "third wave" of democratization in Africa. *Journal of Developing Areas* 29(1).

Shillington, K. (1992). *Ghana and the Rawling's factor*. New York, NY: St. Martin's Press.

Skinner, K. (2011). Who knew the minds of the people? Specialist knowledge and developmentalist authoritarianism in postcolonial Ghana. *Journal of Imperial and Commonwealth History 39*(2) 297–323. Retrieved April 13, 2018, from http://dx.doi.org/10.1080/03086534.2011.568756

Somerset, A. (2007). A preliminary note on Kenya primary school enrolment trends over four decades. London: CREATE Pathways to Access Research Monograph, No. 9. Brighton, UK: University of Sussex. Retrieved March 12, 2018, from https://files.eric.ed.gov/fulltext/ED508694.pdf

Sorensen, G. (2008). *Democracy and democratization: Processes and prospects in a changing world*. Philadelphia, PA: Westview Press.

Tsikata, T. (2006). Challenges of economic reform & democratization: Some lessons from Ghana. In M. Ndulo (Ed.), *Democratic reform in Africa: Its impact on governance & poverty alleviation* (pp. 99–107). Oxford, UK: James Currey.

United Nations Development Program. (1990). The Human Development Index (HDI) is a composite measure of health, education, and income calculated by UNDP since 1990.

Yidana, R. (2012). Socionationalism in Ghana: History, insights, and lessons for Africa. *Journal of Third World Studies 29*(1) 103. Retrieved March 24, 2018, from http://apps.gsw.edu/atws/journal.htm

12 Conclusion

Ghana's exceptionalism in economic reforms? Resolve vs. results

Richard Aidoo

In the past three decades, Ghana has attempted different economic reforms programs and projects, mostly under the guidance of IFIs like the IMF and the World Bank – SAP/ERP, HIPC, and a more recent ECF from the IMF, to help gain a stable and sustainable macroeconomic position which ensures poverty reduction and growth. These economic reform programs have been initiated along with the changing politics of the country, which emerged from its 1957 independence with a leader that desired a one-party state, followed by successive military interventions albeit with brief interludes of civilian rule until the embrace of democratic governance in the early 1990s. Amid these tries at political and economic change, this West African country has received continuous global recognition and praise for its tremendous reform efforts. In a timely contribution titled *Africa's Natural Resources and Underdevelopment: How Ghana's Petroleum Can Create Sustainable Economic Prosperity*, Kwamina Panford (2017, p. 3) shows a list of donors that have collectively and continuously sung the praises of Ghana even when the economic development situation is unfavorable. These mainly include the IMF, World Bank, US government, and affiliate agencies like the US Agency for International Development, government diplomats from France, Britain, Japan, Germany Canada, Australia, and Scandinavian countries like Norway, Sweden, and Denmark. These foreign actors continue to resound past statements of Ghana as a star pupil of the economic reform programs like SAP, and fairly recent reference by the ODI tagging Ghana as a developmental star performer (Overseas Development Institute, 2011). Does some evidence exist to support these accolades and claims with regard to Ghana's economic reform performance in that past three decades? How have external and domestic actors contributed to shaping these reforms and the aftermath of these programs?

Based on the deliberations in this volume, it is quite clear that there is room for a bifurcated response to the above thought-provoking questions by rendering arguments for Ghana's exceptionalism in the area of economic reform experience and some debates against the consideration of exceptionalism. To do so effectively, it is important to argue that most actors (largely external in this case) that have engaged Ghana in economic and political reforms in the past three decades may have been comparatively impressed by the resolve of Ghanaian governments to embrace and attempt the checklist of procedures, precepts, and conditions required in economic reform programs. Alternatively, all stakeholders (domestic and foreign) involved in the processes of reform in Ghana do wonder about the unsustainable results that are often achieved with these attempts. Expectedly, this regularly leads to a blame game where the domestic actors in Ghana – mostly government officials and agencies – point to the pressures and procedures of the external actors, while the foreign actors in turn remind the Ghanaian actors of their obligations and commitments which is often claimed to fall short of what is required to achieve and sustain economic growth. After three decades of economic reforms, Ghana, again, under the John Mahama and NDC administration signed on to an ECF with the IMF to the total of $918m in April 2015 which also consists of a reform package. In the press release that accompanied the agreement, the IMF stated that "Ghana's macroeconomic performance over the years has been mixed. Policy slippages have compounded the adverse impact of the shocks and resulted in significant external and domestic imbalances." According to the IFI, these policy slippages often happened especially during election years. However, the IMF states the commitment of the incoming administration of Nana Akufo-Addo and the NPP (who won the 2016 elections to depose the NDC administration) to follow through and further achieve macroeconomic stability and fiscal discipline (IMF, 2017).

In this book, discussions that underscore the resolve and results of Ghana's attempts at economic and political reforms have been interestingly packaged and presented by the contributors. The volume starts with a broad introduction that lays out the conceptual character and evolution of economic reforms in Ghana in the past generation, which carefully ties in with the Mawuko-Yevugah's theoretical reflection on the political–economic journey through economic reforms in Africa, and Ghana in particular. Chapters in Part II of this volume from external perspectives underscore the resolve argument as these chapters point to significant mileage and achievements in terms of economic cooperation as in the case of Canada, Ghana's attempts to produce some political and economic outcomes in spite of the internal institutional challenges of donor bodies like the EU, and the possibilities that exist for furthering economic growth by embracing known successful models and approaches from Asian partners. These discussions assume or project into the capabilities of Ghana's political economy to achieve the needed results of macroeconomic growth and stability, job creation, balanced trade, and general well-being of the population through recognition of the levels of determination from various Ghanaian administrations over the years, either military of democratically elected regime.

Part III of this volume is packed with research and discussions that highlight the results end of the debate. The chapter contributors turn to reflect on the results – achievements or otherwise – that Ghana has collected in the past three decades. These include a test of the resilience of the country's institutions and policies to render the needed check over foreign oil investments, either by contribution of the foreign investor's fair share to the socioeconomic and cultural advancement of the local populations residing around resource-endowed regions, or leveraging the influence of the Ghanaian state in multinational engagements. Similarly, has the policy reform process with regard to Ghana's economic and political development prepared the state institutions to deal with issues like illegal mining which often result with multiple global initiatives to attract investors in the countries? Chapter 8 reveals that as domestic actors turn to blame the international partners in the political and economic evolution, these internal actors could connive with foreign interests to create local problems that hinder the process of development of a sector or the entire economy. Three other chapters appraise and extol the outcomes of Ghana reform processes over the past three decades. Interestingly, apart from Chapter 9 that traces the journeys of Ghana and Senegal through different economic agendas to measure the challenges these two states have faced and assess the conceptual path to economic autonomy, the contributions of Gambia and Kenya turn out to be overly focused on Ghana's political successes – largely, the attainment of an enviable democratic record. These research and discussions reference the emulation of the results that Ghana has recorded by examining potential lessons that could be gleaned from these achievements though both cases also acknowledge the imperfections of Ghana's results in political reform. Together, the issues raised throughout the book which help underscore or praise the resolve or results of Ghana's engagement of economic and political reform programs over the past three decades highlight the causes for celebration and recognition as well as making the case for some unqualified recognition. Does Ghana's experiences in economic (and political) reform merit exceptionalism? If not, why?

Ghana's exceptionalism in economic reforms in the past three decades simply stems from its relatively stable political environment. Most academics and researchers on Ghana's political economy or African politics in general are quick to perceive Ghana as a safe example for political stability on a continent that has displayed a persistent and pervasive characteristic of several post-independent military interventions, civil wars, politically generated conflicts, and intransigent leaders that extend their tenures beyond the expiration of their term limits. Radelet (2010) points to the emergence of a new era in Ghana from the late 1990s when the economy began to stabilize and expand, and most significantly the country's politics shifted from authoritarian to democratic rule – marked by strengthening of political rights, civil liberties, and basic freedoms (as shown in Figure 1.2). This is a big storyline that has marched along any attempt at economic development or reform. As political confidence in Ghana has grown with its democratic successes, this has often eclipsed erratic and sometimes unsustained results produced by years of economic reform programs that were helped with enormous resources of loans, grants, technical aid, and expertise. As competitive elections have been deemed free and fair, and the transition process from incumbent to opposition described as remarkable, IFIs and other global partners have touted Ghana's political stability as a sign of sturdiness for economic success. However, has this political development materialized in displaying the fruitfulness of economic reforms in Ghana – the often-referenced star reformer? Definitely, there has been some progress in economic development but not sustained enough to equally go along with the story of successful political self-determination. Consider this: If Ghana became politically free along with countries like Malaysia and Singapore that currently have economies that far outpace that of their African counterpart, are attempts at economic reform in Ghana exceptional? In 1960, Malaysia and Singapore had GDP per capita of \$234.9 and \$427.9 respectively, while Ghana registered \$183.0 for GDP per capita. Over five decades later, Ghana's GDP per capita stands at \$1449.7 in 2014, as Malaysia and Singapore report \$11,183.7 and \$56,957.1 individually in the same year (African Development Bank, 2018). With such results, the question then becomes: Does Ghana merit any accolades beyond its democratic stability storyline? For most that have studied Ghana, along with the African continent as a whole, the former's democratic achievement is worth every mention, and because the connection between this progressive democratic record and the erratic economic performance is inconclusive, touting the democratic results is often mixed up with the resolve at attempting various economic reforms.

Linked to the above are the regional dynamics or situations that often make Ghana an elevated sub-Saharan African example. Most references to Ghana's economic reform programs offer some comparative regional perspectives to the African region as a whole – either through sector-to-sector or state-to-state analysis. Ghana's seeming resolve at keeping with externally packaged reform programs and the austere conditions that come with them is often admired along with its democratic credentials. This is particularly so, when one considers that Ghana has had slightly but progressively higher GDP per capita growth rates from the 1990s compared to the sub-Saharan African region as a whole (see Figure 1.1). For instance, in 2011 while Ghana posted an impressive 11.3% GDP per capita growth rate, the sub-Saharan region recorded 1.6%. Though such results and differences in margins may be due to a multiplicity of factors, nonetheless, they offer support for some level of efficacy of economic reforms in Ghana's political economy.

A significant sector in Ghana's economy that has been drawn to this exceptionalism argument, though yet to be proven is the petroleum sector – a newly established sector that tests Ghana's capacity to avoid the resource curse phenomenon and its attendant enclave effects. This is particularly notable, given that most petroleum economies on the African continent have variedly ended up with signs of resource curse and its developmentally deficient outcomes. In an attempt to explicate the resource curse debate in Ghana's newly established petroleum industry, Panford (2017) explored the various institutional and legislative structures that have been put in place to ensure the avoidance of the enclave effects in Ghana's oil and gas industry. Accordingly, since the start of commercial oil and gas production in Ghana, four significant pieces of legislation have been passed in parliament: the Petroleum Exploration and Production Bill (passed August 2016) PRMA (Act 815) (passed March 2011), Petroleum Commission (PC) (Act 21) (passed 2011), and Petroleum (Local Content and Local Participation) Regulations (passed November 2013) (Panford, 2017, p. 108). Despite such popular and political investments in the process to safeguard Ghana's petroleum industry from the known fate of resource curse, Panford (2017) reckons that these institutions and legislation are not sufficient by themselves if attempts are not made to offer for instance real-life practices and policies to augment some of these arrangements, and deal with issues of local content, corruption, and ineptitude in the state's management of petroleum resources in Ghana, much like other parts of Africa. Though the petroleum industry in Ghana is in its incipient stage, the policies, processes, and procedures, both anticipated and established by the various government administrations have generally caught the attention of industry watchers that praise Ghana for its exceptional efforts at putting in place necessary first-step mechanisms to ensure the avoidance of resource curse and enclave economic effects. This includes an ambition to emulate Norway's Heritage Fund to help manage the petroleum proceeds. In Chapter 10 in this volume, Abdoulaye Saine points to the potential of Gambia to glean from Ghana's lessons in oil production as the former attempts to develop its newly found oil resources. So, even if results are yet to be fully determined, Ghana's early strides in petroleum production are noticeably toward proper management practices, which again is relatively different in a region that has witnessed less of such outcomes in the oil industry.

One factor that remains indelible in Ghana's records of economic reforms is simply the strength of an authoritarian regime or more specifically the firm hands of an authoritarian leader – Jerry Rawlings. This is nonetheless a contentious debate. Some across Africa and the world have been drawn to the stable, yet authoritarian leadership of Rawlings, and attribute the accolades of contemporary Ghana to his strong-handed, and no-nonsense rule. Critics on the other hand, see Rawlings as one of the main reasons for a continuously stagnated and underperforming Ghanaian economy despite the bouts of economic reforms, as political expediency was often placed over economic rationality during his era of leadership. As Deepak Lal (1983, p. 33) asserts, "A courageous, ruthless and perhaps undemocratic government is required to ride roughshod over … newly created special interest groups" (cited in Sandbrook, 2000, 75). Hence, Rawlings came to power (energized by two successful coup d'états in 1979 and 1981) with some popular legitimacy which emboldened his capacity to ignore or suppress protests and press on with his reform agenda whatever that may be. The change to democratic rule in 1992 could still not have immediately transformed the political soul of Jerry Rawlings as dictatorial tendencies may still hang on to a democratic convert. As often argued, the reality of democracy in Africa manifest fragility and limits as even elections and multiparty politics may awaken or aggravate clientelism, factionalism, ethnic and regional loyalties rather than ideological differences (Sandbrook, 2000, 77). Thus, Rawlings and his regimes (AFRC, PNDC, NDC) were able to enjoy some rare continuity in reform efforts which display the resolve that many celebrate, instead of the inconsistent and inconclusive results of the country's over three decades of economic reforms.

Given the foregoing discussions, how then is Ghana's exceptionalism status even more complex and often not deserving? First, the challenge of managing both political and economic institutional reforms in an African state setting has wide-ranging impacts on the results. This is attributable to two elements in governance – the role of the state in political and economic development, and the leadership traditions. Bates (1981) cogently contended that African leaders often sacrifice economic development and growth targets for political expediency by emphasizing and catering to the interests of urban constituencies as these urbanites were often key to the regime's survival. Callaghy (1988) also pointed to the fact that African leaders often amassed as much personal wealth as possible to enable them to assuage and withstand any legitimacy challenge from the wealthy class that may attempt to undermine their rule. Given such undercurrents among leadership, scholars are still quite uncertain about fruitful connections between democratic governance and neoliberal reforms (see Jeffries, 1993; Opoku, 2010). Though Bates (1981) used the Acheampong regime in Ghana as an example of an administration that acquiesced to the urban bias thesis as a means of political survival, subsequent administrations after Acheampong – from Rawlings to the current administration of Nana Akufo-Addo – have also catered to the urban population with a sense of creating some certitude with the urban vote. This often means discounting or de-emphasizing the role that the rural economy plays in the process of transforming the national economy. Thus, to achieve the political gain irrespective of the economic cost, the state as the main political institution is used for political preservation of the regime rather for economic change to benefit the general population. This is evident in the past three decades of economic reforms in Ghana, even under democratic rule, as political administrations or incumbents engage state resources in their campaigns to retain political power, and in the process disregard fiscal policies and restraints put in place under previous economic reform attempts. As earlier mentioned, the IMF's review of Ghana's ECF signed on 2015 noted that slippages particularly happened during election years when economic caution is certainly sacrificed for political expediency (IMF, 2017).

Over the past generation, Ghana's economic reforms (much like several across Africa) have often been criticized for having been crafted and supervised by external actors, mostly western financial institutions like the IMF and the World Bank, thus lacking local agency. As intimated by Sandbrook (2000, p. 80), displacing leaders involved in political capitalism may facilitate executive commitment to advancing market reforms, but long-term implementation of controversial programs requires that elected governments and representatives "own" their own projects. This significant critique has led to two major developments throughout the decades – first, a paradigm that projects Ghana's domestic economic challenges onto foreign actors particularly the IMF and the World Bank, and second, the reemergence and embrace of China as an alternative to western dominance in the economic development process. Scholars often argue the demise of the state (particularly in the developing world) and its power in shaping its own economic destiny, as global institutions like the IMF and World Bank settle within the borders or remotely controls business, especially in terms of institution of economic reforms as in the case of Ghana. As often the case, in the desperation for loans and grants to ease economic hardships and pursue development agenda, various governments in Ghana over the past three decades have had little choice but to come to terms with IMF and World Bank demands (Sandbrook, 2000). Nonetheless, this line of argument has been challenged on several fronts including Rothchild and Gyimah-Boadi (1986) who assert that contrary to blaming the global institutions and resources for Ghana's economic challenges, Ghana was ignored by global capitalist interests as a result of strategic insignificance and the lack of government policy support rendered to incoming investments – both common reasons for disinterest in investing and engaging African economies. Juxtaposing the cases of Ivory Coast's economic miracle in the 1970s and 1980s with Ghana's economic maladies in the same periods, Opoku (2010) stressed the important roles played by domestic factors and policies in shaping the divergent economic destinies of both countries. Based on Gyimah-Boadi and Daddieh (1999), Opoku (2010) further asserts that conditions in the late 1970s (i.e., rising oil prices) were rife for both countries to be economic basket cases in Africa, given that they both possess similar human and natural resources. Ivory Coast successfully managed to pay higher prices to its cocoa producers thereby expanding the sector to ramp up cocoa production to the benefit of its economy. Nevertheless, as profound as such challenges may be, they still highlight the significant issue of the overwhelming role and presence of external actors, often minimizing the effects emanating from the activities of local actors. This is even more visible as most of the praise for Ghana's performance comes from the external partners and actors. Sometimes, the dominance of western actors in push for reforms in an African economy can be counterproductive. Sandbrook (2000, p. 80) rightly captures this by arguing that "If Western governments or multilateral agencies push governments too aggressively, they achieve not a political commitment to reform but a shallow and sullen acquiescence." And further typifies his argument with the irate words of Mozambican President Joaquim Chissano venting at western reform process:

> The U.S. said, "Open yourself to OPIC, the World Bank, and the IMF." What happened? … We are told now: "Marxism! You are devils. Change this policy." O.K. Marxism is gone. "Open the market economy." O.K., [the ruling party] Frelimo is trying to create capitalism.… We went to Reagan and I said, "I want money for the private sector.… Answer: $10 million, then $15 million more, then another $15 million. … O.K. we have changed.…" Now they say, "If you don't go to a multiparty system, don't expect help from us."
>
> (cited in Sandbrook, 2000, pp. 80–81)

To avoid such persistent frustration, in the course of the past three decades, leaders from African countries like Ghana have increasingly pursued other options and approaches to attain their development objectives. Enter China!

China's role as political and economic actor in Ghana has gradually expanded over the past two decades as Ghana, like other African countries, has sought elsewhere for an option to the neoliberal economic reforms that have not been capable of producing the required economic gains. With a long post-independent relationship, Ghana and China have endeavored to shift their relations from the predominantly ideological diplomacy to a more pragmatic economic-dominated engagement that values exchange in commodities and services with rather visible economic impact. Even though the relationship has seen its own challenges in the past and present as shown in this volume by the research works by Richard Aidoo and Isaac Odoom, Ghana has perceived China as a useful economic development model as boldly expressed by President Akufo-Addo during his address to the UN 73rd General Assembly in New York:

> We know we must get our population educated and trained.... We must address our infrastructural deficit. The traditional methods of tackling this problem will not provide the answer. We are looking for new ways to resolve it. Ghana, like many countries in Africa, is forging relations with China to make arrangements to help address part of our infrastructure deficit.
>
> (Ghana Government, 2018)

Purposively, this declaration came along with the intent of the Akufo-Addo administration to end existing IMF support of the ECF signed in 2015 (The African Exponent, 2018). As Ghana–China relationships evolve with such affirmations, loans, grants, and other forms of aid, one of the main ideals shaping this relationship is also founded on the capability for Ghana to reform its economy and development course with less external political interference in its domestic affairs – an enhancement of Ghanaian agency – and one of Beijing's often-stated cornerstone doctrines in its relationship with the developing world, particularly African countries (see Aidoo & Hess, 2015; Hess & Aidoo, 2010). China's noninterference doctrine is a major pull factor for African political leaders and elites as the underlying concept of the doctrine offers African countries (like Ghana) the needed support for development without the preconditions and requirements indicative of western economic support. Thus, in concept, African/Ghanaian agency is elevated above external overextension in economic development efforts.

Finally, Ghana's economic reform attempts in the past three decades show some level of deficiency in economic policy planning, especially at the level of political organization, i.e., political parties (see Pitcher, 2012). Ironically, this is particularly noticeable under Ghana's fourth celebrated democratic era as political parties and their leadership are mostly focused on winning elections rather than relishing the opportunity to create and implement policies that will advance the economic well-being of the Ghanaian population, especially the poor. As bluntly put by a former Head of Policy Monitoring and Evaluation in the NDC political party:

> The welfare of the mass population has not mattered much to the political leadership as much as their own parochial welfare and every change of

> government is nothing but a change of an elite to replace the previous administration's elite.... Our congresses never extended to the discussions of policies and programmes. It was only for elections; elections of party officials and flagbearer.... We never had time to discuss policies and programmes.
>
> (Citinewsroom, 2018; Ghanaweb, 2018)

Such candid disclosures denote a character of arbitrariness and narrowness in democratic politics and policy realms, a known and identifiable feature with many past and present governments across Africa, and one that often undermines gains made in past economic reform endeavors. Evidently, such inconsistencies in policy planning and implementation is likely irreconcilable with the image of a star reformer.

As shown by the contributions in this book, as much as Ghana's political and economic courses have been definitely shaped by the different economic reform programs and attempts in the past three decades, the continuation of the impacts of these reforms under different government administrations and on the Ghanaian masses would continuously be dependent on the politics – both structures and processes – at the national, local/traditional levels in Ghana. With a tinge of optimism, Radelet's (2010) assertion succinctly captures Ghana's efforts at economic reforms and the future:

> Ghana's record is far from spotless. The progress over the last 20 years at times has been uneven, and there are still many flaws. Nevertheless, overall progress has been strong, and the major changes in economic policy and governance provide a strong foundation for continued growth in the future.

Whether Ghana's accolades of exceptionalism in reforms and development is informed by its resolve over the decades or the results that have been collected in the past three decades, future political administrations, irrespective of their political and economic ideologies would have to continuously prove themselves worthy of such commendations. Attaining this by taking advantage of reform opportunities to build innovatively beneficial partnerships with the West, recognize the challenges and strengths of global institutions, glean from pragmatic approaches from the East, ensure that crucial sectors of the economy also benefit the local population, and value intra-African partnerships while exercising agency in political–economic policymaking and development of institutions – these are definite hallmarks of any exceptional African reformer, potentially Ghana.

References

African Development Bank. (2018). Africa Information Highway – GDP by country: Statistics from the World Bank, 1960–2017. Retrieved October 20, 2018, from opendata forafrica.org/mhrzolg/gdp-by-country-statistics-from-the-world-bank-1960-2017?country

African Exponent. (2018). Africa beyond aid: Ghana set to exit $1 billion IMF bailout by end of 2018. Retrieved November 20, 2018, from www.africanexponent.com/post/9406-ghana-on-track-to-exit-imf-bailout-sooner-than-expected

Aidoo, R., & Hess, S. (2015). Non-interference 2.0: China's evolving foreign policy towards a changing Africa. *Journal of Current Chinese Affairs 44*(1) 107–139.

Bates, R. (1981). *Markets and states in tropical Africa: The political basis of agricultural policies*. Berkeley: University of California Press.

Callaghy, T. (1988). The state and the development of capitalism in Africa: Theoretical, historical, and comparative reflections. In D. Rothchild & N. Chazan N. (Eds.), *The precarious balance: State and society in Africa* (pp. 67–99). Boulder, CO: Westview Press.

Citinewsroom. (2018). Change of governments in Ghana mean nothing – Tony Aidoo. Retrieved November 10, 2018, from https://citinewsroom.com/2018/10/04/change-of-governments-in-ghana-mean-nothing-tony-aidoo

Ghana Government. (2018). President Akufo-Addo's speech at 73rd UN General Assembly. Retrieved September 30, 2018, from www.ghana.gov.gh/images/documents/president_akufo_speech_73rd_unga.pdf

Ghanaweb. (2018). Tony Aidoo reveals why he stopped attending NDC congresses. Retrieved November 10, 2018, from www.ghanaweb.com/GhanaHomePage/NewsArchive/Tony-Aidoo-reveals-why-he-stopped-attending-NDC-congresses-689734

Gyimah-Boadi, E., & Daddieh, C. (1999). Economic and political liberalization in Ghana and Cote d'Ivoire: A preliminary assessment of implications for nation building. In K. Mengisteab & C. Daddieh (Eds.), *State building and democratization in Africa: Faith, hope and realities* (pp. 125–155). Westport, CT: Praeger.

Hess, S., & Aidoo, R. (2010). Beyond the rhetoric: Noninterference in China's African policy. *African and Asian Studies 9*(3) 356–383.

International Monetary Fund (IMF). (2017). Ghana. IMF Country Report No. 17/262. Retrieved October 25, 2018, from www.imf.org

Jeffries, R. (1993). The state, structural adjustment and good government in Africa. *Journal of Commonwealth and Comparative Politics* 31(1) 20–35.

Lal, D. (1983). *The poverty of development economics*. London, UK: IEA Hobart.

Opoku, D. K. (2010). *The politics of government–business relations in Ghana, 1982–2008*. New York, NY: Palgrave Macmillan.

Overseas Development Institute (ODI). (2011). Mapping progress: Evidence for new development outlook. London, UK: Overseas Development Institute.

Panford, K. (2017). *Africa's natural resources and underdevelopment: How Ghana's petroleum can create sustainable economic prosperity*. New York, NY: Palgrave Macmillan.

Pitcher, M. A. (2012). *Party politics and economic reform in Africa's democracies*. New York, NY: Cambridge University Press.

Radelet, S. (2010). *Emerging Africa: How 17 countries are leading the way*. Washington, DC: Center for Global Development.

Rothchild, D., & Gyimah-Boadi, E. (1986). Ghana's economic decline and development strategies. In J. Ravenhill (Ed.), *Africa in economic crisis* (pp. 254–285). London: Macmillan.

Sandbrook, R. (2000). *Closing the circle: Democratization and development in Africa*. New York, NY: Zed Books.

Index

Abrahamsen, R. 39–40
Accelerated Growth Strategy 20, 158
ACEP *see* Africa Centre for Energy Policy
ACET *see* Africa Center for Economic Transformation
Acheampong, Gen. Ignatius Kutu 15, 17–18, 180, 196
ACP countries 67, 71, 74–75
Adam, C. 68, 74
ADB *see* African Development Bank
AFPRC *see* Armed Forces Provisional Ruling Council
AFRC *see* Armed Forces Revolutionary Council
Africa 5–9, 11–13, 18–21, 37–41, 47–51, 68–74, 76, 86–88, 111–115, 121–123, 128–130, 135, 140–141, 173–176, 195–199; and Ghana's postcolonial economic development vision 24; neoliberal policy reform in 35, 40; political economy of 37, 91–92, 172; pre-1ndependence 164, 171; pre-liberation 166; redefining 171; sub-Sahara 13, 15; *see also* African states
Africa Center for Economic Transformation 111, 124
Africa Centre for Energy Policy 97
Africa Development Fund 113
African, Caribbean and Pacific countries *see* ACP countries
African Continental Free Trade Area 90
African Development Bank 3, 25, 50, 155, 194, 199
African economies 2, 12, 25, 112, 135, 140, 152, 197
African governments 10, 21, 75, 122; *see also* governments
African leaders 6, 9, 35, 83, 87, 169, 174, 196
African nationalism 5–6, 12
African states 11, 13–14, 19, 21, 51, 54, 58, 66, 69–70, 72–73, 75–77, 88, 90, 92, 96, 102, 109, 112–113, 126–128, 129, 138, 158, 174–176, 180, 182, 189, 197–198; Angola 2, 9, 96, 129; Botswana 2, 101; Chad 2; Gabon 2; Ivory Coast 2, 197; Kenya 2, 14, 25, 99, 173–174, 176–178, 180–186; Mozambique 26; Nigeria 19, 54, 58, 66, 88, 90, 92, 96, 102, 109, 126, 129, 158, 189; Sudan 2, 115, 129, 145, 173; Tanzania 2; Uganda 2, 99, 115
AGS *see* Accelerated Growth Strategy
Aguilera, R.V. 99–100
Aidoo, Richard 1–25, 28, 77, 111, 124, 127–141, 170, 172, 191–199
Akuffo, Fred 47, 51–52, 180
Akufo-Addo, Pres. Nana 68, 160, 166, 169–171, 181, 192, 196, 198, 200
Allied Oil (IOC) 99
Angola 2, 9, 96, 129
Ankrah, Gen. J.A. 180
anti-Chinese populism 127, 127–141, 143, 172
Arid and Semi-Arid Lands 179
Armed Forces Provisional Ruling Council 165
Armed Forces Revolutionary Council 15, 54, 181, 195
Aryeetey, Ernest 2, 20, 153
ASALs *see* Arid and Semi-Arid Lands
Ashanti Goldfields Corporation 20
Ashanti tribes 148
Asia 8, 13, 15, 49, 135; oil companies 124; partnerships 12, 81, 83, 85, 87, 89–91, 192
Atuabo Gas plant 118–119
Awaso 127, 130, 132, 134–137, 140–141

Ayelazuno, J. 122

Balladur, Edouard (Prime Minister, France) 153
Bandung Conference 1955 82, 127–128
Bank of Ghana Act 2002 23
Barrow, Pres. Adama 165, 169–170
Bates, Robert 6–7, 9, 15, 128, 178, 196
Bawa, S. 55, 57, 60–61
Bawumia, M. 10, 22, 26
Becker, Gary 33
Beijing 113–114, 116–117, 122, 127–129, 133, 135–136, 139, 198
Berg Report 35, 37
Bittaye, Musa 167
Bloomberg News 129, 133, 135, 139
Boafo-Arthur, K. 37–38, 90, 111, 181–183
Bodenstein, T. 70–72
Botswana 2, 101
BP (IOC) 115–116
Brazzaville Conference 1944 148
Bretton Woods institutions 18, 37, 50, 63, 152, 154, 171
Bretton Woods institutions (IMF and World Bank) 18
Buckley, P.J. 112, 125
Bui hydroelectric project 129
businesses 10, 26–28, 61, 64–65, 96, 99–100, 109, 123, 130–131; controls on 196; core 99, 108; domestic 22; green 54; large Chinese 129; managed 131; small-scale 129; stable 51

CAFTTG *see* Canadian Armed Forces Training Team Ghana
Canada 13, 42, 47–66, 109, 143, 162, 192; and the Canadian government 49, 52, 55, 61, 66; commitment to increase aid by 8% and to provide more funding to African countries 51; engagement in Ghana's economic reforms 47–62; and influencing the shaping of policy in Ghana 52; perspective on the neoliberal agenda 49; and support after the coup 53–54; and support for broad-based reforms 60
Canada Fund for Africa 51
Canadian Armed Forces Training Team Ghana 51
Canadian International Development Agency 50–54, 56–57, 59–60, 63
Canadian International Development Platform 53, 63
Canadian University Students Overseas 53
capitalism 14, 33–34, 41, 159, 177, 197, 200; competitive 34; global 112; political 196; selective 86
Castro, Fidel 6
CDB *see* Chinese Development Bank
Central Bank of West African States 155
Chad 2
Chan, S. 113, 125
Chege, Michael 178
Chenery, Hollis 33
Chevron (IOC) 115
China 12, 23–25, 60, 81–82, 84–89, 111, 113, 115–116, 120–121, 123–124, 127–129, 133–136, 138–141, 169–170, 196–198; and the $3bn loan to Ghana 138; access to Ghana's oil and gas 112, 116, 121; approach to economic reform 13, 113; engagements in Africa 135; evolves away from Nkrumah's socialist–statist ideological relationship to a more market-oriented economic relationship 128; geopolitical interests 81; and Ghana 25, 60, 87, 111, 123, 129–130, 133–134, 171, 198; government of 113–114, 143; involvement in the galamsey crisis in Ghana 35, 130–141; and the noninterference doctrine 198; and subnational China–African competition centers 140
China Development Bank 112, 116, 133
China National Offshore Oil Corporation 112, 115–116, 121–122, 125, 142
Chinese 20, 25, 75, 88, 111–113, 117–123, 125–127, 129–140, 142; actors 111–112, 121–122, 132; companies 23, 114, 116, 121–123, 129, 136; contractors 113, 125; interest in Ghana's oil and gas 111–112, 116, 121; investments 114, 123, 129, 141–142; involvement in "galamsey" activities 130–135, 137–141; involvement in Ghana's economy 111, 114; involvement in unregulated activities (hotels, restaurants, and equipment rental) 131; labor 138; loans 124, 127, 134, 136, 138–139; migrants 131, 137–138; miners 132–133; nationals 133, 135, 137, 139–141; TNCs 113; transnational corporations 113; and western oil companies in Ghana 122; women 136, 138–139, 141
Chinese Academy of Social Sciences 132
Chinese Development Bank 116–117, 119–120, 123–126, 133, 135–136

Chretien, Jean (Prime Minister, Canada) 49
CIDA *see* Canadian International Development Agency
CIDP *see* Canadian International Development Platform
civil society organizations 95, 102, 119, 185
Clinton, Pres. Bill 184
CMB *see* Cocoa Marketing Board
CNOOC *see* China National Offshore Oil Corporation
coalition governments 165
cocoa 2, 6, 12, 17–18, 20, 23, 84, 87, 92, 98, 120, 153, 164, 197; beans 2, 6, 17, 84, 87, 92; exports 23; farmers 18; industry 17; prices 164; producers 197; production 197; revenues 120
Cocoa Marketing Board 20
Cold War period 39–40, 83
Colombo Plan 49–50
Convention People's Party 1, 17, 127, 149–150, 180
Copenhagen Agreement 57
corporate social responsibility 55, 61, 64, 95–97, 99–101, 106–110
corporate social responsibility movement 95
Corporate Village Enterprise 22
Cotonou Agreement 72–74
COVE *see* Corporate Village Enterprise
CPP *see* Convention People's Party
Crawford, G. 67–68, 71, 73
crude oil 114, 118–120
CSOs *see* civil society organizations
CSR *see* corporate social responsibility
CSRM *see* corporate social responsibility movement
CUSO *see* Canadian University Students Overseas

Daddieh, C.K. 166, 170, 197
Dakar 149–150, 158
Danquah, Joseph Boakye (J.B.) 148–149
Dekanozishvili, Mariam 13, 24, 67–77
Del Biondo, K. 73–74
Delputte, S. 70, 72
democracy promotion 68, 71, 73–74, 78; efforts 68, 72, 76; objectives 72; rhetoric 68
democratic development 15, 72, 173, 175–176, 181–183
DFRD *see* District Focus for Rural Development
Dione, Saliou 145–161
Diop, M.C. 153, 155–158
Diouf, Pres. Abdou 151–152, 155–156, 162
District Focus for Rural Development 178, 189
Dreyer, J.T. 86, 88

EC *see* Electoral Commission
ECF *see* extended credit facility
ECK *see* Electoral Commission of Kenya
Economic Community of West African States) 85, 169
Economic Partnership Agreement 67, 72–73, 75, 80, 101, 107
economic planning 21, 116, 120
Economic Recovery Programme 2, 7, 19–21, 37–38, 152–153, 165, 168, 182
economic reforms 1–2, 4–5, 7–9, 11–16, 22, 24, 26, 41–43, 53–59, 75–76, 162, 165–166, 182–183, 191–196, 198–200; critical 18; discourse of 13, 16; diverse 1; domestic 15; experiences of 4, 14–15, 191; general 108; initiatives 7; ongoing 101; persistent 9; radical 181; structural 178
economic reforms of policy 31, 42
economic strategies 86, 150, 152, 161
ECOWAS *see* Economic Community of West African States
EDF *see* European Development Fund
Electoral Commission of Kenya 39, 79, 179, 182–184
electoral fraud 181
electoral malpractice 184
Ellimah, R. 55, 61
Engler, Y. 52–53, 56
EPA *see* Economic Partnership Agreement
ERP *see* Economic Recovery Programme
Esipong stadium 129
EU Emergency Trust Fund for Africa 74
EU–Ghana Joint Cooperation Strategy 2017–2020 68
Europe 13, 17, 78–80, 126, 135, 141, 147, 162, 170, 177; and the concept of nation-state 145; farms 177; political systems 67; reconstructing war-devastated 148
European Commission 67, 69–70, 76, 78
European Development Fund 67, 70, 73, 79
European Union 13, 24, 67–68, 78–80
extended credit facility 14, 23, 118, 192, 198

ExxonMobil 115–116, 121

Faletto, Enzo 6, 33
Fanti tribes 148
farmer-based organizations 55, 59
FBOs *see* farmer-based organizations
FDA *see* French Development Agency
FDI *see* foreign direct investment
Financial Sector Reform Programme 10, 22
Financial Sector Strategic Plan 10, 22
FINSSP *see* Financial Sector Strategic Plan
Fourth Republic 9, 39, 181
France 65–66, 145, 147–148, 150, 153, 155, 157–158, 161–162, 191
French Development Agency 150
Friedman, Milton 34, 37, 99
fuels 107, 123, 137
Furness, M. 71

Gabon 2
GAC *see* Global Affairs Canada
galamsey 25, 130–141; activities 130, 132, 141; and anti-Chinese populism 136; crisis 131, 133, 135–136, 143; operations 134, 140; operators 131, 137; politics of 127–141; practice of 132, 137
Gambia 14, 25, 164–172, 193, 195; culture of 167–168; economy of 165; gas production in 171; and Ghana collaboration 2, 164–171; government of 170; independence of 167; and the *National Development Plan 2018–2021* 170; and newfound oil wells 169; reducing state vulnerabilities of 170
GDP 3, 7–8, 16–17, 20–21, 25, 38–39, 56, 59, 150, 153, 194
gender equality 48, 51, 54, 56–57
general elections 53, 117, 173, 179–180, 184
Ghana 1–16, 18–28, 31, 37–43, 47–49, 51–93, 96–103, 105–162, 164–176, 180–200; anti-Chinese populism in 127–141; and the Canadian mining companies 55, 57, 61; and China 25, 60, 87, 111, 123, 129–130, 133–134, 171, 198; and cocoa sector reforms 12; and corporate social activities 99; debt sustainability 118, 123; and economic independence 149, 161; and economic reforms 26, 47–62, 66, 170, 183; economy of 2, 5, 7, 10–11, 20, 22–23, 52, 55, 111, 122–123, 129, 137, 164, 194; and the energy sector 25, 111, 115; eschews donor state dependency 81; government of 55, 115, 118, 127, 133–137, 154–155, 198, 200; independence of 12, 164–165, 167, 186; and the Jubilee Oilfield 108, 110, 112, 114–115; and the mining industry 63, 130; and the oil industry 95, 97–107, 110–111, 114–115, 121, 126; perceives China as a useful economic development model 198; and perspectives on corporate social activities 99–100; policy reform in 37; policymakers 122–123; political economy of policy reform in 37–40; and political independence 1, 17, 31, 37, 111, 127; politics 11, 16; politics of 7, 15, 25, 38, 40, 151, 187; population of 1, 154, 198; post-Independence 10, 22, 111; reform processes 193; relations with Canada 50–53, 59, 63, 140–141, 166–167, 170–171; relationship with Gambia 25, 165; and the role of Chinese transnational oil corporations 111–124, 136, 194; and Senegal 145, 145–161, 163; and the textile industries 22, 130, 137–138, 143; trade unions 82; western region of 95, 97, 101, 108, 130, 132, 137, 140
"Ghana Boys" 167
Ghana Cocoa Board 153
Ghana Electoral Commission 53
Ghana Gas Company 119
Ghana Grains Development Project 59
Ghana Investment Fund 22
Ghana National Petroleum Corporation 97–98, 101, 106, 109, 114–116, 118, 121
Ghana Poverty Reduction Strategy 43, 54, 156–157, 162
Ghana Shared Growth and Development Agenda 157, 162
Ghana Stock Exchange 20
Ghana Telecom 129
Ghana Trades Union Congress 82, 92
Ghanaian agency 11–12, 25, 111, 122, 198
Global Affairs Canada 51–53, 55–61, 64
GNPC *see* Ghana National Petroleum Corporation
GOIL (IOC) 99
Gold Coast 17, 127, 148–149, 164; *see also* (present name) Ghana
governments 10, 32–37, 49, 51–53, 63–64, 74–75, 89–91, 113–122, 125–128, 132–138, 149–158, 164–166, 177–183,

185, 195–200; African 10, 21, 75, 122; recipient 36, 68, 70–71, 74; Western 197
GPRS *see* Ghana Poverty Reduction Strategy
Great Britain 26–28, 41–43, 50, 52, 54, 60, 62, 80, 125–126, 147–151, 161–163, 165, 167, 187–189, 200; and the colonial government 145; and Margaret Thatcher 35; postwar politics and consensus failure 148
GSGDA *see* Ghana Shared Growth and Development Agenda
GTUC *see* Ghana Trades Union Congress
Guyo, Fatuma Boru 14, 25, 173–186
Gyimah-Boadi, E. 6–7, 15, 40, 184, 197

Handley, A. 10, 15
Hardus, S. 115–116, 118, 121, 123, 136
Harper, Stephen 49
Hayek, Frederick 34
Heavily Indebted Poor Countries 2, 21–22, 50, 60, 84, 156, 162, 191
Herbst, J. 9–10, 13, 86, 128
Hess, S. 129, 140–141, 170, 198
Higgot, Richard 5
HIPC *see* Heavily Indebted Poor Countries
human rights 48–49, 51–53, 55–56, 58, 61, 65, 67, 73, 75–76, 159, 171
Huntington, Samuel 14
Huq, M.M. 16–17
Hutchful, E. 18–20, 38, 47, 57, 83, 111, 138, 164

ICFG *see* Integrated Coastal and Fisheries Governance
IEBC *see* Independence Electoral and Boundaries Commission
IFCTU *see* International Federation of Christian Trade Unions
IFIs *see* international financial institutions
IMF 16, 18–19, 22–23, 33, 35–38, 47–48, 63, 98, 118, 152, 154, 156–157, 162, 191–192, 196–197; backed SAPs 161; board 118; conditionalities 59, 91; intervention 36; review of Ghana's ECF 196; sponsored SAPs 19; and World Bank demands 197; and World Bank imposed reforms 153; and World Bank institutions 12; and World Bank-sponsored Structural Adjustment Program 7
independence 1–2, 5, 27, 31, 81, 84, 145, 147–152, 161, 164, 166–167, 170, 177, 180, 184–185; of Gambia 167; of Ghana 12, 164–165, 167, 186; judicial 173, 186; political 13
Independence Electoral and Boundaries Commission 173, 184, 186, 188
instability: macroeconomic 21; political 31, 151, 164, 182
Integrated Coastal and Fisheries Governance 105
Inter-Party Advisory Committee 182
International Federation of Christian Trade Unions 82
international financial institutions 4–6, 12–13, 48–49, 56, 62, 83, 86, 111, 150, 155, 165, 171, 178, 182, 191–193
International Monetary Fund *see* IMF
international oil companies 95, 97, 99, 102–104, 106–107, 115
IOCs *see* international oil companies
IPAC *see* Inter-Party Advisory Committee
Islam 167–168
Ivory Coast 2, 197

Jallow, Tamsir 167
Jammeh, Pres. Yahya 165, 167–169
Japan 24–25, 81–82, 84–88, 117, 191; acts as a model for East Asian states in the region 85; adopts a state-led development 86; and the aid disbursements 87; overseas development assistance 87; slides from international prestige in 2003 86
Japan Bank for International Cooperation 90
Japan External Trade Organizations 90
Jawara, Pres. Dawda Kairaba 165–168
JBIC *see* Japan Bank for International Cooperation
Jeffries, R. 6–7, 15, 40, 196
JETRO *see* Japan External Trade Organizations
Jubilee Project 103, 115
"Junior Jesus" 11

KADU *see* Kenya African Democratic Union
Kalabule 2
Kalenjin ethnic groups. 177
KANU *see* Kenya African National Union Party
Kelsall, T. 17–18, 23
Kemmerling, A. 71–72
Kenya 2, 14, 25, 99, 173–174, 176–178, 180–186; citizens of 178; democratization of 185; economy of 179

Kenya African National Union Party 179
Kenya African Democratic Union 177
Kenya People's Union 177
Kenyatta, Pres. Jomo 177–178, 182
Keohane, Robert 9
Kibaki, Pres. Mwai 179
Kikuyu ethnic groups 177
Knight, J. 102, 104
Koch, S. 68–70, 74
Kosmos Agreement 114–116, 121
Kosmos Energy Company 98–99, 125
KPU *see* Kenya People's Union
Kufuor, Pres. John 2, 10, 21–23, 83, 128, 156–158, 181
Kuznets, Simon 33
Kyoto Protocol 54

Land Tenure Reform Project 60
Latin America 8, 15, 26, 33, 41, 48–49, 57, 125, 141
Lee, M.C. 129–130, 138, 140
Lehman, H.P. 87, 90
Lewis, Arthur 5, 33, 42
Lumumba-Kasongo, T. 84, 87

Mahama, Pres. John 119–120, 128, 133, 139, 181, 192
Malaysia 13, 194
Marxism 5, 8, 149, 153, 197
Master Facility Agreement 116–122
Mawuko-Yevugah, Lord 24, 31–42, 192
McKinsey Global Institute 57, 65
MDGs *see* Millennium Development Goals
MDRI *see* Multilateral Debt Relief Initiative
MFA *see* Master Facility Agreement
Millennium Development Goals 66, 126, 157–158, 175, 189
Mills, Pres. John Evans Atta 115
Ministry of Economy, Trade and Industry 86
Moi, Pres. Daniel Arap 178
Molenaers, N. 69–70
Mozambique 26
Multilateral Debt Relief Initiative 22, 50, 159, 162
multinationals, state-owned 122
Mutua, M. 177–178

NAFTA *see* North American Free Trade Agreement
NARC *see* National Alliance Rainbow Coalition
National Alliance Rainbow Coalition 179
National Commission for Democracy 183
National Democratic Congress 10, 15, 23, 117, 124, 134, 136, 143, 181, 192, 195, 198
National Democratic Party 134
National Development Plan of Gambia 2018–2021 170
National Development Planning Commission 154
National Liberation Council 53, 180
National Redemption Council 180
NDC *see* National Democratic Congress
neo-Marxism 5–6, 15
neoliberal reforms 14
NEPAD *see* New Partnership for Africa's Development
New Partnership for Africa's Development 158
New Patriotic Party 2, 10, 21–23, 68, 117, 124, 136, 139, 181, 184, 192
Niger Delta 96, 108
Nigeria 19, 54, 58, 66, 88, 90, 92, 96, 102, 109, 126, 129, 158, 189; and the African states 19, 54, 58, 66, 88, 90, 92, 96, 102, 109, 126, 129, 158, 189; and neighboring Ghana 38; and the oil sector 19
Nkrumah, Pres. Kwame 1, 5, 11–12, 17, 53, 63, 82–84, 119, 127–128, 147–151, 161, 164, 167, 180–181, 189; administration and the socialist–statist agenda under 128; administration overthrown in a military takeover 128; campaign for the reinstatement of China at the United Nations 128; and the Convention People's Party 1, 17, 127, 149–150, 180; and the CPP government 180; Gold Coast government issues a white paper proposing the end of colonization 145, 149; and his postcolonial aspirations 180; and his vision of Ghana's role in Africa 171; and the post-Nkrumah government 153; self-reliance approach involving a reduction of Ghana's economic dependence on Britain 151; toppled by the military in 1966 180
NLC *see* National Liberation Council
North America 13, 17, 135, 141; *see also* US
North American Free Trade Agreement 49
Norway 100–101, 169, 171, 191
NPP *see* New Patriotic Party

NRC *see* National Redemption Council
Nugent, P. 11, 151

Obeng-Odoom, F. 95, 122
ODI *see* Overseas Development Institute
Odoom, Isaac 13, 23, 25, 81, 87–88, 92, 111–124, 126, 189, 198
OECD 49, 54–55, 58–59, 61, 65–66
Official Development Assistance Act 2008 54
oil 10, 23, 25, 27, 35, 83–86, 95–126, 132–133, 136, 142–143, 147, 149–150, 156–157, 169, 194–195; activity in Ghana 97; barrels of 98, 114; commercial 194; companies 95, 97, 99, 101, 103–104, 121, 125, 142; crises 83, 86, 150; crude 114, 118–120; discoveries 10, 27, 84, 95, 102, 105, 124, 157; exploitation 96, 98; exploration 96, 98, 102, 104, 108; and gas in Africa 126; industry 23, 25, 95, 195; infrastructure 95, 107; offshore 115; palm 106, 147; prices 114, 120, 150, 157, 197; production 97, 101, 106, 108, 114, 122, 195; resources 98, 114, 133, 195; revenue 101, 107, 109; sector 95, 99, 101–102, 104, 107, 169; and social responsibility in Ghana 95–108
oilfields 115, 132
"One-China policy" 128
OPEC *see* Organization of Petroleum Exporting Countries
Opoku-Boateng, Ernest 13, 24, 47–62
Organization of Petroleum Exporting Countries 35
Ottawa 47, 53
"Ottawa consensus" 56–58, 60
Overseas Development Institute 2, 27, 191, 200
Oyelaran-Oyeyinka, B. 89

PAC *see* Parliamentary Accounts Committee
palm oil 106, 147
PAMSCAD *see* Programme of Actions to Mitigate the Social Costs of Adjustment
pan-Africanism 83
Panford, K. 47–48, 55, 57–58, 98, 101, 106–107, 194–195
Paris Agreement 57
Parliamentary Accounts Committee 60
Peet, Richard 33, 35
People's National Party 181
PES *see* Plan for an Emerging Senegal
Petroleum Commission 97, 101–102, 107, 194
PIAC Public Interest & Accountability Committee 97–98
Plan for an Emerging Senegal 160
PNDC *see* Provisional National Defence Council
PNP *see* People's National Party
policy reform 31–32, 37, 40, 43; economic 31, 42; far-reaching economic 36; process 193
political economy 7, 9, 24, 26–27, 32, 40–43, 127, 141–143, 146–147, 160, 162, 176, 192–194
political independence 13
political parties 10, 139, 148–149, 154, 173, 176–177, 179–181, 198; Convention People's Party 1, 17, 127, 149–150, 180; Kenya African National Union Party 179; Kenya African Democratic Union 177; Kenya People's Union 177; National Alliance Rainbow Coalition 179; National Democratic Congress 10, 15, 23, 117, 124, 134, 136, 143, 181, 192, 195, 198; National Democratic Party 134; New Patriotic Party 2, 10, 21–23, 68, 117, 124, 136, 139, 181, 184, 192; People's National Party 181; Progress Party 17, 180; United Democratic Party 165; United Gold Coast Convention 149
post-Cold War era 2, 7, 9, 12–13, 39
Poverty Reduction Strategy Paper 157
Pratt, C. 49–50
Presidential Special Initiatives 22
Preventive Detention Act 1959 180
Private Sector Development Strategy 22–23
Programme of Actions to Mitigate the Social Costs of Adjustment 20, 50, 183
Progress Party 17, 180
Provisional National Defence Council 2, 7, 10, 15–16, 19, 22–23, 37, 101, 152, 164, 172, 181, 183, 186, 195
PRSP *see* Poverty Reduction Strategy Paper
Przeworski, A. 175–176
PSDS *see* Private Sector Development Strategy
PSI *see* Presidential Special Initiatives

Quijano, A. 146, 160

Radelet, S. 2, 9, 193, 199

Rawlings, Pres. Jerry 2, 5–7, 10–12, 14–19, 21–22, 27–28, 37, 83, 128, 151–152, 164–165, 168, 181–184, 186–187, 195–196; capitulates to the international financial institutions as lenders of last resort 83; era of 18, 23, 184; extreme anti-private sector measures 10; and his role in economic reform 15, 28; leftist polices of 182; legacy of 14; and the military takeover 18; reflects the proto-revolutionary movements 18; regime of 2, 15, 83, 182; revolutionary rhetoric of 164
Reagan, Pres. Ronald 36, 197
recipient governments 36, 68, 70–71, 74
reform agendas 1, 4–7, 13, 35, 41, 96, 106, 195
reform efforts 2, 4, 16, 22, 74, 191, 195
reform packages 12, 23, 48, 192
reform policies 12–13, 23, 31, 37–38, 40–41, 150, 154
reform programs 1–3, 12, 19, 21, 47, 74, 191–194, 199
reforms 2–4, 9–11, 13, 15, 23, 25–27, 31–32, 42–43, 47–50, 74–75, 77, 147–149, 152–153, 191–193, 197–199; comprehensive legal 23; constitutional 184; economic liberalization 112; electoral 52, 187; exchange rate 19; human rights 57; ideological 11; institute 9, 165; market-led 37, 196; market-oriented 83; neoliberal 7, 14, 27, 37, 47, 49, 196; security sector 169; social 56; state-wide 169; tax 35, 48
regional trade agreements 12
regionalization 5, 12–14; dates back to the post-Independent era 12; and globalization 13; politics of 12
regions 4, 13, 25, 33, 84–85, 95–97, 101–102, 104, 108, 112, 128, 132, 141, 177; autonomous 177; developing 181, 183; emerging 92; gold-rich 130; oil-producing 97; resource-endowed 107, 192; resource-rich 96; underdeveloped 4
Rift Valley 177–178, 189
Risse, Thomas 14
Rodney, Walter 112, 159
Rosenstein-Rodan, Paul N. 33
Rothchild, D. 197
Rothschild, Donald 39
RTAs *see* regional trade agreements
Rupp, D.E. 99–100

Saad-Filho, Alfredo 48–49, 57
Sachs, J.D. 85
Sackeyfio, Naaborle 81–91
SAF *see* Structural Adjustment Facility
Saine, Abdoulaye 14, 25, 164–171
Sakho-Loum Plan (emergency plan) 154–155
SAL *see* Structural Adjustment Lending
Sandbrook, Richard 1, 2, 16, 28, 195, 196, 197, 200
SAPs *see* Structural Adjustment Program
Schultz, T.W. 33, 43
Sekondi-Takoradi 95, 129
Senegal 14, 145–146, 148, 150–158, 160–161, 193; contemporary 147; economy of 147, 155, 159; and Ghana 145–153, 155, 157–161, 163; strategy of 157
Senegalese 146, 148, 155–156, 159; bureaucracy 151; and Ghanaian peoples 155, 159; government 158
Senghor, Pres. Léopold 145, 147–148, 150–151, 161
sentiments 1, 11, 136, 139; anti-Chinese 137–138, 140–141; expressed on increased rents and the high costs of land in the region 95
Shillington, K. 15, 17, 181
Sino-African partnerships 88
Sino-Ghanaian relationship 88
Sinopec International Petroleum Corporation 119, 122
SMC *see* Supreme Military Council
Smith, Adam 32–33, 35, 37, 145
social responsibility 25, 95, 97, 99–103, 105–109; decisions 108; and Ghana's oil sector 95; guidelines 61; projects 108
Société Française de Pétrole 98
SOEs *see* state-owned enterprises
South Africa 9, 88, 90, 158
Soviet Union 127, 148
stability 7, 39, 50, 187, 192; economic 48, 90, 171; long-term 173; macroeconomic 3, 23, 157, 192; microeconomic 39; political 8, 50, 53, 166, 183, 193; social 32
Star Oil (IOC) 99
state-owned enterprises 7, 36, 57, 113, 119, 182
state-owned multinationals 122
state-owned power companies 158
state subsidies 36
Structural Adjustment Facility 20
Structural Adjustment Lending 21, 50
Structural Adjustment Programs 8, 12–13,

21, 35–36, 38–40, 48, 50, 54, 62, 152–154, 157, 161, 174–175, 182, 188
structural reforms 19, 47, 49–51, 53, 57, 62, 155
subsidies 35–36, 47–48, 55, 58, 72, 153, 182
Sudan 2, 115, 129, 145, 173
Supreme Military Council 17, 180

Tanzania 2
textile industries 22, 130, 137–138, 143
Tinbergen, Jan 33
TNCs *see* transnational corporations
Total (IOC) 99, 115
trade unions 82, 148, 154
transnational corporations 111–115, 122
tribes 148; Ashanti 148; Fanti 148
Tsiboe-Darko, Antoinette 23, 95–108

UDP *see* United Democratic Party
Uganda 2, 99, 115
UGCC *see* United Gold Coast Convention
UK *see* Great Britain
UNIGOV *see* Union Government
Union Government 180
United Democratic Party 165
United Gold Coast Convention 149
United States *see* USA
USA 21, 35, 47, 49–50, 52, 54, 58, 60, 136, 160; and Chinese inaction 54; embassy in Accra 115; government 116, 191

Volta River Project 83, 102

Wade, Pres. Abdoulaye 156–158
WAEMU *see* West African Economic and Monetary Union
Washington Consensus 7–8, 14, 24, 26, 28, 33, 36, 39, 43, 47–50, 56–57, 62, 66, 83
Watson Commission 149
West Africa 52, 59, 72, 76, 110, 124, 150, 166, 171, 187, 189
West Africa Constabulary Force 167
West Africa Oil Company Limited 98
West African Economic and Monetary Union 155
Williamson, John 8, 36, 48
World Bank 20–23, 25–26, 32–33, 35–40, 42–43, 48–50, 52–54, 56, 59–60, 150, 152, 156, 158, 163, 196–197; and the *Berg Report* 35, 37; demands of 197; institutions 12; research department 33; Structural Adjustment Program 7
World War II 85, 145–146, 148, 167

York, G. 51

Kolibri 360 GmbH
Ferdinand-Jühlke-Straße 7
99095 Erfurt, Deutschland
produktsicherheit@kolibri360.de